D1020162

North Korea
THROUGH THE LOOKING GLASS

Kongdan Oh and Ralph C. Hassig

BROOKINGS INSTITUTION PRESS
Washington, D.C.

Copyright © 2000
THE BROOKINGS INSTITUTION
1775 Massachusetts Avenue, N.W., Washington, D.C. 20036
www.brookings.edu

All rights reserved

All photographs, except as noted, copyright © by Frank Hoffmann
Reprinted by permission

Library of Congress Cataloging-in-Publication data

North Korea through the looking glass / Kongdan Oh, Ralph C. Hassig.
p.   cm.
Includes bibliographical references and index.
ISBN 0-8157-6436-7 (cloth) — ISBN 0-8157-6435-9 (pbk.)
1. Korea (North)—Politics and government. I. Oh, Kongdan. II. Hassig,
Ralph C.
DS935.5 N673 2000
951.93—dc21   00-008812
                                                   CIP

9 8 7 6 5 4 3 2 1

The paper used in this publication meets minimum requirements of the
American National Standard for Information Sciences—Permanence of Paper
for Printed Library Materials: ANSI Z39.48-1984.

Typeset in Minion

Composition by Oakland Street Publishing
Arlington, VA

Printed by R.R. Donnelly and Sons
Harrisonburg, VA

ON THE COVER: Detail from statue of a court official standing before Tangun's tomb, completed in 1994 near Pyongyang. The North Korean government says that the tomb houses the 5,000-year-old bones of the founder of the Korean people, bolstering Pyongyang's claim to be the historical capital of Korea. Most Korean historians outside the DPRK consider Tangun a symbolic yet mythical figure.

Ḃ THE BROOKINGS INSTITUTION

The Brookings Institution is an independent organization devoted to nonpartisan research, education, and publication in economics, government, foreign policy, and the social sciences generally. Its principal purposes are to aid in the development of sound public policies and to promote public understanding of issues of national importance.

The Institution was founded on December 8, 1927, to merge the activities of the Institute for Government Research, founded in 1916, the Institute of Economics, founded in 1922, and the Robert Brookings Graduate School of Economics and Government, founded in 1924.

The general administration of the Institution is the responsibility of a Board of Trustees charged with safeguarding the independence of the staff and fostering the most favorable conditions for scientific research and publication. The immediate direction of the policies, program, and staff is vested in the president, assisted by an advisory committee of the officers and staff.

In publishing a study, the Institution presents it as a competent treatment of a subject worthy of public consideration. The interpretations or conclusions in such publications are those of the author or authors and do not necessarily reflect the views of the other staff members, officers, or trustees of the Brookings Institution.

Board of Trustees

James A. Johnson
Chairman

Leonard Abramson
Michael H. Armacost
Elizabeth E. Bailey
Zoë Baird
Alan R. Batkin
James W. Cicconi
Alan M. Dachs
Kenneth W. Dam
D. Ronald Daniel
Robert A. Day

Lawrence K. Fish
Cyrus F. Freidheim Jr.
Bart Friedman
Stephen Friedman
Henry Louis Gates Jr.
Brian L. Greenspun
Lee H. Hamilton
William A. Haseltine
Teresa Heinz
Samuel Hellman
Shirley Ann Jackson
Robert L. Johnson
Ann Dibble Jordan

Marie L. Knowles
Thomas G. Labrecque
Jessica Tuchman Mathews
David O. Maxwell
Constance Berry Newman
Steven L. Rattner
Rozanne L. Ridgway
Judith Rodin
Warren B. Rudman
Joan E. Spero
John L. Thornton
Vincent J. Trosino
Stephen M. Wolf

Honorary Trustees

Rex J. Bates
Louis W. Cabot
A. W. Clausen
William T. Coleman Jr.
Lloyd N. Cutler
Bruce B. Dayton
Douglas Dillon
Charles W. Duncan Jr.
Walter Y. Elisha
Robert F. Erburu
Robert D. Haas
Andrew Heiskell
F. Warren Hellman

Roy M. Huffington
Thomas W. Jones
Vernon E. Jordan Jr.
Breene M. Kerr
James T. Lynn
Donald F. McHenry
Robert S. McNamara
Mary Patterson McPherson
Arjay Miller
Maconda Brown O'Connor
Donald S. Perkins
Samuel Pisar
J. Woodward Redmond

Charles W. Robinson
James D. Robinson III
Howard D. Samuel
B. Francis Saul II
Ralph S. Saul
Henry B. Schacht
Michael P. Schulhof
Robert Brookings Smith
Morris Tanenbaum
John C. Whitehead
James D. Wolfensohn
Ezra K. Zilkha

To our parents for their love and support

Mi Ryo Park and
the memory of Chung Do Oh

Margaret Dixon Hassig and
Carl E. Hassig

Foreword

Fifty-five years after its founding at the dawn of the cold war, and ten years after the end of that war, North Korea is an anachronism. Whether its leaders are trying to bring the country into step with the global community is debatable. Kongdan Oh and Ralph C. Hassig doubt that the recent modest changes in this modern-day hermit kingdom signal a commitment to the kinds of reform that most other communist and former communist states have adopted.

North Korea's official ideology of Juche, repeated endlessly in classrooms and in the media, emphasizes national self-reliance, independence, and the worship of the supreme leader, General Kim Jong Il. Political pluralism and globalization are roundly condemned. Although North Koreans often fail to follow the teachings of Juche in their everyday lives, the ideology remains a powerful influence on their domestic and international policies. The socialist economy, guided by political principles and bereft of international support, has collapsed. The supreme leader is remote from his struggling citizens, to whom he has never given a public speech. The military, benefiting from the leader's "military first" policy, represses the people and threatens foreign nations. North Korea's foreign policy is cautious and idealistic—seeking diplomatic recognition from the world but limiting the people-to-people contact that would threaten the leader's hold on his people.

As an impoverished, middle-sized, xenophobic state, North Korea would not figure largely in U.S. foreign policy but for Pyongyang's pursuit of nuclear weapons and ballistic missiles, and its continued threat to a staunch U.S. ally, South Korea. Although they sympathize with the difficulties that American policymakers encounter in trying to halt North Korea's proliferation of weapons of mass destruction and keep peace in the region, Oh and Hassig believe that a long-term solution to the perennial challenges posed by the Kim regime requires a more active attempt to open this Orwellian society to the outside world. For example, greater efforts should be made to monitor the distribution and identify the source of aid donated to the DPRK, and a multifaceted plan to circumvent the Kim Jong Il regime's control of mass media and open the DPRK's borders to the movement of people should be formulated.

The authors want to thank the many people who have given them support and assistance during the writing of *North Korea through the Looking Glass*. In the United States, Samantha Ravich at the Center for Strategic and International Studies, Francis Fukuyama at George Mason University, Richard Haass at the Brookings Institution, and Mike Leonard and Philip Major at the Institute for Defense Analyses supported Kongdan Oh throughout the project. Frank Hoffmann generously offered to let the authors browse through his extensive collection of North Korean photographs. Hy-Sang Lee and several anonymous reviewers read early drafts of the manuscript and offered valuable suggestions. Scott Snyder, Larry Niksch, Rinn-Sup Shinn, James Lilley, Bates Gill, Peter Beck, Selig Harrison, Mel Gurtov, Jim Cornelius, John Merrill, Michael Green, William Drennan, Charles Armstrong, Robert Ross, WheeGook Kim, Chae-Jin Lee, Hong-Nack Kim, Samuel Kim, Victor Cha, Jaehoon Lee, and Kay Cho helped the authors over the years in their study of the two Koreas.

At the Republic of Korea's Ministry of Unification in Seoul, Lim Dong-Won, the authors' long-time senior colleague and friend, often shared his vision and strategic thinking about North Korea and Korean unification. Lee Kwan-Sei procured necessary materials and set up numerous meetings at the ministry, as did his colleague Rhee Bong-Jo. Lee Jong-Ryul was instrumental in setting up meetings with defectors. Doowon Lee of Yonsei University was a constant and reliable source of information and materials. Many others in Korea deserve a word of thanks, including Kim Hyung-Gi, Yang Young-Shik, Moon Moo-Hong, Chung Suk-Hong, Park Song-Hoon, Song

Sung-Sup, Yang Chang-Seok, Shin Ui-Hang, Kim Chun-Sig, Lee Duk-Haeng, Song Min-Soon, Park Yong-Ok, Kim Kyu-Ryoon, Choi Jinwook, Kim Kook-Shin, Suh Jae-Jean, Park Youngho, Yoo Young-Ku, Kil Jeong-Woo, Kim Sang-Yohl, Kim Kyung-Hee, Kim Seung-Han, Kim Taeho, and the Koreans from the North who granted interviews, including Hwang Jang Yop and his colleague Kim Duk-hong.

In Japan, Yoshi Imazato set up numerous meetings for research on the book. Yutaka Yokoi also assisted at various stages in the book research and always showed a deep interest in Korean unification. The research in Japan profited from the assistance and cooperation of Eiji Yamamoto, Akio Miyajima, and Shigekatsu Kondo.

Several scholars in China provided the Chinese view of North Korea, including Ye Ru'an, Jin Zhenji, Ma Jisen, Qi Bioliang, and Zhang Shoushan.

The authors are grateful to many others who in their conversations and writings on Korea gave them ideas to pursue. The authors take full responsibility, however, for any errors that may have crept into their account of what is admittedly an opaque communist state and for the views expressed in this book, which they have tried to make consistent with the truth as they see it.

At Brookings, Theresa Walker edited the manuscript, and Susan Jackson and Jungyon Shin verified it; Carlotta Ribar proofread the book, and Susan Fels prepared the index.

Brookings and the authors are grateful to the Smith Richardson Foundation for its support of this effort.

The views expressed in this volume are those of the authors and should not be ascribed to the trustees, officers, or other staff members of the Brookings Institution or any other organizations with which the authors are associated.

MICHAEL H. ARMACOST
President

MAY 2000
Washington, D.C.

Contents

Preface

In another moment Alice was through the glass, and had jumped lightly down into the Looking-glass room. The very first thing she did was to look whether there was a fire in the fire-place, and she was quite pleased to find that there was a real one, blazing away as brightly as the one she had left behind. Then she began looking about, and noticed that what could be seen from the old room was quite common and uninteresting, but that all the rest was as different as possible.[1]

Three years ago, when we first proposed to write this book, one of our colleagues sought to dissuade us on the grounds that North Korea would collapse before the book reached the printer. This was not an uncommon expectation in the years immediately following the 1994 death of North Korea's founder, Kim Il Sung. We had earlier predicted that his son and successor, the reclusive Kim Jong Il, would be unable to hold on to power for long. In any event, North Korea still survives, muddling along in a considerably weakened state. But even should North Korea collapse in the near future, we believe that a better understanding of the country and its people will help the world deal with a Korea struggling to reunify. The title we have chosen—used by us once before in a 1996 article and coincidentally used as a North Korean section title in a 1999 *Economist* survey of the two Koreas written by Edward Carr—expresses one of our main themes: that North Korea is strikingly different from other countries, in large part because its leader and people are living in their own "separate reality."[2]

The years since the fall of the Berlin Wall have been a time of eager anticipation for most Koreans in the southern half of the peninsula (in the northern half most people still do not fully understand the circumstances of German unification). But the hope of reuniting millions of Korean families from the North and the South has been disappointed. North Korea is in serious decline, with thousands, perhaps millions, of people dying of starvation. Yet rather than initiate the sort of reforms that were implemented, however imperfectly, by communist governments in Eastern Europe, the former Soviet Union, Southeast Asia, and China, the North Korean leaders have remained faithful to their command economy and military-first policy. It is this paradox of stubbornness, this seeming desire to escape today's reality, that we investigate in this book.

For indeed we decided to write a book, summarizing more than ten years of study on North Korea (formally known as the Democratic People's Republic of Korea, or DPRK). We want to provide an overview for readers who are unacquainted with this remote and peculiar country and share our opinions and interpretations of North Korea with those who have a special interest in that country. Our research is based on sources in English, Korean, and Japanese, supplemented by meetings and interviews with specialists and government officials who deal with North Korea, including meetings with North Korean government delegations visiting the United States. We have also learned much from interviews with two dozen North Koreans who have come down to the South during the 1990s. These interviews, conducted in Seoul in December 1997, were emotionally moving and intellectually stimulating, reminding us of the human side of the North Korean tragedy. The decision to defect from their homeland was a difficult one for these people, a decision that some of them are constantly reliving. If more North Koreans had the courage to take exit or voice action in the face of the totalitarian North Korean regime, Korean reunification would come sooner rather than later.

Our research makes extensive use of English-language translations and transcriptions provided by the Foreign Broadcast Information Service (FBIS), a U.S.-government-funded organization that culls foreign broadcasts and print outlets all over the world for information of potential use to U.S. government officials. Until September 1996, North Korea articles were included in the FBIS's *Daily Report: East Asia*, available in hard copy at most research libraries. Since the discontinuation of that *Daily Report*, a greatly reduced sampling of North Korean articles may be found on the World News Connection website (http://wcnet.fedworld.gov/), which is available by subscription.

The North Korean media are long on propaganda and short on news. Some news is released to the foreign community but withheld from the domestic audience. Other news is released domestically but not made available to foreigners, except as they are able to eavesdrop through such channels as FBIS. In this book, source citations attributed to KCNA were broadcast in English, exclusively for a foreign audience, except for those news pieces that KCNA picked up from the North Korean press (for example, *Nodong Sinmun*, the Korean Workers' Party newspaper, or *Minju Choson*, the official government newspaper). KCBN, however, provides a window on what the North Korean people hear. We have made a point of frequently quoting from these media to provide the reader with verbal snapshots of how North Korea officially talks and thinks. The DPRK government treats most information about its country as a state secret, a precautionary measure to preserve state security. Because of this secrecy some of our descriptions of North Korea may be inaccurate in detail, but we believe that, taken as a whole, our depiction of North Korea is true to reality.

We would gladly see our book overtaken by a North Korean transformation and subsequent reunification with South Korea, but our pessimistic analysis of the thoughts and perceptions of the North Korean leaders suggests to us that this state, an anachronism at the end of the century, is likely to endure for some time. If that is the case, there will continue to be an urgent need in Washington, Seoul, and other capitals to develop policies to prevent the North Korean leaders from threatening the stability of the post–cold war era and to alleviate the suffering of the benighted North Korean masses.

A final note, on the spelling of Korean words and names. We have not strictly adhered to the McCune-Reischauer method of transcribing Korean into English, because the resulting spellings often lead to mispronunciations (for example, Chuch'e rather than the more common-sense Juche). We have also dispensed with diacritical marks. In FBIS references, we have kept the exact FBIS title spellings to enable the interested reader to retrieve the article by title words. Throughout the book, Korean names are given family name first, with the first and middle names hyphenated, except when common usage or the individual's preference dictates otherwise.

CHAPTER ONE

Looking
Backward

Without Pyongyang, Korea would not exist,
and without Korea there would be no earth.[1]

North Korea, known officially as the Democratic People's Republic of Korea, or DPRK, is a fiercely proud nation of some 23 million people living in a mostly mountainous area the size and approximate latitude of New York state. North Korea shares a border on the north with China, and for a few miles on the northeast, with Russia. It is separated from South Korea, officially known as the Republic of Korea or ROK, by a no-man's-land called the demilitarized zone, which separates two armies poised to resume or prevent—depending on one's point of view—the hostilities interrupted by the 1953 cease-fire agreement ending the Korean War. In comparison to its modernized, democratized, wealthy neighbor to the south, North Korea is in important respects a throwback to earlier times, a country with a past but no future.

A nation's development is commonly described in terms of movement (some might say "progress") along such dimensions as tradition versus modernity, agrarian versus industrial society, monarchic versus democratic-parliamentary governance, closed versus open borders, and colonialism versus independence. North Korea has failed to develop along many of these lines. Rather, the country, entering the twenty-first century, seems stuck in the past, or to be more accurate, in two pasts. On the one hand North Korea is a case study of totalitarian communism reminiscent of the days of Stalin. On the other hand it displays many of the characteristics of a traditional, premodern, communal, closed society. In both senses it is out of step with the world of the new millennium.

North Korea lives a schizophrenic existence in which dreams of creating a totalitarian socialist utopian community under the stern but benevolent rule of a modern-day emperor are pursued with the calculations of domestic and international power politics. How North Korea developed into such a peculiar retrograde state amid the modernization of the rest of East Asia is one of the stranger and sadder stories of the last half of the twentieth century.

North Korea's vision of a "socialism in our own style" is not without its virtues, even though that objective is pursued by harsh totalitarian means. Dismissing the DPRK as a "rogue state" is not helpful in understanding what the country is and what it wants to do. Utopian visions are rarely accepted in their day, even though some parts of those visions later become accepted in mainstream thinking. It is timely, for example, to recall a socialist utopian work published in the United States by Edward Bellamy in 1887. Bellamy's *Looking Backward*, written as a retrospective view from the year 2000, was widely read in its day. Today it is largely lost to memory, but many of the socialist ideas presented in the work such as government intervention in the economy have become a part of Western capitalist culture. In the present context, "looking backward" suggests that although it is regrettable that the North Korean people, through no democratic choice of their own, are forced to look to the past for guidelines to their future, the vision their leaders present of an independent socialist economy existing within a peaceful community of nations practicing full equality of international relations is not without allure. Whether the North Korean leaders truly believe in a "socialism of our own style" is one of the topics taken up in this book. That they might have sound reasons to seek their vision should not be disputed.

A Brief History

The first step toward an understanding of the combination of utopianism and *realpolitik* that coexists in North Korea today is to look at the country's past, especially its experiences in the nineteenth century. In those days, not unlike today, Korea was a nation struggling to maintain its place in a fast-changing and increasingly hostile world, prevented by historical circumstance from participating as an equal in the international community.[2]

Today's Kim dynasty—established by Kim Il Sung when the northern half of Korea was liberated from the Japanese at the end of World War II and handed down to his son, Kim Jong Il—shares important traits with earlier Korean dynasties. In 1997 it adopted a "dynastic calendar" counting from the birth year of its founder (1912) and named after his ideology of Juche (the year 2000 is Juche 89). It is from the Old Choson dynasty (Choson meaning "morning freshness or morning calm") of the fourth and third centuries B.C. that the North Koreans take the name of their people (*Choson saram*, or Choson people) and the name of their country (*Choson Minjujuui Inmin Konghwaguk*, that is, Democratic People's Republic of Korea). As an indigenous Korean state, Old Choson was appropriated as a model for modern-day nationalistic North Korea. The Republic of Korea, however, uses the Korean name *Taehan Minguk* (The Great Korean Republic), an expression derived from the Chinese, and the South Korean people refer to themselves as *Hanguk saram*, from the Chinese name for the Han or Korean people. Taking the name of their country and their people from an older and more independent Korean dynasty than do the South Koreans, the North Koreans make a claim of having greater political legitimacy.

North Korean historiography traces the DPRK's lineage from the founder of Korea—the (probably mythical) Tangun—through Old Choson, to Koguryo, the northernmost of the Three Kingdoms (first through seventh centuries A.D.).[3] Koguryo fought fiercely to keep its independence from China, whereas its fellow Paekche in the southeast part of the Korean Peninsula maintained a cordial relationship with the Japanese, and Silla in the Southwest joined forces with Tang dynasty China to eventually defeat Paekche and Koguryo. When Silla weakened two hundred years later, a regional warlord expanded his influence and took over the state, naming his new state Koryo, derived from the name of the Koguryo dynasty, which the warlord claimed he was re-establishing, thereby providing him with instant legitimacy. In recognition of the claimed heritage of the Koryo dynasty, the DPRK's unification formula calls for the formation of a confederated Korean state to be called *Koryo Yonbang Konghwaguk* (Federation of the Koryo Republic).

Nearing the end of the Koryo dynasty, almost five hundred years later, General Yi Song-gye, sent by the Korean court (which was loyal to the old Chinese Yuan dynasty) to attack the forces of the new Ming dynasty, instead sided with the Ming and turned against his own government, a traitorous feat that while it resulted in his becoming the first king of a new dynasty, would earn him the enmity of later North Korean historians. Yi took the name of the original Choson dynasty for his own, and he and his successors ruled the (later) Choson dynasty for more than 500 years (1392–1910), until Korea was annexed by Japan.

North Koreans do not trace their origins to this dynasty, the longest surviving in Asian history, because throughout most of its existence Choson maintained a vassal relationship with its powerful neighbor, China, a principal reason why it was able to survive for so long as a separate state. Moreover, with the establishment of the Choson dynasty, the capital was moved south from Kaesong to present-day Seoul, thus withdrawing legitimacy from the northern half of the peninsula and conferring it on the southern half (although the two halves did not of course exist as separate governments at that time).

Yet it is from the Choson dynasty that North Korea's style of governance is derived: Choson was ruled by a succession of Confucian monarchs supported by a small class of *yangban* nobility, a class structure not unlike North Korea today, where the new *yangban* are the cadres of the Korean Workers' Party and the supreme leader is Kim Jong Il. An important difference is that, as James B. Palais has argued, the power of the Choson monarch was constrained by court politics and the power of local lords.[4] All the evidence available suggests that in North Korea today, Kim Il Sung and his son have exercised almost total power. There can be no doubt that Confucianism has strongly influenced the ruling style of the Kim family, and it is a credit to Kim Il Sung and his son that they have been able to combine communism with Confucianism. Kim Il Sung adopted the title of *oboi suryong* (supreme and benevolent leader, teacher, father), as befitting a Confucian emperor who was a man apart from the people. *Oboi* is also the honorific for the head of the Confucian household, who holds the same position in the family as the Confucian ruler holds in his kingdom. Despite having limited formal education, Kim also took on the Confucian role of great teacher, dispensing wisdom on any and all subjects as he visited the countryside on his famous on-the-spot guidance tours. As the cult of the ruler was augmented by North Korean propagandists, Kim became transformed from a brave guerrilla fighter attached to the Chinese and Soviet armies to a supernatural being who could even command the weather and transcend time and space. By all accounts the Korean people accepted his claims of quasi divinity, revealing a popular mentality that, to Westerners, is more attuned to the Middle Ages than to the twentieth century, with striking similarities to the reverence accorded by the Japanese to Emperor Hirohito in the 1930s and 1940s.[5]

Kim Il Sung's ability to ideologize and isolate North Korea is all the more remarkable because during the Choson dynasty the people living in the northern part of Korea were more pragmatic than those living in the more isolated southern part. Since Korea's principal trade routes lead north to China, the Koreans living in the North were the travelers and traders of Korean society. Northern border cities like Uiju (now called Sinuiju, or "new Uiju") provided a gateway to China. Kaesong, located in the southern part of North Korea, was a lively city noted for its shrewd merchants. The center of Confucianism, however, was much farther south, in the present-day province of Kyongsang in the southeast corner of the peninsula. Kim succeeded in turning North Korea into the more isolated and ideological part of Korea, smothering its traditional pragmatism. But even here one finds a paradox, because in order to distance himself from international communism, Kim espoused his own brand of ideology called Juche, whose principal theme was that communism be adapted to the Korean situation.

If Choson Korea provided a model for the Kim dynasty, the period of Japanese colonial rule following the collapse of the Choson dynasty provided Kim with a negative example to legitimize his rule. During their thirty-five-year occupation of Korea the Japanese not only took political control of the country, building a social and industrial infrastructure for the purpose of supplying the Japanese islands with Korean goods and labor, but also set out to uproot Korean culture.[6] Koreans were required to worship at Shinto shrines, a burden on everyone but particularly on Korea's 450,000 Christians, whose teaching forbade worship of non-Christian images.[7] Japanese rather than Korean became the standard language in education and business, and to this day many Koreans who were forced to learn Japanese refuse to speak it. Koreans were given fabricated Japanese-style names.[8] The Japanese modernized Korean industry and bureaucracy but not Korean politics, and their forced departure created a political vacuum in Korean leadership and a people anxious to be independent but inexperienced in the process of political participation. The Japanese colonial experience bred a strong feeling of nationalism in the Korean people, who vowed never again to be dominated by another country. During the colonial period Korean socialists, communists, and nationalists were driven underground, across the border into China or Russia, and overseas. When Japan invaded China, many Koreans joined the Chinese army to fight the Japanese. In the late 1930s and early 1940s, the Japanese army chased many of these Korean fighters out of China into Siberia. Of the more than 200,000 Koreans who fought against the Japanese in China, the soldier destined to become most famous was Kim Song-Ju, who took the name of a legendary Korean hero, Kim Il Sung.

The Japanese destroyed Choson dynasty society but did not construct a new Korean society. As soon as the Japanese surrendered in 1945, Korean political factions of all stripes began vying for power. Koreans who had fled to China, Russia, and the United States returned to the fray of Korean politics. The American and Soviet troops that accepted the Japanese surrender south and north of the 38th Parallel tried to impose some social and political order in their respective jurisdictions, initially at least with the prospect of preparing the Koreans to rule themselves. In the southern half of the peninsula the seventy-year-old Princeton- and Harvard-educated Syngman Rhee received the grudging support of the Americans. In the North, thirty-three-year-old Captain Kim Il Sung, late of the Soviet army, was backed by the Russians to form a communist society in Korea compatible with Soviet interests.[9]

When repeated attempts by moderates in the northern and southern halves of the newly divided peninsula failed to create the foundation for a unified Korea, separate Korean elections were held. Kim Il Sung gained control of the levers of power in the North through his astute political maneuvering, backed by Soviet administrators and their troops and by the small but loyal band of soldiers who had returned with Kim from Russia. In the South the strong-willed President Rhee became the Americans' reluctant choice for president, but during the first years of the republic Rhee was unable to achieve the same measure of control Kim achieved in the North, having to contend with armed resistance in many villages and rebellions by nationalists and communists on Cheju Island and in the southwestern region of the country.[10] By the time Rhee had gained the upper hand, thanks largely to the advice and support of his American advisers, Kim Il Sung had already consolidated his control over North Korea and was planning to extend his control over the entire Korean Peninsula.

Kim and his war planners overestimated the likelihood that South Koreans would rise up against the Rhee government when Kim's troops marched south. Kim also underestimated the determination of the Americans to defend the anticommunist government in the South—an understandable mistake given the contradictory signals coming out of Washington.[11] The North Korean attack of June 25, 1950, ultimately failed, and Kim's forces were driven into the North Korean hinterlands and toward the Chinese border. Kim viewed the "Fatherland Liberation War" as a just war whose laudable goal was to save the South Korean people from an oppressive foreign-dominated government.[12] In the post–World War II years, this goal of communization seemed well within his grasp as communism spread throughout the world. The entry of the United States into the war was counted as a great treachery, for which the North Korean people have yet to deliver retribution.

Kim's government was saved by a million Chinese soldiers who took the lead in prosecuting the war against the troops of the United Nations. Failing to unify Korea by force, Kim had to settle for an armistice signed by North Korea, China, and by the United States representing the UN forces. South Korea's Syngman Rhee refused to sign, holding open the option of launching a punishing attack on North Korea to reunite the country, after the manner of Chiang Kai-shek's plan to retake the Chinese mainland. The Korean War destroyed much of North and South Korea's infrastructure, and more tragi-cally, killed more than a million people: 294,000 North Korean soldiers; 225,000 South Korean soldiers; 184,000 Chinese soldiers; and 57,000 UN soldiers, mostly Americans.[13] These figures do not include several hundred thousand Korean civilians killed in combat-related actions. Eleven million Korean fam-ilies were separated by the war, with many North Koreans (especially men) fleeing to the South under the misapprehension that their families would later join them. A much smaller number of South Koreans fled to the North to escape persecution by the anticommunist South Korean government.

The Korean War shaped North Korea as much as did its enduring cold war commitment to communism. The two Korean states (for that is essentially what they became) harbor deep distrust toward one another. Both Korean govern-ments, using the rationale of national security, adopted draconian measures to suppress dissent. Both governments devote a large share of their national income to maintain their military forces (an estimated 25 percent of the North's GNP compared with 5 percent of the South's much larger GNP).[14] Whereas the commitment of the United States to the defense of South Korea remained firm, North Korea could not count as heavily on the support of China and the Soviet Union, necessitating a policy of self-sufficiency in politics and national defense. Finally, the Korean War, even if it was viewed as a civil war in North Korea, placed North Korea firmly in the communist camp in the eyes of the rest of the world. Despite the desire of Koreans in both halves of the penin-sula to reunite, the two Koreas became caught on separate sides of the global struggle between communism and democracy. Only as the cold war ended forty years later did it become possible to view North Korea not as a frontline communist state but as a country that was being transformed into a dynastic kingdom under Kim Il Sung and his son.

Following the Korean War, Kim Il Sung's first order of business was to hold power by refusing to accept responsibility for starting the war. Three days after the armistice was signed, a show trial was convened to prosecute a dozen high party officials for allegedly aiding and abetting the enemy and plotting to replace the Kim regime with one headed by Pak Hon-yong, the leader of the southern communists. All twelve were convicted and presumably executed, as was Pak in a separate trial two years later.[15] Throughout the 1950s leaders of domestic political factions with links to the Russians (who had withdrawn in 1948) and to the Chinese (after they withdrew in 1958) were purged. Even some members of Kim's own guerrilla band who had fought alongside him in China during the Japanese occupation were purged, leaving Kim the undisputed master of his country. Throughout the cold war North Korea remained only loosely aligned with other communist states, favoring whichever country was willing to provide Pyongyang with economic and military aid.

While cleaning up the domestic political landscape, Kim directed the rebuilding of the North Korean economy following the Soviet strategy of mobilizing manpower and building heavy industry. Kim's faith in communist totalitarian methods of industrialization was not misplaced: until the 1970s North Korea's economy grew faster than South Korea's. As Kim's political and economic successes multiplied, he allowed (or encouraged) his propaganda organs to create an ever more elaborate cult of personality.

Rather than conforming to communist-style politics by choosing a successor from the party powerful, Kim followed the path of dynastic rulers by appointing his first son to succeed him. Widespread speculation among foreign observers centered on why Kim Jong Il became the chosen successor. The official North Korean explanation was that Kim Jong Il was better acquainted with his father's Juche philosophy than anyone else. Certainly Kim was a bright and energetic individual, a quick study and fond of art and amateur philosophizing. Yet he lacked one important attribute of leadership in a totalitarian state: charisma. Quite the contrary: he has always avoided public meetings, even on the most important state occasions. Within his coterie of followers he is feared, and by that token, not well liked. His younger brother (by his father's second marriage) was the more handsome and popular, but Confucian tradition dictates that the eldest son succeed the father. Official propaganda supports the assumption that the senior Kim desired above all to appoint a successor who would carry on his work and secure his reputation. Choosing his eldest son, who has the Confucian duty to obey his father's wishes, would seem the safest course. And so North Korea's fate was placed in the hands of someone who was so loyal to Kim Il Sung's flawed policies that—out of respect or out of fear—he continued those policies decades after they had lost their effectiveness. In a fitting homage to his father, Kim Jong Il in 1998 proclaimed that North Korea would revert to the economic policies of the 1950s, that is, mass mobilization, concentration on heavy industry, and increased ideological indoctrination. Thus has North Korea become a nation out of step with the times, following the dictates of a leader who, despite his formidable political skills, is living in a bygone era.

The Kim Il Sung Nation

Kim Il Sung's vision of his nation—what the North Korean press often refers to as the "Kim Il Sung nation"—was a combination of a Confucian kingdom and a twentieth-century totalitarian socialist state. There was never any question of adopting true socialism or communism. The North Korean ideological theorist Hwang Jang Yop, who escaped to South Korea in 1997, describes North Korea as a feudal state.[16] Kim Jong Il can call on the Korean tradition of Confucianism to induce the people to accept a strict hierarchical social order (masses, party cadres and, at the top, Kim himself) and to solicit absolute loyalty and respect for the ruler. Confucianism also grants to the ruler exclusive rights to contact foreigners and speak for the people. According to the benevolent values of Confucianism, the ruler must show concern for the people, as Kim Il Sung did when making on-the-spot guidance appearances. Kim's portly figure dressed like modern-day royalty in perfectly tailored, color-coordinated, Western-style business attire (by the 1980s he had discarded his Mao jacket) gave the poor farmers and factory workers a glimpse of the glory of their kingdom.

The North Korean people have been woefully deprived of the opportunity to advance socially and politically. When the Choson dynasty collapsed, Japan immediately took control over Korea, instituting its own autocratic regime. When the Japanese left, Kim Il Sung imported Stalinism. The North Korean people were never challenged to think for themselves. Many of those who came into contact with other societies, even as part of their assigned duties, were later purged or banished to the countryside. The top cadres who were permitted to stay in Pyongyang to work in foreign affairs were kept under strict surveillance. Even in the 1990s gaining a position in which one is able to contact the outside world is a hazardous affair: positions in foreign trade and diplomacy offer opportunities to accumulate wealth, but they also come with the constant danger of being purged.

In the early years, Kim Il Sung may have genuinely believed he could build an independent and strong nation by combining the methods of Stalin and the teachings of Confucius. He may have believed that a people inspired by his charismatic leadership could overcome any hardships and accomplish any goals he set for them. In the early years, when he was young and active, North Korea did make great strides. But beginning in the 1970s it became clear to objective observers that North Korea was going to fall far short of Kim's dreams. As the disparity between dream and reality grew, Kim distanced himself from the day-to-day affairs of his country, enjoying the role of a retired gentleman at his lavish country estates, meeting the occasional dignitary from second or third world countries, and letting his son run the country. The young Kim, growing up as a dictator's son who was denied nothing, placed even greater emphasis than his father on ideological indoctrination as the key to achieving North Korea's goals. He tried to run the country as he had run his personal affairs, by ordering people around. But the people failed to respond whole-heartedly to his ideological exhortations, and North Korea fell farther and farther behind South Korea.

North Korea is a land of illusions. An ideology that places the leader above the people and the nation. An economy built on the assumption that people can lead selfless, communitarian lives. A ruler and his top policymakers who rarely travel outside the country or meet foreigners. A military that boasts of being the mightiest in the world. A social control system that seeks to keep 23 million people isolated from the outside world. And a foreign policy based on the premise that by threatening other nations North Korea can become a respected member of the international community. Underlying these illusions is the desire to turn back the clock to a time when the prevailing form of soci-ety was the independent, largely self-sufficient state ruled by a king whose subjects believed in the notion of divine right of rule.

To be sure, the situation in North Korea is more complicated than this pic-ture. No individual or nation can exist for long by completely ignoring reality. Although members of the political elite in Pyongyang resist change, they are acutely aware of their nation's domestic and foreign problems, but they are plagued by fear and bafflement. Their supreme leader, Kim Jong Il, can dis-cover no way to extricate himself from his predicament. His associates fear that if they point out their leader's failures, they will lose their privileged posi-tions, be banished, or even executed. The consequence is policy paralysis.

All the while, 20 million North Koreans seek to survive, living their diffi-cult lives with the same hopes and fears, pleasures and pains of people everywhere. One of the defectors interviewed for this book observed that whereas many foreigners believe North Koreans live a life of drab uniformity, like every society North Korea is a human society in which people drink, dance, sing, fight, make love, and get divorced.[17] Although North Korea's problems are addressed as if they were the problems of a state rather than a people, in the final analysis North Korea is millions of human beings who have, in most cases through no fault of their own, fallen on exceedingly hard times.

For the ruling elite, especially the supreme leader, Kim Jong Il, the para-mount goal is to preserve and enhance political power. Any leader in any capital of the world can understand this motivation. Kim differs from most leaders in that his power is relatively unconstrained by any institutional checks and balances. And yet for all his power, he is a very insecure ruler because he knows his people are not satisfied. How to change or replace the Kim Jong Il regime is a question that foreign governments and organizations have grappled with for years. This question, which is at the heart of foreign policy toward North Korea, will be taken up in the final chapter of the book.

Before then, North Korea's economy, the nature of the leadership, and the policies the government employs to pursue domestic tranquility and national security must be studied. The dual themes of this book are persistence and illusion. Why does the North Korean regime persist in policies that have clearly failed to serve the welfare of the people and, consequently, which threaten the future of the regime? It will be suggested that part of the answer can be found in the tremendous difficulty of overcoming the inertia built up over many years and spreading throughout North Korean society. Another part of the answer is that the North Korean elite and the masses, cut off as they are from the international community, live in "a reality sealed off from the outside"—essentially, a fantasy world, where an autarkic, isolated existence seems possible.[18] To the extent that this view of North Korea is true, it can be predicted that even after the inevitable fall of the Kim regime and the extension of South Korean governance over the North, it will be many years before the North Korean people can function in a liberal, democratic society.

CHAPTER TWO

The Power and Poverty
of Ideology

Some countries are known for economic prosperity and others for military strength and still others for rich cultural assets. But our country is the only country known for its ideological power.[1]

The red electric torch glowing atop the 150-meter Tower of the Juche Idea in the heart of Pyongyang is a striking testimonial to the importance and omnipresence of ideology in North Korea. According to Carl J. Friedrich and Zbigniew Brzezinski, "It would be impossible to write a meaningful history of the USSR without giving sustained attention to ideological issues."[2] This is even more true of North Korea, whose ideology shares much in common with other communist ideologies. The difference is that under the custodianship of Kim Il Sung and Kim Jong Il the North Korean brand of ideology has been inflated beyond what was found even in the heyday of Stalin or Mao. Certainly no other country today puts as much effort into the production, elaboration, and dissemination of ideology as does North Korea.

To the extent that ideologies are "sets of ideas which have their unity not in the ideas themselves, but in the collective or individual unconscious," they can reveal important insights about the people who subscribe to them.[3] Ideology serves as a guide for behavior; it is, according to the North Korean press, "a compass showing the course for a country and its people to follow, a foundation on which an entire nation comes together in a wholehearted unity, and a banner of victory that leads a nation to infinite prosperity and development."[4] Ideology provides clues as to why North Korea has failed to pursue pragmatic domestic and foreign policies. In their extensive examination of North Korea, Robert A. Scalapino and Chong-Sik Lee note, "Ideology erects perimeters; it channels and interdicts as well as stimulates thought, and thus it inhibits any rapid adjustment to changing realities."[5] North Korea's unitary ideology is indeed a serious barrier to progress. As the French philosopher Alain said, "Nothing is more dangerous than an idea, when you have only one idea."[6] For North Koreans, that one idea is Juche. Article 3 of the socialist constitution proclaims, "The DPRK is guided in its activities by the Juche idea, a world outlook centered on people, a revolutionary ideology for achieving the independence of the masses of people."[7]

North Koreans proudly refer to Juche socialism as a thoroughly scientific theory, but Juche is not by any stretch of the imagination a set of empirically related propositions to be tested and then revised or discarded according to observations of reality. Even though Marx's predictions have fallen wide of the mark, Marxism-Leninism remains a cornerstone of North Korean ideology. North Korea's ideology is neither theory nor science but rather doctrine and dogma assumed to be true because of the authority from whence it comes. In North Korea, all ideology flows from the allegedly omniscient authority of the founder and his son; disputing or revising ideology thus constitutes an attack on their authority, inviting certain punishment. Ideologies and the myths associated with them are weapons of the political leaders and a prison in which they are confined. This truth helps explain why even though Kim Il Sung and his son created North Korea's ideology, they cannot easily adapt it to changing conditions.

A useful working definition of political ideology is "a belief system that explains and justifies a preferred political order for society ... and offers a strategy ... for its attainment."[8] The ideology of a totalitarian state like North Korea provides guidelines for virtually all fields of human endeavor, from poetry to potato farming. The ideology prominently includes ideas for transforming the nature of human beings and their society into a utopian community.[9] In this important sense it is revolutionary in nature, vigorously attacking the status quo. North Korea's ideology provides no rest for the weary, as one economic "speed battle" is followed by another, and the "victorious conclusion" of the "arduous march" ushers in a "forced march for final victory," which turns into a "march to paradise," even though paradise remains as distant as ever to the North Korean people. Only when they have been transformed into loyal followers of Kim Jong Il, when South Korea has been communized, and when the international system has been democratized will the North Korean people be permitted to rest. Certainly the march will be far longer and more arduous than Kim Il Sung expected in the first decade after he had taken control of North Korea and the international communist movement was gaining momentum.

North Korean ideology sounds strange to most foreigners. The myths embedded in North Korean ideology are backward-looking: stories "concerned with past events, giving them a specific meaning and significance for the present."[10] The myths are part fabrication, part reorganization, and part reinterpretation of historical facts. For example, the core communist myth is the Marxist model of history, a story of the irrevocable march of history culminating in a global classless society in which the storehouses are bursting with goods produced and distributed "from each according to his ability, to each according to his need." The uniquely North Korean myths overlaid on Marxism trace the history of North Korea from its alleged founding by Tangun, the offspring of a god and a bear-woman, to the coming of demigod Kim Il Sung and his revolutionary family.[11] The role of these myths is not to describe reality but to glorify tradition and inspire the masses.

North Korea's adherence to a failed and fantasized ideology is not as irrational as it might first appear if one distinguishes between what works for the masses and what serves the interests of the ruling elite. Ideology may have destroyed the economy and isolated the country, but it has strengthened the power of the Kim family by glorifying their leadership and by serving as a spiritual substitute for economic success, as the quotation at the beginning of the chapter illustrates.

Heeding Friedrich and Brzezinski's advice to give sustained attention to ideology, what should one look for in terms of linkage between ideology and life? North Korea's ideology has developed over half a century into such a fantastic set of assertions that it is difficult for outsiders to take them seriously—or to imagine that the North Korean people or their leaders do. Taken seriously or not, the people are forced throughout their lives to devote many hours a week to reading, memorizing, and discussing the teachings of Kim Il Sung and his son. To what extent is ideology an epiphenomenon, something separate from everyday concerns? A major hypothesis in this book is that ideology holds North Korea back from developing into a modern society.

Ideology must say something about how the leaders think, and about their estimation of the intellectual sophistication of their followers. As it has developed over the years, Juche reflects the changing concerns of the leaders, and the problems that they seek to solve in the path toward constructing their ideal of a totalitarian socialist state. Some problems, like poor worker motivation, are ever-present. Others, like grief over the loss of Kim Il Sung and a weakening loyalty to his son, are triggered by specific events.

As Juche has developed, it has addressed several major issues. First, the problem of maintaining North Korea's independence in the international community. Second, remolding people into ever-loyal disciples of the leader but at the same time giving them a sense of individual purpose as "masters of society." Third, glorifying the solidarity of the people as a modern Confucian national family around the party and its leader. Fourth, defending North Korea's brand of socialism in the face of declining living conditions and the collapse of the international communist bloc. And fifth, under increasingly miserable conditions in the wake of Kim Il Sung's death, giving people a reason to die, if not to live, for the regime.

Juche: The Early Years

Here is the North Korean socialist dream: a communal society, blessed with an abundance of goods produced and exchanged without the need for money. These happy people are bound together like a great national tribe, insulated from the economic and political strife of the international community by the fact that the nation is economically self-sufficient. Being productive and self-sufficient, the people are the equal of any nation on the globe, large or small. They envy no one, for they live in an earthly paradise.

The pair of ideas that form the basis of North Korea's utopian ideology are as appealing as they are impractical. Socialism (as a precursor of communism) is the method by which this paradise is to be achieved, and Juche is its guiding principle. Juche is the absolute given of North Korean life, the defining characteristic of the nation and of any "good" North Korean. A person without Juche is worthless; a state without Juche is a colony. Juche is North Korea's gift to the world, a world that is reluctant to accept it because (according to the North Koreans) the "imperialists" led by the United States are actively scheming to defeat Juche and make the working people slaves to the capitalists.

The essence of Juche is difficult to grasp, either because it is so simplistic as to be unbelievable or so complex and culture specific as to be untranslatable. A starting point is to define the core meaning as a combination of national self-reliance and Korean nationalism. Bruce Cumings, a scholar who has come closer than most Westerners to understanding Koreans, says of Juche that "it is less an idea than a state of mind. The term literally means being subjective where Korean matters are concerned, putting Korea first in everything."[12] Cumings adds, "The term is really untranslatable; for a foreigner its meaning is ever-receding, into a pool of everything that makes Koreans Korean, and therefore is ultimately inaccessible to the non-Korean."[13] Indeed, it may not be accessible even to many Koreans. Han Shik Park, a Korean-American academic who has specialized in the study of Juche, recounts an interview he had in 1981 with a Juche theoretician at Kim Il Sung University:

> In a three-hour marathon session with him, I was not only thoroughly frustrated by his lengthy reiteration of well-known propaganda lines, but I also had considerable difficulty in grasping the logical and philosophical aspects of the ideology. When he sensed that I was somewhat mystified by his exposition of the doctrine, he sought to comfort me by saying the idea is such a profound "eternal truth" (*yongsaeng pulmyol ui chilli*) that it is not meant to be fully comprehensible![14]

The phrase "eternal truth" that the North Korean used is the same phrase that (South) Korean Christians use when they refer to their religious beliefs. It may not be a coincidence that Kim Il Sung, the founder of North Korea and originator of Juche, came from a Christian family and thus recognized the persuasive power of Christian beliefs.

In an attempt to explain Juche to the modern-day surfer on the World Wide Web, the Korean Central News Agency has tried to clarify matters in its website (which, contrary to Juche logic, originates in Japan, owing to lack of computer infrastructure in North Korea):

> Juche is [a] Korean word. It means the subject in English. ["Korean subjectivity"?] "The revolution in each country should be carried out responsibly by its own people, the masters, in an independent manner, and in a creative way suitable [to] its specific conditions." It raised the fundamental question of philosophy by regarding man as the main factor, and elucidated the philosophical principle that man is the master of everything and decides everything.[15]

North Koreans have written volumes on Juche, prompting foreign observers to devote many articles to the concept as well. Arriving at a satisfying definition is difficult for at least two reasons. First, the Juche idea has gathered around it layers of meaning to adapt it to the changing needs of the ruling elite. Second, Juche is not a particularly profound or cohesive set of ideas. The core of the Juche idea is national pride, which is a laudable sentiment among any people, and especially appropriate for Koreans, who live in a land surrounded by greater powers. But national pride hardly counts as an original ideology. Juche ideology is credited to Kim Il Sung, who is characterized in the 1998 socialist constitution (and elsewhere) as "a genius ideological theoretician." The first syllable, *ju*, means "the main or fundamental" principle; the second syllable, *che*, means body or self or the foundation of something—the same as the Chinese word *ti* in the famous phrase, "Chinese learning for the foundation and Western learning for application."[16] Kim introduced Juche (the word had existed before but was given a new political meaning) in a speech to Korean Workers' Party (KWP) propaganda and agitation workers on December 28, 1955, during the early years when he was still working to eliminate potential political rivals. This speech has gained increasing importance in retrospect and may have undergone revisions in the intervening years to make it compatible with subsequent interpretations of Juche. It is not unusual in North Korea (as in the former Soviet Union and other totalitarian states) to revise original texts for later publication to make them consistent with more recent ideological thought or even to fabricate text and "discover" it many years later.[17] According to Suh Dae-Sook's biography of Kim Il Sung, some fifteen speeches referring to Juche that the North Korean press attributes to Kim from as far back as the 1930s are sheer fabrications, never having appeared until their publication in the 1970s. Looking back almost half a century to the 1955 speech, its title, "On Eliminating Dogmatism and Formalism and Establishing Juche in Ideological Work," is pure irony, for the imitation of foreign ways that Kim criticized has been replaced by a far more slavish adherence to his own failed Juche policies. The political context of the speech was Kim's campaign to purge political rivals, especially those in the Soviet and Chinese factions of his party, although criticism in the speech is primarily directed against the Soviet faction, since Stalin was already dead and Chinese troops who had participated in the Korean War were still in North Korea and would not be completely withdrawn until 1958.

Kim's speech sets forth the core Juche idea of national self-reliance and pride. North Korea must adapt Marxist-Leninist principles to Korean conditions, rather than swallow them whole: "We are not engaged in any other country's revolution, but solely in the Korean revolution."[18] Kim's appeal to nationalism is awkward in light of the fact that the Russians had backed his bid to rule North Korea in 1945, and the Chinese had saved the North Korean army from advancing UN troops in the Korean War. As a practicing communist, Kim attempts to reconcile nationalism with communist internationalism: "Internationalism and patriotism are inseparably linked with each other.... Loving Korea is just as good as loving the Soviet Union."[19] His rationale for this assertion is that by strengthening the revolution in

Korea, the international communist revolution is strengthened.[20] Kim's speech closes with two typically communist-utopian themes: an appeal to the people to have faith and optimism in the revolution, and—in anticipation of what was later to become the centerpiece and supreme irony of Juche—an appeal to the people to believe that power is in their hands, that they are "masters in everything."[21]

At its inception, Juche was pragmatic in two respects: as a political tool for Kim to preserve his power and as a declaration of North Korea's intention to adapt foreign imports to Korean conditions. In a phrase as pithy as the injunction China's Deng Xiaoping, another pragmatist, used years later, Kim says, "It does not matter whether you use the right hand or the left, whether you use a spoon or chopsticks at the table. No matter how you eat, it is all the same insofar as food is put into your mouth, isn't it?"[22] This sentiment has been periodically echoed, with an increasing lack of sincerity, as when Kim Jong Il in 1986 boasted that "the Juche idea categorically rejects narrow-minded chauvinism in the ideological domain. The Juche idea fairly evaluates and assimilates the ideas capable of making even the smallest contributions to enhancing man's position and role in the world, no matter which nation or people have evolved them."[23] But over the years the use of Juche as a means to legitimate the Kim dynasty has completely crowded out the pragmatic aspect of Juche. In fact, any idea not originating with the Kims, father or son, is condemned as heresy. Virtually every article in the North Korean press begins with the phrase, "As Kim Il Sung (or Kim Jong Il) has indicated," whether the article deals with pig farming or foreign policy.

The breadth of the Juche idea and the possibilities for its endless elaboration and application are revealed in a statement Kim Il Sung made in 1972 during an interview with members of the Japanese press: "You requested me to give a detailed explanation of the Juche idea. But there is no end to it. All the policies and lines of our Party emanate from the Juche idea and they embody this idea."[24] This admission, perhaps unwittingly, indicates how the Juche idea can be used as a tool for political dueling and social control by making the correct interpretation of Juche the criterion for patriotism.[25] North Korea's prison camps are filled with people who, in a moment of frustration or forgetfulness, criticized the prevailing Juche line.

It is easier to understand North Korean's dedication to Juche if one remembers that it provides an implicit criticism of South Korea. The opposite of self-reliance is *sadaejuui*, translated as "servility," "reliance on others," or "flunkeyism." As long as U.S. troops remain in South Korea, North Korea can hold the moral high ground by claiming to be the only independent state on the Korean peninsula. Of course there are other measures of dependence, such as reliance on foreign powers for economic aid and military support. On these measures North Korea has fallen woefully short of the Juche idea. But "on the ground" North Korea has Juche and South Korea does not.

For North Koreans, Juche is inseparable from socialism, considered the only means by which the masses can gain their independence. Whatever changes have been made in the Juche concept over the years, North Korea's commitment to socialism as an organizational principle has never changed. By the late 1950s all industrial facilities were state owned and most farms had been transformed into party-guided cooperatives, although the goal of transforming the cooperatives into state-run farms (known as "resolving the rural problem") has yet to be achieved.

Juche Becomes a Philosophy of Man

Not content with proposing a practical guide for the adaptation of Marxism-Leninism to Korean conditions, the Kims expanded the Juche idea into a philosophy of man, introducing a basic contradiction with Marxism-Leninism. Marx's historical insight was that social and economic conditions (feudalism, capitalism, socialism) shaped human beings. Structural "contradictions" in one stage of economic development inevitably give rise to a dialectical resolution achieved in the next stage. Only with the establishment of communism, in which there would be no competing classes—the working class having taken control of the means of production—would contradictions disappear. Kim Il Sung, and more important Kim Jong Il, attributed free will to human beings, thereby freeing them from the restraints of economic and political forces. In his published answers to questions submitted by the major Japanese daily *Mainichi Shimbun* in 1972, Kim Il Sung explained, "The idea of Juche means that the masters of the revolution and the work of construction are the masses of the people and that they are also the motive force of the revolution and the work of construction. In other words, one is responsible for one's own destiny and one has also the capacity for hewing out one's own destiny."[26]

Throughout his lifetime, Kim struggled to imbue the cadres and the masses with the selfless can-do spirit of Juche socialism, yet he never figured out how to make people altruistic. Kim's quixotic solution to the motivational problem is to posit that man is the center of the universe, needing no motivation other than his own innate desire to work to the maximum and contribute to society.

By the 1970s two catchwords had appeared in the Juche lexicon: "independence" and "creativity." "Independence is what keeps man alive. If he loses independence in society, he cannot be called a man; he differs little from an animal."[27] Independence is achieved through individual creativity: people solving problems on their own. Both themes can be traced back to Kim's 1955 speech. The independence theme is the core of the original Juche concept. Creativity, that is, each individual adapting work principles to the situation in order to discover solutions, is the means to independence. This call for creativity was at best insincere and at worst delusional. Under socialism's "democratic centralism" the party provides guidelines for all aspects of life, and any adaptations of these guidelines to specific circumstances risk party censure. Kim's creativity and independence themes are not new or unique to communist thought. In the former Soviet Union the masses had also been urged to employ their "creative energy and initiative" as masters of their fate under the strict guidance of the leader and the party.[28] In North Korea, censure for transgressing against the party is a fact of life, where everyone from the lowliest peasant to the most decorated general must submit to an almost daily ritual of other- and self-criticisms employing the standard of whether his or her actions have conformed to the Kims' interpretation of Juche. The party rules on the correctness of the adaptation; whether or not desired results are obtained by the action is of secondary concern. Everything is recorded in one's personnel record for possible use in the future. As the sole authorized interpreters of Juche, only the two Kims are exempt from criticism.

Since it has always been apparent that most people are poorly motivated by the prospect of working for the group rather than for themselves, they must be constantly persuaded of the value of collectivism. The great problem of the Korean revolution became how to inculcate Juche ideology into people, for Kim was not simply building the nation, but "remolding" people.[29] A new type of Korean must emerge, just as Soviet leaders over the years sought to create a new Soviet man, and Mao envisioned a new Chinese. Kim had been able to motivate his small band of guerrilla fighters; could he motivate an entire nation in peacetime?

With the introduction of the idea of the "sociopolitical life," Kim moved Juche closer to a religion. "We might say that the socio-political life is more valuable to a man than physical life.... If he is forsaken by society and deprived of political independence, though he seems alive, he is virtually dead as a social human being. That is why the revolutionaries [for example, Kim's guerrilla band] deem it far more honorable to die in the fight for freedom than to keep themselves alive in slavery."[30] This appeal for a collectivist spirit helps clarify what is meant by independence in North Korea: not individual freedom but a national independence that can only be achieved by people working together under party guidance.

Kim Jong Il Interprets Juche

Thanks to the efforts of Kim Jong Il, Juche was transformed from a nationalistic ruling ideology to a cult ideology, marking a break between political persuasion and religion. Kim Jong Il, who worked in the KWP's Propaganda and Agitation Department early in his career, was secretly and unofficially designated as Kim Il Sung's successor in 1972 or 1973, and formally introduced to the nation as successor in 1980.[31] Not being a soldier, a statesman, or an economist, the junior Kim's self-appointed role was to interpret and propagandize Juche ideology and oversee cultural affairs. Once he got his hands on the concept, Juche became increasingly alienated from the real world, more "pure ideology" than an "implementing ideology."[32] Kim claims authorship of more than 400 papers, many dealing explicitly with Juche and almost all of them touching on the subject. Unconstrained by the need to achieve results in economic construction, since he was accountable to no one except his father, Kim made Juche an article of faith rather than a guide to practice.

Whereas Marxism was said to be correct in predicting the inevitable triumph of communism over capitalism, according to Kim Jong Il the Marxist materialistic outlook "was not free from historical limitations."[33] It was not until his father formulated the Juche philosophy of man that Marxism-Leninism was perfected. Kim Jong Il observed that "man is neither a purely spiritual being nor a simple biological being. Man is a social being who lives and acts in social relationships."[34] This revelation is cited as the basis for the claim that Juche is "an absolutely scientific" theory. "The chuche [or Juche] idea indicated, for the first time in history, that a man has a sociopolitical integrity, as well as a physical life. . . . True human life . . . can only be realized admirably in a socialist society based on collectivism. In this society, people are free from all manner of exploitation and oppression, domination and subordination and can lead an independent and creative life."[35]

Like his father, Kim junior wrestled with the problem of reconciling the claim that Juche was man centered with the Marxist idea that objective economic conditions determined the nature of the social consciousness. In a 1986 talk, "On Some Problems of Education in Juche Idea," Kim invents this unsatisfying explanation:

Some officials have a misunderstanding that the Juche philosophy has nothing to do with the general principles of dialectical materialism because it is a man-centered philosophy. . . . It is clear that [Juche] conforms to the basic principles of materialism and dialectics that man, the most developed material being, holds the position of master towards the less developed material beings.[36]

Thus the insight of the human-centered nature of Juche made it complete and self-sufficient: "Our party does not need any other ideological system than the system of the Juche idea."[37] And since unity is posited as one of the key strengths of North Korea, the entire nation must be "dyed in the same ideological color." Reference to Marxism-Leninism was dropped from the 1980 charter of the Korean Workers' Party and from the 1992 version of the constitution, which states: "The Democratic People's Republic of Korea makes Juche ideology, a revolutionary ideology with a people-centered view of the world that aims towards the realization of the independence of the masses, the guiding principle of its actions." Moreover, it turns out that the only hope the people have of correctly understanding and implementing Juche is to follow the party and the leader. "For the popular masses to be an independent subject of the revolution, they must be united into one organization with one ideology under the leadership of the party and the leader. Only the masses, who are united organizationally and ideologically, can shape their destiny independently and creatively."[38]

Bruce Cumings has maintained that North Korea's version of socialism with Confucian overtones is a form of state corporatism. In the Confucian tradition, society is viewed as one big family headed by a wise, stern, benevolent father to whom unconditional respect and gratitude are owed. In Juche terminology, "The leader, the party and the people form one sociopolitical organism, and share the same destiny."[39] The leader is said to be the "nerve center" and "top brain" of the nation. "Children love and respect their parents not because their parents are always superior to those of others or because the children receive benefits from them, but because the parents are the benefactors of their lives who gave birth to them and have brought them up. . . . All the communist revolutionaries of Korea have been accorded immortal political integrity by the fatherly leader. . . . Therefore, the loyalty of our party members and working people to the great leader is . . . unconditional."[40] And if the leader is the father of the people, their mother is the party: "If politics of love and trust is to be exercised in socialist society, the socialist party in power must be built into a motherly party."[41]

As life became more difficult for the North Korean people in the 1980s and 1990s, a "politics of benevolence" theme was emphasized. According to Juche, the people are "heaven." Hence the party and the leader must listen to them to learn of their needs and wishes. In communist jargon this is known as the "mass line," the one breath of democracy in the system. "The working class party must always go among the masses and listen to their desires." In a capitalist society, where individual motivation is provided by money, people are treated as commodities. Under socialism, people are to be treated as the masters, with the party and the leader as their servants. "Serve the people" has been one of Kim Jong Il's mantras. As for the leader, "In order to realize genuinely benevolent politics in socialist society, a political leader who unfailingly loves the people must come forward. A political leader of socialism should be a master in leadership but, first of all, he must be a man of virtue who loves the people boundlessly."[42]

The correct Juche view of the leader is known as the "revolutionary view of the leader." In a scripted question-and-answer program broadcast on North Korean television, this view is explained, "Above all, the leader [*suryong*— absolute leader, a phrase reserved for Kim Il Sung] holds an absolute status that cannot be compared to anyone else in the revolutionary struggle. So-called extraordinary individuals have existed throughout history, but they have remained only individuals, they cannot be compared to the leader."[43] Just as socialist consciousness does not automatically arise from social conditions, a true socialist leader does not arise from social conditions:

> The previous theories [for example, Marxism-Leninism] said that only if an historical inevitability is created on the basis of an objective condition, a leader will necessarily emerge. . . . This kind of opinion is theoretically wrong, and is practically very extremely harmful. . . . The ideology about the nature of a revolutionary view of the leader elucidates that the leader is not any individual, but one who possesses extraordinary traits and qualifications, which just any individual cannot have; and because of this, he holds an absolute status and plays a decisive role in the revolutionary struggle. . . . Today, the world's people are consistently envious of our people, calling our people the people blessed with the leader.[44]

The leader is virtually a divine gift to the people, like the divine right of kings in Western tradition and the Confucian belief that a virtuous king ruled with the mandate of heaven. There is no social contract between leader and follower, and loyalty should not be made contingent on anything the leader does. Absolute loyalty, love, and obedience is to be given unconditionally to the leader—a view of the leader as one who transforms followers rather than who must please and satisfy them.[45]

Consistent with the Juche view of leadership, in 1997 Kim Jong Il acceded to the general secretaryship of the party not by election, as provided for in the charter of the Korean Workers' Party, but by "declaration" of the KWP's Central Committee and Central Military Commission, following a series of staged meetings throughout the country in which resolutions recommending Kim Jong Il's election received "unanimous approval."[46]

Through propaganda, the reclusive Kim Jong Il assumed the role of benevolent leader. While his father the "great leader" was alive, the junior Kim was called "dear leader," a more familiar and endearing form of address. To prove himself a "dear leader," Kim Jong Il presented himself as a promoter of the people's standard of living, for example, by organizing the August Third Movement, whereby consumer goods would be manufactured locally. In 1993 the North Korean propaganda machine began to characterize Kim Jong Il's ruling style as one of "benevolence," "boldness." and "broad scale," reminiscent of earlier campaigns describing the peasant soldier Kim Il Sung as personifying the Confucian traits of benevolence and virtue.[47] Certainly one indication of the younger Kim's boldness was his adoption, after his father's death, of the appellation "respected and beloved general," in the face of strong evidence that he had no military training and was neither respected nor loved by his countrymen. Kim Jong Il's love and concern are said to be all-encompassing. He "respects the aged fighters," "regards young functionaries . . . as precious treasures of the revolution." "He is taking good care of people from different strata—including workers, farmers and intellectuals," and "especially, the dear comrade leader is looking after those who have a shameful past."[48] Not to put too fine a point on the matter, Kim Jong Il "put[s] up the people as the most beautiful and excellent beings in the world and deeply worships them."[49]

Kim Jong Il's cult of personality has grown apace since his father's death in 1994. Early on Kim Il Sung had boasted that his family, as far back as the nineteenth century, was a heroic revolutionary family, his purpose being to establish a ruling dynasty that would make his own position unassailable and guarantee his son's succession. Within months of taking the post of KWP general secretary in October 1997, Kim Jong Il's propaganda people began a campaign to place his diseased mother, Kim Jong Suk, in the first rank of revolutionary immortals, completing the roster of the "three generals" of Mount Paektu: father, son, and now mother (Kim Il Sung's second wife, who is living, is a political nonperson). The little Kim was born to the purple. "Slogan trees," whose bark is said to have been carved with slogans by Kim Il Sung's band of revolutionary fighters in the 1930s and 1940s, are still being "discovered" (that is, carved). These slogans "prove that the succession to the cause of the Korean revolution was ensured in those days."[50] Examples of carvings lauding the "bright star" Kim Jong Il who was destined to succeed his father, the "sun," include "Birth on Mount Paektu of the Bright Star, Heir to General Kim Il Sung" and "Longevity and Blessing to the Bright Star above Mount Paektu Who Will Shine with the Beam of the Sun." Granite mountainsides in North Korea are similarly defaced with propaganda slogans lauding the two Kims.

Juche on the Defensive

The Marxist myth of the inevitable victory of socialism was seriously damaged when the communist governments of Eastern Europe and the Soviet Union collapsed in the late 1980s and early 1990s. First the North Korean elites, and later the masses, had to be given an explanation. On May 5, 1991, Kim Jong Il gave a talk to senior party members, "Our Socialism for the People Will Not Perish," in which he rebuts the criticisms that the capitalist democracies were leveling at socialism. [51] On the alleged superiority of capitalism: "The imperialists and reactionaries, loudly advertising the 'advantage' of private ownership, are urging socialist countries to abandon social ownership and restore private ownership. . . . The people in our country experienced through their actual lives that social ownership alone provides them with an abundant and cultured life." On alleged human rights violations: "In our socialist society which regards man as most precious, human rights are firmly guaranteed by law; even the slightest practice infringing upon them is not tolerated. In our country all people's rights ranging from the rights to employment, food, clothing and housing to the rights to free education and medical care are fully guaranteed." On alleged restrictions of political freedom: "The imperialists and reactionaries disparage political life in the working-class party and other political organizations led by the party as if it were the 'restraint' of freedom . . . If people in socialist society do not lead political life properly in the working-class party and other political organizations led by the party, they cannot preserve their socio-political integrity." On alleged lack of ideological freedom: "The U.S. imperialists and their stooges are saying that we have no ideological 'freedom'. . . . Our people have accepted the Juche idea . . . as their conviction, of their own accord, and from their vital need."

If socialism offers such benefits, why has it yielded to capitalism in other countries? "Of course it is not easy for the revolutionary idea of the working class to hold undivided sway in socialist society because this society still retains survivals of obsolete ideas and is subject to the ideological and cultural infiltration of imperialism. Although man's ideological consciousness is influenced by socio-economic conditions, the establishment of a new socio-economic system does not change people's ideological consciousness automatically."

The following year, as the "yellow wind of capitalism" continued to blow in North Korea's direction, Kim delivered another major address in defense of socialism.[52] After reminding his audience, "It is an inexorable law of historical development that mankind advances toward socialism," he addressed the question of how to view "the recent frustration of socialism and the revival of capitalism in some of those countries which had been advancing along the road to socialism." "The path to socialism is an untrodden path that has to be blazed" and "therefore, difficulties and trials are inevitable . . . and an unexpected situation may also crop up." "The frustration of socialism . . . is only a local and passing phenomenon. However, we can never regard this as an accidental phenomenon, nor can we consider that this has been caused merely by an external factor."

Kim continued, "As the great leader always says, when anything is wrong with us, we must find the reason in ourselves, not elsewhere. . . . The basic reason for the frustration of socialism in some countries which had been building socialism is that they did not put the main emphasis on strengthening the motive force of building socialism and on enhancing its role because they failed to understand [that is, preserve] the essence of socialism by centering on the popular masses." Marxism, it seems, was a good basis for establishing socialism but not for continuing the revolution. Socialist leaders in other countries had concerned themselves only with the material, failing to transform the mental states of their people. "It is wrong to think that a change in the social system and material conditions will inevitably be followed by a change in the ideological consciousness of people." "The main emphasis in the ideological revolution should be put on educating everyone to remain boundlessly faithful to the party and the leader and to serve the masses devotedly."

Given the inherent weakness of socialism compared with capitalism (as it would seem), political pluralism cannot be tolerated. "Historical experience shows clearly that if anti-socialist ideas are disseminated by liberalizing ideology, and the activities of anti-socialist parties are guaranteed through the tolerance of 'multi-party democracy,' the class enemies and reactionaries will raise their heads, commit anti-socialist acts and come to drive the working-class party out of power." "The socialism of a country will ruin itself without even exchanging one gunshot in confrontations with imperialists no matter how strong its economic power and military capacity are."[53] That is, ideological change provokes political change, which in turn threatens the regime.[54]

To prevent socialism from being polluted by capitalism, "In socialist society, transitional society where the class struggle continues, the state must also exercise dictatorship against the anti-socialist elements." "If we weaken the dictatorial function of the government . . . we can not provide the people with democratic freedom and rights, defend our revolutionary achievements and we can leave the socialist system itself endangered."[55]

"Socialism in our own style" (reminiscent of a similar idea that had been adopted by the Soviet Union years earlier) became the new slogan in the late 1980s, as North Korea sought to distance itself from other socialist and formerly socialist countries—in fact, from everyone. In a 1997 work, "On Preserving the Juche Character and National Character of the Revolution and Construction," Kim sounded a strong nationalistic note, erecting an ideological wall around North Korea. "The Juche idea clarified that the country and nation are the basic unit for shaping the destiny of the masses." This idea replaces the Marxist principle that "the working class has no motherland." What "socialism in our own style" means (apart from being autarkic and totalitarian) is of little consequence. The point is that North Korea's brand of socialism is not to be lumped together with the socialisms that have already collapsed or are in the process of collapsing.

Resisting Imperialist Pollution

Inevitably, word of the changes occurring in other socialist countries has begun to permeate North Korea's borders, finally coming to the attention even of farmers in the remote rural areas. How is this news to be handled? One of the paradoxes of socialism is that, despite its proponents' claim of superiority to individualistic capitalism, practicing socialists tend to lapse in their faith. After an early burst of enthusiasm in the 1950s, a time when forced collectivism in North Korea imposed order on the society and economy, producing remarkable economic gains, cracks in the socialist economy began to appear, widening as the years passed. It turned out that the selfish nature of human beings was not so easily changed. North Korea's leaders have attributed the instability of socialist ideology to three circumstances: individualist ideas are still harbored in the unreformed masses; the imperialists are craftily seeking to overthrow the new socialist order; and the imperialists' agents (that is, domestic elements critical of the Kim regime) seek to undermine socialism from within.

Until socialism began to collapse in Europe in the late 1980s, campaigns to combat and eliminate individualism were undertaken as a form of rear-guard action, a matter of weeding out hostile elements and drumming the virtues of socialism into the masses. But the downfall of socialism abroad demonstrated how shallow socialism's roots were. Kim Jong Il began to devote more attention to reinforcing the faith. The campaign to demonstrate the superiority of socialism employed three themes: the shortcomings of capitalism; the narcotic allure of capitalism; and the consequences of recidivism in the former socialist states.

First, the sum and substance of capitalism's shortcoming is the "bourgeois mentality": an individualistic and egoistic striving for money. Capitalist society is frequently described as following the law of the jungle in which human "wolves" prey on one another in a state of anarchy, with the powerful surviving and the weak perishing in the vicious pursuit of money. Human relations and culture are dead. The workers live short, brutish, meaningless lives. Unemployment is endemic; those lucky enough to have a job work for slave wages. The weakest members of society, the children, suffer most. Since no human law or order is imposed on society, evils proliferate: murder, robbery, fraud and swindling, lust, depravity, and dissipation are on the short list. Most important, people in a capitalist society have no control over their lives; they are "latter-day slaves to the capitalist owners of production."[56]

Even in North Korea's controlled information environment the people, especially the elite, have heard rumors of the more glamorous aspects of the outside world. To lessen the impact of this information, the party has resorted to the technique of attitude inoculation, admitting that capitalist society has at least the semblance of economic success and political freedom but warning that appearances are deceiving.[57] For example, the argument is made that whereas capitalists may enjoy a more lavish lifestyle than North Koreans, they are spiritually impoverished. As for the apparent wealth of capitalist states, only a small core of capitalists, owning most of the property, are said to enjoy such wealth. Thus if a North Korean should hear of the bustling capitalist cities with their gleaming buildings and streets full of cars, they should infer that these cities are populated by the lucky few. Obviously a contradiction lurks within this argument, since many buildings and cars presuppose many owners or renters. When a North Korean delegate to the Red Cross talks visited Seoul in 1972, he accused the South Koreans of collecting all the cars in the country to put on Seoul's streets to impress their guests; Lee Bum Suk, a South Korean delegate to the talks, facetiously answered that they had also put wheels on the buildings to bring them into Seoul.[58]

Another shortcoming attributed to capitalism is that its freedoms are specious. As for freedom of speech, North Koreans are told, again somewhat contradictorily, that the ruling capitalist class "ensures unlimited freedom for the ideological activities to champion and propagate the bourgeois ideas which represent its class interests" but "mercilessly suppress[es] such ideas as are considered to be a threat to its ruling system."[59]

Capitalism has been likened to a drug which will paralyze the political consciousness of the North Korean people.[60] An article in the party newspaper *Nodong Sinmun*, "The Imperialists' Wily Strategy of Disintegration," explains, "The main object of this strategy is the mind of people. In other words, imperialists are seeking to get the normally sound mind of people in revolutionary and progressive countries to degenerate."[61] A North Korean who first encounters, say, the wealth of the average South Korean citizen (who is supposed to be an impoverished slave) is likely to be startled and confused. But the inoculation prepares him by providing a ready-made "narcotic" explanation for his confusion. Capitalist ideas are said to have long-term effects, crowding out socialist ideas. Kim Jong Il explains, "[Capitalist ideas] destroy [North Koreans'] national culture and paralyze the consciousness of national autonomy and the revolutionary spirit."[62] It is dangerous to yield even slightly to the capitalist's temptations, because "if one retreats one step from the imperialists, one is doomed to retreat two more steps, and one will be finally forced to retreat 100 steps. If one makes one concession on one thing today, one will have to make a concession on everything tomorrow."[63]

Yet attributing such potency to the drug of capitalism raises a troublesome issue: if the drug is so powerful, if it has already intoxicated most of the socialist countries, how are the North Korean people supposed to resist it? As the international situation worsened for North Korea in the 1990s, Kim Jong Il tried to tone down the threat by teaching that capitalism is not to be feared: "Imperialism is by no means an object of fear; it is doomed as the refuse of history. If you are afraid of confrontation with imperialism and abandon the anti-imperialist struggle, you will never free yourselves from its domination and control. The revolutionary parties and peoples must see through the vulnerabilities of imperialism."[64]

The third means of demonstrating the superiority of socialism is to point to the plight of those who have abandoned it. According to North Korean propaganda, the Soviet Union and Eastern Europe sowed the wind and reaped the whirlwind. "Former socialist countries drove their economies into catastrophic crises by bringing in the capitalist economic system and management style under an illusion about them. . . . They do not operate the economy or man-

age production under unified state plans. Instead, they go their own ways producing anything they find profitable, changing production at will and thus
plunging the national economy into chaos."[65] Of course, North Korea's economy by this time was moribund, as any North Korean could clearly see. Could
things be worse elsewhere? Yes they could: "Workers are forced to give capitalists all their labor for their pursuit of profits . . . and many of them are sold
to capitalist countries as latter-day slaves."[66] It is said that specially made videos
of life scenes in postcommunist economies, depicting former high-level officials selling hot dogs on the street, are widely shown.[67]

To appreciate the argument that foreign capitalism is poison, it is necessary
to recall North Korea's history. Before liberation most people did live a relatively miserable existence, often lacking adequate food, clothing, and housing,
just as they do today. The difference is that in the past they worked for Korean
or Japanese landlords, whereas today they work for themselves, that is, for the
government. Life may be the same, but its interpretation is different, illustrating the philosopher Gilbert Ryle's definition of myth as "the presentation of
facts belonging to one category in the idioms appropriate to another."[68]

Much of North Korean propaganda, like good propaganda anywhere, is
exaggeration built around a kernel of truth. Capitalism does have flaws, the
capitalists do indeed desire to bring their market system to the socialist countries, and the newly reformed economies of the former communist states are
certainly struggling. At times, North Korean propaganda takes a bolder tack
by turning the truth on its head and then accusing the capitalists of lying. The
greatest falsehood, which many defectors say simply stunned them when they
learned the truth, is that the Korean War was triggered by an American–South
Korean invasion of the North. To keep the people from ever again trusting
Americans, North Korean propaganda warns, "By 'peace' the imperialists
mean aggression and war, by 'disarmament' they mean arms buildup and by
'détente' they mean tension."[69] According to this logic, the more cooperative,
helpful, and peace loving the capitalists seem, the more deceiving and aggressive they are.

The portals through which foreign ideology and culture can flow into North
Korea are so varied that the only means of keeping out all foreign ideas is to
completely cut the people off from the outside world. The North Korean government has come closer than any other modern government to achieving this
goal. Yet a little information does seep in. The authorities have warned against
pollution from radio (dials on North Korean radios are fixed, but some people alter their radios and manage to receive foreign broadcasts), films, music
(although South Korean songs are very popular in North Korea), dance, liter-

ature, tourists, economic and cultural exchange delegations, foreign aid teams, and foreign business people.

Much as the regime desires to isolate its people, the need for foreign aid, business investment, and tourism revenues has provided a modest opening for information to flow into the country. Realizing that acceptance of foreign aid is an explicit admission of the failure of Juche, and fearing that the people will begin to wonder whether the capitalist foreign aid donors are as evil as they are supposed to be, the government has mounted a vigorous campaign to explain the nature of capitalist foreign aid. In a major talk, Kim Jong Il said:

> Aggression and plunder are the real nature of imperialism. No matter how the international situation may change, the dominationist ambition of the imperialists will not change. Nothing is more foolish and dangerous than pinning hopes on the imperialist 'aid,' unable to see through the aggressive and predatory nature of imperialism. The imperialist 'aid' is a noose of plunder and subjugation aimed at robbing ten and even a hundred things for one thing that is given.[70]

This theme is constantly presented to the North Korean people, embellished to make the message more vivid: "A huge monster called imperialism tries all kinds of magic to catch countries moving toward independence with a fishing rod of temptation. The market economy is one of the fishing rods of temptation. Hanging from the fishhook are two specious baits called 'economic cooperation' and 'aid.'"[71]

If North Korea's agricultural sector improves to the extent that people can survive at a subsistence level with domestic harvests supplemented by Chinese aid, the contradiction of accepting capitalist foreign aid may disappear. But North Korea's ideologues have dug a deeper hole for themselves in their attitude toward capitalist trade and investment. While vigorously soliciting foreign business deals (and trying to keep foreign business segregated from the mainstream economy), the authorities warn their people to treat all foreigners with suspicion:

> Technical cooperation, joint ventures, and joint management are frequently used in developing economic relations between countries. Such economic exchanges bring in various delegations, inspection teams, and visitation delegations. In such cases, scientists, technicians, and a certain number of personnel will stay in other countries for a short or long time. Waiting for this critical moment, the imperialists have slyly placed impure elements in delegations, groups of visitors, inspecting teams, tourists

entering other countries, and manipulated them in order to use them to infiltrate ideological culture. These people cunningly maneuver to create a fantasy about capitalism through contacts with the people in a given country.[72]

Juche *in Extremis*

As the economy ground to a halt in the 1990s and hundreds of thousands of North Koreans faced hunger, disease, and death, the North Korean media redoubled their emphasis on the importance of relying on ideology to effect a turnaround in the economy and to bolster morale. Economic managers were urged to mobilize "inner reserves," a resource never clearly identified. "The reserves for production growth are in the heads of the people. When functionaries and working people are motivated to generate new ideas, reserves will emerge from here and there as a matter of course and the work of exploring and enlisting reserves could take firm root as people's own work."[73] This loaves-and-fishes approach was the best economic plan the government could come up with. Unfortunately, it contradicted the long-held policy of democratic centralism, whereby the people were expected to follow unquestioningly the orders of the party and in turn receive its benefits. Kim Jong Il's instruction to party officials to "nudge the masses to handle enterprise management" was unlikely to produce results after years of collectivization.

To breathe new life into the discouraged masses, the martial themes of the "red flag" and the "arduous march" were emphasized. Although references to the red banner or red flag of communism had been as common in North Korea as in other communist countries, an ideology taking that name apparently first appeared in the 1996 New Year's joint editorial, "Let Us Advance Vigorously in the New Year, Flying the Red Flag."[74]

The road to victory would not be easy: "[the revolutionaries] sacrifice themselves on the glorious road of revolution with a clean revolutionary conscience because they also firmly believe that the revolutionary cause led by their leader is most just."[75] As for the Arduous March, as late as October of 1997, it was "the unshakable determination of our party to bring the 'Arduous March' to a victorious end this year without fail,"[76] but as North Korea entered another hungry winter, the only thing that ended was the Arduous March, to be replaced by the "forced march to final victory" in the new year, which was later optimistically referred to as the "march to paradise."

In recognition of the people's discouragement, party organizations were urged to "spruce up the streets of their towns and villages, their homes, and their workplaces all the more and lead a more cultured and aesthetic life. By so doing, we will make the whole society be firmly dominated by a merry and lively atmosphere to suit the demands of the realities of the new age of the juche-oriented revolution we are in."[77] Perhaps the most pathetic ideological campaign during the lean years of the 1990s was the attempt to turn people's attention away from their miserable physical existence and toward the hereafter, an admission that North Koreans had more to die for than to live for. Typical slogans included "living today for tomorrow," "devote everything to handing over greater and more brilliant assets for the next generations," and "the more our generations undergo sufferings and shed sweat, the happier our future generations will be."[78]

As living conditions failed to improve approaching the millennium, with Kim Jong Il presumably growing more concerned about the legitimacy of his rule and the possibility that foreign powers would take advantage of North Korea's growing weakness, the guns-and-bombs-to-protect-the-leader campaign was intensified, reminiscent of the Kamikaze ethic employed by Japan in the final days of World War II. A graphic rendering is the following: "Self-detonating explosion [chap'ok] demands a resolute and pathetic decision [pijanghan kyolsim]. The spirit of suicidal explosion can be cherished only by those who thoroughly resolve to voluntarily choose death for the sake of the party and the leader."[79]

Believing in Juche

It is easy for outsiders to criticize Juche for its lack of validity, internal logic, and value as a practical guide for living. But how do the North Koreans view Juche? By forcing people to engage in endless study and self-criticism, Kim Il Sung and Kim Jong Il have tried to create a new socialist human being who is infinitely loyal to the leader and the party, but how well have they succeeded?

This is a complex question, because at the very least one must distinguish among beliefs in different components of Juche thought on the part of different segments of North Korean society. A similar question has been asked about the dedication of the citizens of former communist regimes in Eastern Europe and the Soviet Union to their ideology, and the answers to that question may shed some light on the North Koreans' depth of faith in Juche, despite obvious differences in culture and circumstances. Although commitment to socialism was strong in the Soviet Union in the 1950s, by the 1960s a strong note of criticism was discernible, coming first from Soviet intellectuals.[80] In East Germany in the 1980s the breakdown in belief in Soviet-imposed communist ideology was becoming apparent. Reinhart Schönsee and Gerda Led-erer describe the commitment to official ideology of five political classes in East Germany.[81] The leadership elite (nomenklatura) were cynical; the bureau-crats and intellectuals, some of whom were directly responsible for creating and disseminating ideology, engaged in doublethink in order to outwardly sup-port the ideology that guaranteed their special privileges; the middle-class professionals believed even less in the ideology, although they too were aware of the advantages to be gained by supporting the status quo; the masses out-wardly accepted the ideology but offered passive resistance to its teachings by refusing to live like "good" communists; the outcast class met secretly to com-plain about the system. Thus an entire political-social structure was grounded on the false premise that people believed in communism. Only the outcasts showed any form of resistance—a resistance that would later grow into broad social pressure for change. North Korea differs from Eastern Europe and the former Soviet Union in at least one important respect; namely, the greater social control that the government exercises over the people prevents the formation of organized resistance groups.

The main goals of the interviews of defectors conducted for this book were to assess belief in Juche and satisfaction with the Kim Jong Il regime. Even among a group of only twenty defectors differences of opinion existed about the beliefs of the general population, so the conclusions drawn in this chap-ter should be treated as hypotheses. To simplify matters, the beliefs of two social groups—the masses and the elite—on the following dimensions of Juche will be considered: socialism; Juche national self-reliance and independence; peo-ple as the masters of society; the importance of the sociopolitical life; the revolutionary view of the leader; belief in the personality cults of Kim Il Sung and Kim Jong Il; and confidence in the future of socialism.

The Masses

Despite boasts made in the North Korean press that the entire North Korean people are heart and soul behind Kim Jong Il and the party, continual calls in the press for greater efforts at ideological education indicate an absence of total commitment. This conclusion is supported by testimony from defectors. It seems that the average North Korean citizen believes socialism as an economic model is superior to capitalism (which has not been experienced) and that the capitalists are vigorously working to subvert socialism in the few countries in which it remains. Some defectors to South Korea, even after many years, voice strong complaints about the capitalist system and the materialism of South

Korean society. One defector complained that the South Korean people lie, act aggressively, and spend money with abandon. He said that although his relatives in South Korea knew of his defection, not one offered a penny to help him get on his feet (the South Korean government grants a modest stipend to defectors).[82] Surveys conducted in the former Soviet Union reveal this same commitment to socialism in the abstract.[83] In North Korea, the socialist spirit appears to be modestly realized at the local level. Defectors echo the official press when they affirm that, on the whole, North Korean people are more likely to help one another than are the capitalist southerners. Yet this commitment to a communal principle is accompanied by a reluctance to embrace the virtues of communal work. Even when the government was providing regular rations, people had to be cajoled to put effort into communal work.

It seems that most people also support the idea of Juche as a principle of national sovereignty, pride, and self-sufficiency. Pride in one's own country and the desire to preserve its independence characterize all nations. The goal of national self-sufficiency appeals to everyone, but people with sufficient knowledge of economics realize that, in the modern world, national economies must operate interdependently. The applications of Juche to agricultural and industrial production are probably less appreciated. "Juche" as a label has been attached to any idea hatched by the Kims. Juche farming, for example, prescribes when and how crops are to be planted. Juche steelmaking dictates the steelmaking process. In all cases the goal of the Juche method is to make local production units self-sufficient or to make the entire nation self-sufficient. Since these methods are handed down by the party, often without a thorough understanding of the technical aspects of a task (although party cadres are supposed to consult with local workers), production methods often lead to failure, one example being intensive terrace farming, which denuded the hillsides. Yet as party policy attributed to the teachings of Kim Il Sung or Kim Jong Il, these production guidelines must be followed.

The more philosophical aspects of Juche later added by Kim Jong Il are not likely to be understood well by the average North Korean. People as the masters of a society in which they have no voice must make little practical sense. The idea of the sociopolitical family may sound comforting in principle, but one wonders how many people truly believe that living for the "national family" under the fatherhood of Kim Jong Il is preferable to living for oneself and one's immediate family.

Defectors from North Korea unanimously agree that the vast majority of North Koreans harbored great love and respect for Kim Il Sung as the man who freed them from the Japanese, defeated the Americans in the Korean War, and built the foundations of the national economy. The tears shed for the Great Leader when he died were real. Many of the stories that make up the Kim Il Sung myth are believed. He was their George Washington, Abraham Lincoln, Franklin Delano Roosevelt, and Dwight D. Eisenhower all rolled into one. He was the only Korean leader they had known. Except for the most ignorant and superstitious, most of the masses probably did not believe that Kim could control the weather or work miracles, but they could accept such statements as being worthy of him. They also believed he was recognized throughout the world as an outstanding man of his time.

It is hard, however, to find a defector who has anything good to say about Kim Jong Il. In Pyongyang he was referred to as "that man" (*ku saram*).[84] Perhaps if the Kim Jong Il myth continues to be drummed into the people for another twenty years, and the economy improves, people will begin to believe. But by cause or coincidence, just around the time in the early 1980s that Kim Jong Il was introduced to the people as their future leader, the North Korean economy began to decline. Despite waves of propaganda that declare the post-Kim Il Sung years to be an era of heroic achievements, people have found life under Kim Jong Il increasingly difficult to bear. One wonders what conclusions the less-educated segment of the population drew from the series of devastating natural disasters—floods, droughts, and tidal waves—that struck North Korea beginning in 1995, the year after the Great Leader's death. The Korean phrase "tiger father, dog son" must be in everyone's minds.

Do the masses believe in the future of "socialism in our own style," given that they are told that North Korea is the last bastion of socialism? Do they likewise see any hope of a victorious conclusion to the forced march? Do they believe the New Year's predictions that perennially predict a "turnaround" in the North Korean economy? Little evidence can be found for such beliefs. They may believe that socialism is bound to triumph in the end, but in the depths of a depression, their thoughts are mostly fixed on survival.

Yet even in hard times they accept or at least tolerate socialism and Juche and the greatness of the leaders who brought them to ruin. How does one account for this persistence? First, the North Korean masses have never experienced political or social freedom. During the Choson dynasty many of them worked for landlords. Shortly after the turn of the century, the entire country's economy was geared to supply the Japanese. After the war the communists imposed their centralized form of nonparticipatory government. To the North Korean people, life in an autocratic society is business as usual. And this life is backed by centuries of Confucian teaching that ordinary people have their proper station in life and should subject themselves to the will of their superiors, who in principle rule as benevolent fathers. Since political ideas are handed down to the people by the omniscient Kim Il Sung and Kim Jong Il, there is no room for discussion or debate, only interminable explanation and elaboration.

The masses in North Korea differ from those in the former Soviet Union and Eastern Europe in one important respect—they are cut off from outside information. Although the people have been told that unspecified countries have abandoned socialism and are now suffering the consequences, they have no access to firsthand information to judge foreign conditions. And certainly they have little information about life or thought in noncommunist countries such as South Korea, Japan, or the United States. It is difficult for outsiders to imagine how people can evaluate good from bad, useful from useless, when they have such a limited standard of comparison. If the North Korean people do not believe what they are told, they have nothing else to believe.

Finally, defectors say that even though they were unconvinced on some ideological points, and actively disbelieved others (such as the Kim Jong Il cult), they had no energy to pursue their thoughts and certainly no opportunity to discuss them. So, to avoid complicating their lives, they abandoned political thought and resigned themselves to repeating the political lessons they were taught. This is not a case of fearing to voice doubts or ask questions in public; this is a case of not even raising questions in one's mind. The average North Korean has become politically disengaged. Similar responses to totalitarian communist regimes have been reported in the former communist countries of Eastern Europe and the Soviet Union. Eric Scheye quotes Czech citizens on the psychological mood under communism: "People did not hear or listen to what went on outside themselves. Everyone was in their own small world."[85] As one defector from North Korea said, "If a normal desire to learn the truth survived in their minds, the distortion of history could not have continued this long."[86] Yet alongside this lack of belief—and even interest in—political thought is a strong emotional attachment to things North Korean. This defector recounts how, as a resident of North Korea, he was moved to tears by a North Korean film, heavily laden with propaganda; when he saw the movie again after fleeing to South Korea (the South Korean government has relaxed its restrictions on the import of North Korean cultural works), the work struck him as absolutely silly.[87]

The Elite

In the context of a discussion on ideological belief, the elite population is defined as the several thousand top party, government, and military officials living in Pyongyang who have access to foreign information, for example, by being included in the distribution list of *Chamgo tongsin* (Reference News), a government publication covering international and domestic news stories not available to the public. Some of the elite have also had the opportunity to travel outside the country for education or for their official work. For these people, is Juche primarily a tool used to control the masses, or do they truly believe in its principles? If they do believe, less change can be expected in North Korean thought and practice than if they use ideology merely as a tool to get what they want. A tentative conclusion is that, in the words of Reo M. Christenson and others, ideology "captures and is captured by leaders."[88]

Members of the elite believe in socialism as a utopian idea but probably see little hope for its realization in the foreseeable future. They are like many people in capitalist countries who recognize the beauty of a truly cooperative lifestyle but have no expectation of realizing it. With their limited knowledge of the outside world, they realize that North Korea is virtually the last country trying to make socialism work. And if they examine their lives, they will realize that they have used their positions to acquire whatever goods they can obtain on the black market, a very capitalist endeavor.

The elite population probably also firmly believes in the importance of national pride, independence, and economic self-reliance, for like all citizens they have a strong patriotic streak and generally lack an appreciation of the interdependent nature of the national economy.

On most other points of ideology, it is likely that elite citizens are nonbelievers. The sociopolitical life probably sounds too much like a pseudophilosophical justification for blind loyalty to the Kims. The idea of people as masters of society who completely subordinate themselves to the will of the party and the leader is recognized as contradictory. Kim Il Sung was respected as a great leader, even by those who knew that much of his personality cult was manufactured. Kim Jong Il is feared but not respected.

Squaring the Circle

Unlike the masses, who by lack of information, lack of education, and lack of opportunity "enjoy the strange luxury of not having to think" (to quote Blair Ruble's characterization of Soviet citizens under Stalin), the elite population faces a cognitive dilemma.[89] These people recognize the contradictions in Juche ideology, and because of their white-collar work and their relatively more affluent lifestyle, they have time to think about contradictions. Yet they have even less freedom to discuss issues than the masses because they are more closely watched by each other and by security personnel. To some degree the indoctrination may have gotten to them, especially in the form of self-criticisms they must undergo, which must at least sound genuine. They are also more involved in teaching and modeling the ideology.

To some degree the elite citizens may live a double mental life, one public and the other very private, like the intellectuals in the former Soviet Union as described by David Remnick. "Gorbachev, me, all of us, we were double-thinkers, we had to balance truth and propaganda in our minds all the time."[90] Schönsee and Lederer portray the elite of East Germany in the same way: privately cynical and corrupt, engaging in Orwellian double-think.[91] Most likely, the elite population as well as the masses rarely engages in political thought, thereby avoiding the discomfort of cognitive contradictions. When a contradiction arises, people do their best to justify and rationalize, like people everywhere. Besides, even elite members of society, with their greater but still fragmentary knowledge of the workings of capitalism and liberal democracy, have little in the way of alternative ideologies to contemplate. They may be dissatisfied and puzzled about the contradictions in their ideology, but they are not in a position to contemplate a different ideology. And behind any fear of voicing antistate thoughts is the greater fear that if capitalism sweeps away socialism, they are most likely to lose their privileged positions.

For the masses, the basis of Juche ideology is plausible. It is a myth in which they are accustomed to living. In this sense, the masses are not a revolutionary force but a great conservative impediment to change in North Korea. The elite know better, but their interest lies in preserving the status quo. This is especially true of Kim Jong Il, who is the only one with the authority to revise Juche. But even if he were to attempt such a revision he would risk being accused by the masses of being unfaithful to his father's wishes. Thus the elite and the masses are bound by fifty years of ideology and myth.

Juche ideology functions as an anchor to keep the North Korean state from moving with the times. As outlined in this chapter, the emphasis of Juche has changed over the years, or more accurately, new concepts have been incorporated into Juche, but the basic concepts that hold back the Korean people remain: the commitment to socialism, insistence on achieving economic self-sufficiency, the leader's cult of personality. In a larger sense, the content of Juche is not its most constricting feature; rather, it is ideology.

If Juche could function in the background of North Korean life, as a creed and associated myths to be pointed to with pride but honored often in the breach (like democracy in the United States), it would serve a useful function of providing North Korean society with identity and cohesiveness. But the central place Juche has been given in North Korean society, as a subject of countless hours of study and discussion and as a political tool, has made North Korea a caricature in the international community.

CHAPTER THREE

The Turning

Point Economy

The might of our economy is basically the might of ideology and unity.[1]

The refusal of the Kim regime, under both father and son, to discard an unworkable ideology and adapt to a changed international environment has destroyed the North Korean economy and the lives of millions of people. The condition of the economy will determine the country's fate: survival as a sovereign state or absorption by South Korea.

Economic planning in North Korea is at the mercy of Kim Jong Il's pursuit of regime security and his continuing attempt to apply an economic plan grounded in ideology and wishful thinking. The economy has predictably suffered. Weakened by years of mismanagement and the disappearance of the international socialist trading system, North Korea's broken economy has become a seemingly insurmountable challenge, forcing the masses to engage in nonsocialist economic activities and threatening the long-term security of the Kim regime.

The Economy in the Late 1990s

The economic statistics, as well as they can be estimated by outsiders (since the North Korean government stopped publishing economic statistics in the

Table 3-1. *North Korea's GNP, 1985–98*

Year	GNP (billions of dollars)	Real GNP growth (percent)	Per capita (dollars)
1985	15.1	2.7	757
1986	17.4	2.1	853
1987	19.4	3.3	936
1988	20.6	3.0	980
1989	21.1	2.4	987
1990	23.1	-3.7	1,064
1991	22.9	-5.2	1,038
1992	21.1	–7.6	943
1993	20.5	–4.3	904
1994	21.2	–1.7	923
1995	22.3	–1.8	957
1996	21.4	–3.7	910
1997	17.7	–6.8	741
1998	12.6	–1.1	573

Source: Ministry of Unification, Republic of Korea.

mid-1960s), are alarming. From 1990 to 1998, GNP is estimated to have declined by 55 percent from an already low $23 billion (table 3-1). Foreign trade declined by 70 percent in the same period as the country's economy contracted and trade relations with the former socialist economies dwindled (tables 3-2 and 3-3). In 1998 the country's foreign debt, in default since the 1980s, amounted to almost $12 billion, not a large figure for most countries but equaling 96 percent of the country's GNP (table 3-4). The nation's factories (except munitions factories) appear to be operating at no more than 25 percent of capacity. The health care system has virtually ceased to operate, and food distributions are sporadic, forcing the people to fend for themselves.

It is difficult for foreigners, including those few who are permitted to make brief visits to North Korea, to form an accurate picture of the entire economy, since so much of it is hidden by the government for security reasons or operates on an ad hoc basis. Even in a relatively healthy state the socialist economy is not easily described by the economic statistical methods developed for market systems. To complicate matters, in the domestic economy several parallel economic systems exist. In the external economy, North Korea's decline in foreign trade, based on foreign trade statistics, is difficult to estimate. Considerable trade with China (both official and unofficial cross-border trade) goes unreported, and North Korea's sales of military weapons (part of the military economy) are often hidden.

Table 3-2. *North Korea's Foreign Trade Balance, 1985–98*
Billions of dollars

Year	Trade volume	Exports	Imports	Balance
1985	3.095	1.314	1.781	−0.467
1986	3.572	1.507	2.065	−0.558
1987	4.147	1.647	2.500	−0.853
1988	5.240	2.030	3.210	−1.180
1989	4.800	1.910	2.890	−0.980
1990	4.720	1.960	2.760	−0.800
1991	2.583	0.944	1.639	−0.695
1992	2.470	0.916	1.554	−0.638
1993	2.640	1.020	1.620	−0.600
1994	2.108	0.838	1.270	−0.432
1995	2.052	0.736	1.316	−0.580
1996	1.976	0.727	1.249	−0.522
1997	2.177	0.905	1.272	−0.367
1998	1.442	0.559	0.883	−0.324

Source: Ministry of Unification, Republic of Korea.

What *is* apparent to any observer is that the country's infrastructure is crumbling. Workers are idle, factories are shuttered, electricity is sporadic, trains and tracks are broken, and among the relatively few vehicles on the roads, some in the countryside have even been converted to run on charcoal for lack of gasoline. Surely the most tragic indicator of North Korea's economic problems is the widespread hunger and starvation of the North Korean people, a direct consequence of years of economic mismanagement and the decline in economic assistance from North Korea's socialist (and formerly socialist) trading partners, compounded by adverse weather conditions since 1995. The government's response has been totally inadequate: denial and commands to the people to tighten their belts. Pyongyang has also been reluctant to permit foreign aid organizations to monitor food distributions, resulting in a lessening of donor enthusiasm. In the early 1990s the "let's eat only two meals a day" campaign was launched. By the end of the decade, even two daily meals had become an impossible dream for many North Koreans.

Juche Economics

North Korea's economy is subject to the guidance of Juche principles, even when those principles are only honored in the breach. These principles, as laid

Table 3-3. *North Korea's Foreign Trade Partners, 1985-1998*
Billions of dollars

	Item	Russia[a]	China	Japan	Other
1985	Total	1.315	0.506	0.429	0.845
	Exports	0.504	0.268	0.181	0.361
	Imports	0.811	0.238	0.248	0.484
	Balance	−0.307	0.030	−0.067	−0.123
1986	Total	1.689	0.548	0.356	0.979
	Exports	0.630	0.288	0.173	0.416
	Imports	1.059	0.260	0.183	0.563
	Balance	−0.429	0.028	−0.010	−0.147
1987	Total	1.947	0.518	0.454	1.228
	Exports	0.682	0.239	0.241	0.485
	Imports	1.265	0.279	0.213	0.743
	Balance	−0.583	−0.040	0.028	−0.258
1988	Total	2.632	0.579	0.564	1.465
	Exports	0.886	0.234	0.325	0.585
	Imports	1.746	0.345	0.239	0.880
	Balance	−0.860	−0.120	0.086	−0.295
1989	Total	2.393	0.562	0.496	1.349
	Exports	0.895	0.185	0.299	0.581
	Imports	1.498	0.377	0.197	0.818
	Balance	−0.603	−0.192	0.102	−0.237
1990	Total	2.564	0.483	0.476	1.197
	Exports	1.047	0.125	0.300	0.488
	Imports	1.517	0.358	0.176	0.709
	Balance	−0.470	−0.233	0.124	−0.221
1991	Total	0.365	0.610	0.508	1.100
	Exports	0.171	0.085	0.284	0.364
	Imports	0.194	0.525	0.224	0.572
	Balance	−0.023	−0.440	0.060	−0.208

out in the DPRK constitution, were formulated by Kim Il Sung and hold the status of infallible doctrine. The fundamental principle, stated in article 20 of the 1998 revision of the constitution, stipulates that "the means of production are owned solely by the State and cooperative organizations." All industrial facilities and commercial enterprises are state owned. Most farms are still operated as collectives under the strict guidance of the party. However, if the "rural

	Item	Russia[a]	China	Japan	Other
1992	Total	0.292	0.697	0.480	1.001
	Exports	0.065	0.156	0.257	0.389
	Imports	0.227	0.541	0.223	0.456
	Balance	−0.162	−0.385	0.034	−0.067
1993	Total	0.227	0.899	0.472	1.042
	Exports	0.039	0.297	0.252	0.402
	Imports	0.188	0.602	0.220	0.531
	Balance	−0.149	−0.305	0.032	−0.129
1994	Total	0.140	0.624	0.493	0.851
	Exports	0.040	0.199	0.322	0.244
	Imports	0.100	0.425	0.171	0.513
	Balance	−0.060	−0.226	0.151	−0.269
1995	Total	0.083	0.550	0.595	0.824
	Exports	0.015	0.064	0.340	0.294
	Imports	0.068	0.486	0.255	0.447
	Balance	−0.053	−0.422	0.085	−0.153
1996	Total	0.065	0.566	0.518	0.827
	Exports	0.029	0.069	0.291	0.322
	Imports	0.036	0.497	0.227	0.443
	Balance	−0.007	−0.428	0.064	−0.121
1997	Total	0.084	0.656	0.489	0.948
	Exports	0.017	0.121	0.311	0.275
	Imports	0.067	0.535	0.178	0.460
	Balance	−0.050	−0.414	0.133	−0.185
1998	Total	0.065	0.413	0.395	0.570
	Exports	0.008	0.057	0.220	0.274
	Imports	0.057	0.356	0.175	0.296
	Balance	−0.049	−0.299	0.045	−0.022

Source: Ministry of Unification, Republic of Korea.

a. Succeeding the Soviet Union.

question" is finally resolved according to Kim Il Sung's wishes, the collectives will be converted into state farms where worker-farmers receive state wages rather than a portion of the fruits of their collective labor. This conversion is provided for by article 23 of the constitution: "The state strengthens and develops the socialist cooperative economic system and gradually transforms the property of collective organizations into the property of all the people on the

Table 3-4. *North Korea's Net Foreign Debt, 1985–98*

Billions of dollars

Year	Debt	Percent of GNP
1985	2.90	19.2
1986	4.06	23.4
1987	5.21	26.9
1988	5.20	25.2
1989	6.78	32.1
1990	7.86	34.0
1991	9.28	40.5
1992	9.72	46.1
1993	10.32	50.3
1994	10.66	50.3
1995	11.83	53.0
1996	12.00	56.1
1997	11.90	67.2
1998	12.10	96.0

Source: Ministry of Unification, Republic of Korea.

basis of the voluntary will of the entire membership." The stipulation that any change will be voluntary should not be given undue weight. Since the collectives are now controlled by the state, conversion to state ownership would likely have little practical impact on agricultural productivity or on the lives of farm workers, but the change would be important in principle since it would cut the bond between farmers and their land. The only legal and politically acceptable alternative to state or collective ownership of the means of production is the farming of small garden plots for personal consumption and sale in local markets. The revised article 22 of the 1998 constitution, while reasserting the eventual goal of nationalizing the collective farms, also adds that besides the products of the garden plots, "Income from other legal economic activities shall also belong to private property," although little reason exists to trust that this legal right will be respected any more faithfully than other human rights guaranteed by the constitution but never realized, such as freedom of speech, assembly, demonstration, and association.

A second basic economic principle is central planning: "The State shall formulate unified and detailed plans and guarantee a high rate of production growth and a balanced development of the national economy" (article 34). In practice, the military has first call on available resources, while producers of consumer goods are last in line. When the economy began to contract in the

1990s, even the military felt the pinch. Yet these dismal economic results have not shaken official faith in the alleged virtues of the command economy.

A third economic principle is the Juche idea of economic self-sufficiency. Beginning with the 1992 revision of the constitution, Juche received prominence as the first article (article 19) in the economics chapter: "In the Democratic People's Republic of Korea, socialist production relations are based upon the foundation of an independent national economy." In accordance with the Juche principle, North Korea's foreign trade amounts to only around 10 percent of GNP, far below that of most other economies; South Korea earns more than 50 percent of its GNP through trade. One reason for Pyongyang's emphasis on Juche in the economy is to boast that North Korea is a truly independent state compared with South Korea, whose economy is heavily dependent on foreign trade. Yet in violation of the Juche principle, North Korea's economy has always depended on socialist foreign aid and trade with other socialist economies. Even when North Korea turned to a (misleadingly named) "trade first" economic policy in 1993, the principle of Juche was honored. Kim Jong Il, in typical doublespeak, claimed that engaging in foreign trade, far from invalidating Juche, helped strengthen Juche policy.

When the state owns the means of production and pays workers a set wage regardless of their production, worker motivation must reside in the "all for one—one for all" spirit of socialism, a notoriously weak motivator. Members of the North Korean elite have tried to motivate the masses without using the kind of material incentives that the elite itself seeks. Some work responsibility and collective profit plans have been adopted at the local level, and the size of work teams on collective farms has been reduced. But for the most part, the Kim Jong Il regime has tried to energize workers by staging mass-motivation campaigns, first seen in the *chollima* [flying horse] campaign of 1958, as inspired by the Stakhanovite movement in the Soviet Union and the Great Leap Forward in China.[2] Kim Jong Il's "speed battles" have lasted from a few weeks to an entire decade, as in the "speed of the '90's." In 1998, the government, lacking material resources, launched a "new Chollima" campaign with a view to "turning impossibility into possibility and working miracles in the present difficult situation."[3] Workers are spurred by drum-beating political officers who visit the work site.[4]

Year Plans

The history of the DPRK's economic development describes a pattern of early success followed by a gradual slide into failure, and then a sharp drop when the life support system of socialist trading relations was cut off in the early 1990s. That North Korea experienced rapid growth in its early days has given the leadership false confidence in Juche socialism.

When Korea was liberated by American and Soviet troops after World War II, the northern part of the peninsula possessed 76 percent of Korea's mining production, 92 percent of its electrical generating capacity, and 80 percent of its heavy industrial facilities.[5] The southern half of the peninsula, however, had most of the rice production. These differences can be attributed to climatic and topographical differences (the North is colder and more mountainous than the South) and to thirty-five years of Japanese colonial developmental strategy, when the Korean Peninsula was treated not as an independent economic entity but as a resource to be exploited for the Japanese homeland. The northern half of Korea had the potential to respond to the Stalinist methods of mass mobilization and strong organization and guidance. In 1946, even before North Korea had declared itself a state, authorities distributed 1 million hectares of farmland to landless peasants and began the process of nationalizing industry.

In 1947 the first in a series of Soviet-style economic plans was initiated (figure 3-1).[6] The goal of the 1946–47 plan was to nationalize major industries, with the process continuing in the 1948–49 plan. Starting from a low postwar base, industrial production reportedly increased 54 percent and 38 percent respectively during these two plan periods. A Two-Year Plan for 1949–50 further consolidated industrial organization, and productivity surged, pushing the DPRK well ahead of the ROK in industrial development. Kim Il Sung became convinced that the organized and industrious North Koreans had the means to defeat the South Koreans in a civil war, which he duly launched on June 25, 1950.

Kim's war plans misfired. Within three months of the outbreak of hostilities, U.S. troops led by General Douglas MacArthur, fighting under the UN banner, had repulsed the North Korean invaders and were pushing them toward the Chinese border before falling back under a Chinese counterattack. During the war American bombing wreaked havoc on North Korea's infrastructure, and the fighting killed 300,000 North Koreans, crippling the North's labor supply. After the truce was signed in July 1953, capital and technology assistance from the Soviet Union and its Eastern European allies, combined with manpower from the Chinese "volunteer" soldiers, helped the North Korean economy recover during the Three-Year Plan of 1954–56. By the end of the plan, industrial output surpassed prewar levels.

In 1956, a year after Kim Il Sung proclaimed Juche as the guiding principle of North Korean politics and culture, Juche was applied to the economy, set-

Figure 3-1. *North Korea's Economic Development Plans*

Plan	Goals and events	Results (DPRK figures)
1-Year Plans (1947, 1948)	Nationalize major industries Increase production of basic necessities	Industrial production: 1946-47: 54% increase 1947-48: 38% increase
2-Year Plan (1949-1950)	Consolidate economic foundation	Industrial production: 3.4 times greater than 1946 level
3-Year Plan (1954–1956)	Production of basic necessities Juche introduced Nationalize and collectivize farms	Industrial production: Annual growth rate: 41.5%
5-Year Plan (1957–1961)	Complete nationalization Production of basic necessities Chollima movement Chongsan-ni and Taean systems	Industrial production: Annual growth rate: 36.6% Industries and farms nationalized
First 7-Year Plan (1961–1967) (extended to 1970)	Continued emphasis on heavy industry Military buildup More emphasis on Juche	Industrial production: Annual growth rate: 13% Bottlenecks appear Stop publishing statistics
6-Year Plan (1971–1976) (extended to 1978)	Improve technology Improve light industry Purchase foreign plants Three-Revolution Team Movement Speed battles	Industrial production: Annual growth rate: 16.3% Default on loans
Second 7-Year Plan (1978–1984) (extended to 1986)	Frugality/conservation plans August 3 Consumer Goods Movement Independent Accounting System Foreign Joint Venture Law Ten major targets for 1980s	Industrial production: Annual growth rate: 12.1%
Third 7-Year Plan (1987–1993) (extended to 1995)	Ten major targets for 1980s Open foreign economic trade zone Pass more joint venture laws Socialist trade relations end	Industrial production: Annual growth rate: 12.2% Admitted failure of plan in 1993 Shortages in many sectors GNP decline beginning in 1990

Source: Doowon Lee, "North Korean Economic Reform: Past Efforts and Future Prospects," in John McMillan and Barry Naughton, eds., *Reforming Asian Socialism: The Growth of Market Institutions* (University of Michigan Press, 1996), pp. 317–36.

ting economic self-sufficiency as a long-range goal. Heavy industry was to be developed as quickly as possible to provide the basis for a self-sufficient economy. Consistent with the Juche principle of national independence, Kim also decided not to join the Soviet-controlled Council for Mutual Economic Assistance (CMEA), even though the Soviet Union and its allies were the DPRK's major trading partners.

The North Korean peasants, who had welcomed the redistribution of farm land from Japanese and Korean landlords in 1946, had their farms taken from them in a process of collectivization begun in 1954. The collective farms originally constituted approximately 80 households working 130 hectares of land, but their size later increased to an average of 300 families from neighboring villages working 500 hectares.[7] The party leaders who ran the new collectives in the name of "the people" became the new landlords. Each family was permitted to farm a small garden plot (initially up to 260 square meters, later reduced to 100 square meters). But except for that small plot nothing tied the farmer to the land, since he worked wherever in the collective he was needed.

During the early years of the next economic plan (1957–61), nationalization of all remaining industries and collectivization of all farms was completed. Foreign aid from the DPRK's allies began to decline, and the last of the Chinese soldier-laborers returned home in 1959. To squeeze out more productivity from the economy, a countrywide manpower mobilization movement under the *chollima* banner was launched in 1957. Speed battles, then and now, are designed to boost output by increasing worker motivation. The results have been predictable: short-term gains in quantity at the expense of quality, distortion of the economy as resources are shifted to the sectors targeted by the battle, and eventually human exhaustion. At first the economic gains seemed to justify the means: North Korea's economy pushed ahead so strongly that the goals of the Five-Year Plan were reportedly reached in only four years, with an annual industrial growth of 36.6 percent.[8] Looking back on the accomplishments of the half-dozen years after the Korean War, Kim Il Sung could be justly proud of his economic leadership and realistically entertain visions of even greater progress in the future. What he did not recognize was that the economic policies of nationalization and collectivization, central planning, and mass mobilization that had worked so well in the early stages of economic development were quickly reaching the limits of their effectiveness. The great oak tree of colonial feudalism had been felled and the logs cut, but the carpentry that remained to be done required a more deft style of economic management than a grade-school-educated soldier could provide.

In the First Seven-Year Plan (1961–67), Kim Il Sung continued to emphasize heavy industry and labor mobilization. However, little labor remained to be mobilized, and as resources were stretched to their limit, bottlenecks appeared in the economy as a result of shortages of arable land, skilled labor, energy, transportation, and minerals. These bottlenecks, so typical of a command economy, clearly warned that it was time to diversify production, rely on the market rather than unitary planning to adjust supply and demand, and emphasize technology as a means of increasing productivity. But Kim Il Sung had no economists who were willing or able to tell him that his economic plans had to be changed. The economy also suffered as more resources were diverted to the military to enable North Korea to meet the dual threats posed by South Korea's growing military strength under the presidency of former general Park Chung Hee and the influx of U.S. troops sent to Asia to fight the Vietnam War. After the early 1960s the DPRK stopped publishing economic statistics except for percentage increases over previous periods, and although the First Seven-Year Plan was officially declared a success, the extension of the plan to 1970 suggested that some economic targets had not been met. During the plan years, industrial output had reportedly increased an average of 13 percent a year, slowing during the later years.[9]

The Six-Year Plan, initiated in 1971 (economic plans varied in length and did not coincide with the economic plans of the Soviet Union, North Korea's major economic benefactor), focused greater attention on light industry, technological modernization, self-sufficiency in raw materials, improvement of product quality, and of course reduction of the bottlenecks of the 1960s. A North Korean delegation (absent Kim Il Sung) visited Seoul in 1972 and saw the economic strides that were being made under the capitalist system. In recognition of the limitations inherent in its home-grown technologies, the DPRK purchased some $500 million worth of industrial plants, mostly from Japan.

At this point North Korean economic planners encountered some bad luck. The first oil shock of 1973 sent international oil prices skyrocketing, although since most of the DPRK's oil was imported on "friendship" terms from the Soviet Union and China, the effects on the Korean economy were buffered. · However, the global oil shock did depress the price of the minerals that the DPRK exported. Caught in a credit squeeze, Pyongyang began to default on its debts in late 1974, halting the importation of Western technology. By the end of the decade the North Koreans were forced to stretch out debt payments; almost all foreign debt payments were halted in 1985 when its foreign debt stood at $5.2 billion. A group of Western banks declared the debt in default in

1986; by 1990, 100 creditor banks from seventeen nations had filed suits against the DPRK; and by 1997 the debt had increased to an estimated $11.9 billion, of which $4.55 billion was owed to Japan, Germany, France, and other Western nations, and $7.35 billion to Russia.[10] Throughout the 1970s the bulk of North Korea's resources continued to be devoted to heavy industry, and apart from Soviet aid and the technology purchases from the capitalist economies, autarky continued to be pursued in all sectors of the economy. Military expenditures also remained at a high level.

To put new life into the stagnating socialist economy, Kim Jong Il launched the Three Revolution Team (TRT) Movement, his first major undertaking. The TRT teams of young party members visited farms and factories throughout the country, carrying technological, ideological, and cultural ideas to fight bureaucratism, encourage innovation, and instill communist enthusiasm—a kind of economic Red Guard campaign. The TRT teams were also spreading Kim Jong Il's influence to every corner of the country, preparing the groundwork for his eventual succession. Kim Jong Il's "bold thinking" also fostered new speed battles (the first one lasting seventy days), which exhausted the workers and did little for the long-term growth of the economy. Kim Jong Il's contributions were ideological rather than economic. As a consequence, even the relatively modest goals of the Six-Year Plan were not achieved. Although the plan was declared completed more than a year ahead of schedule, with an annual growth of 16.3 percent, the next plan did not begin until 1978, suggesting that the now-familiar adjustment period was needed to attain the plan's goals.

The Second Seven-Year Plan of 1978–84 was a make-or-break plan for North Korea. Throughout the two preceding planning periods resource bottlenecks, obsolete technology, and poor worker motivation had persisted. The choice for Kim and son was clear: radically change economic policies or find a way to live within the constraints imposed by autarkic socialism. The Kims (for presumably the junior Kim was making many of the decisions by this time) chose to stick with Juche economic principles. Accordingly, one of the themes of the new Seven-Year Plan was frugality, that is, doing more with less. This goal, embodied in Kim Jong Il's August 3 Consumer Goods Movement, has become a permanent fixture of North Korean life, most distressingly with the promotion in the early 1990s of the slogan, "Let's eat two meals a day." By the end of the decade so few resources were left to call upon that Kim was entreating the people to rely on their "inner reserves."[11]

In 1980 Kim Il Sung put forth a grand plan to achieve "Ten Major Targets for Socialist Construction in the 1980s"—essentially an update of the goals of the Second Seven-Year Plan—for electricity generation, coal, steel, cement and mineral production, fertilizer and grain production, fabric production, and tideland reclamation. The DPRK embarked on several large-scale projects dictated as much by political motives and nationalistic pride as economic wisdom. Several "nature-remaking" projects were initiated, the most ambitious being the construction of the $4 billion West Sea Barrage to reclaim tidal land. Of much less practical economic significance was an estimated $4.5 billion spent on the construction of facilities for the Thirteenth World Festival of Youth and Students, a socialist athletic gathering hosted by Pyongyang in August 1989.[12] Lavish celebrations were held annually on Kim Il Sung's birthday, and grand monuments to his accomplishments were built in every part of the country, especially on his sixtieth (1972) and seventieth (1982) birthdays.

In the final years of the 1978–84 plan two economic adjustments were made. The Independent Accounting System gave more responsibility to state enterprises at the local level, and a 1983 *Nodong Sinmun* editorial entitled "Let Us Bring about an Epochal Turning Point in Improving the People's Living Standard" signaled the beginning of Kim Jong Il's campaign to endear himself to the people by improving their standard of living. Although the party declared that the goals of the 1978–84 plan had been met on schedule, with an annual growth of 12.1 percent, little celebration attended the plan's completion, and the start of the next plan was delayed until 1987.[13]

Another Seven-Year Plan (1987–93) targeted Kim Il Sung's ten major goals of the 1980s for completion. More emphasis was placed on the development of new technologies and on foreign trade and investment (a foreign trade zone was opened in 1991 and new foreign investment laws were passed in 1992 to supplement the original 1984 laws), but the loss of socialist trade and aid owing to radical transformations of the socialist economies in the Soviet Union and Eastern Europe and the gradual transformation of China's economy to a "socialist market economy" ruined any chance that North Korea would achieve the ten major goals. In fact, after 1990 the DPRK's economy began to shrink. An official communiqué released during a plenary meeting of the KWP Central Committee in December 1993, while trying to put the best possible face on the situation, made an unprecedented admission of failure: "A new great progress has been made in all fields of socialist construction, though the targets of the whole scope of industrial production and some major indices including electric power, steel and chemical fibre envisaged in the third Seven-Year Plan failed to be attained due to international events and the acute situation created in Korea."[14]

An adjustment period of "two or three years" was set aside to concentrate on agriculture, light industry, and foreign trade, although those sectors were not designated as failures. The communiqué gave no hint of any changes in economic strategy: "These brilliant achievements [of the third Seven-Year Plan] are a powerful demonstration of the undisputed superiority and might of our socialist system not affected by any economic blockade of the imperialists and the fluctuation of the international situation, and a clear proof of the vitality of our socialist economy which develops in a planned way on an independent foundation."[15]

With the death of Kim Il Sung in 1994, the third Seven-Year Plan and the ten major targets of the 1980s were forgotten in the struggle to avoid economic collapse. No important economic statements were announced until the publication in September 1998 of the *Nodong Sinmun-Kulloja* joint editorial entitled "Let Us Adhere to the Line on Building a Self-Reliant National Economy to the End."[16] The editorial opens with the usual North Korean take on world affairs: "The economic crisis has worsened today in Asia and various other regions of the world. As the economic chaos worsens, people are growing to reject the rule and subjugation by the imperialists and to demand economic self-reliance. This is clear proof of the justness of our party's line on building a self-reliant national economy."

Then the editorial calls for a return to the DPRK's economic policies of the 1960s, namely, priority for heavy industry and the military. North Korea's economic problems are blamed on others: "The superiority of the socialist self-reliant economy was and is absolute. Economic difficulties are not the results from any problems in self-reliance in our economy." The editorial promotes the idea, introduced in a *Nodong Sinmun* editorial on August 22—two weeks before the tenth term of the Supreme People's Assembly (SPA) convened—to build North Korea into a militarily strong and economically prosperous state (*Kangsong Taeguk*). The SPA ratified a new constitution, which gave only the slightest hints of loosening state control over the economy.

When the second session of the tenth SPA was convened in April 1999, the finance minister announced the results of the 1998 budget and plans for the 1999 budget, the first budget statements since 1994.[17] The 1999 budget was set 50 percent below the 1994 budget. At the second SPA session a "Law on People's Economic Plans" was also promulgated. The law essentially said that it was the duty of all organizations and individuals to fulfill the economic plans handed down by the state, although state planners were encouraged to take "actual conditions" into consideration when formulating plans.[18] Neither the economic law nor the budget as published stipulated the same explicit economic goals that had characterized the previous multiyear plans.

In short, the North Korean response to economic failure has been primarily political in nature. Foreign governments (especially the United States) are accused of strangling the North Korean economy with an economic embargo. Bad weather is blamed for agricultural failures. Ideological indoctrination is being stepped up to help the people endure increased economic privations and keep them from thinking about alternative economic systems.

Living Standards

Although North Korea is more egalitarian than most capitalist societies, gaps in the standard of living do exist between political classes, and these gaps have reportedly increased since the 1970s.[19] In a socialist welfare state, most individual material needs are, in principle, satisfied by the state.[20]

North Korean wages are paid in the North Korean won, with an official exchange rate of 2.1 won to the dollar, although on the black market the rate was closer to 200 won to the dollar in the late 1990s. The income gap between the richest and the poorest has been estimated to be a relatively egalitarian factor of five. As the primary economy collapsed in the 1990s, official salaries paid in won declined in value, state stores were unable to offer goods at any price, and the prices in the people's markets put many goods out of range of the average North Korean. People survive by barter; for example, by trading household goods to farmers for food. Party and government officials frequently demand bribes for performing their duties; those bureaucrats who have access to special rations can sell them in the black market for substantial sums.

Before severe food shortages hit the country in the mid-1990s (earlier in some outlying areas), biweekly food rations were distributed to each family, including grains and supplemental food items such as soy sauce, bean paste, and salt. Each household has a ration card indicating the amount and mixture of grain to which it is entitled. Authorized travelers carry a special ration card (*yanggwon*, or "grain card") to obtain food from distribution centers in other communities. Even before the food distribution system broke down, food rations were Spartan. In principle, they are based on one's age and occupation; in practice, political position and connections play an important role. Preschool children are supposed to receive 200 to 300 grams a day; primary and secondary students, 400 grams; workers in light-labor occupations, including office work and professionals, 700 grams; pilots, seamen, and special duty military personnel, 800 grams; workers in heavy industries, 900 grams.[21] Six hundred grams equals about three medium bowls of cooked rice or mixed grains (barley or corn). The grain would be supplemented with a few vegetables. A percentage of the ration (10 to 20 percent in the 1970s and 1980s but in the 1990s up to 50 percent) is withheld by the government as a form of reserve for emergency situations, with such slogans as "Produce one bullet for our guns by sacrificing one chicken."[22] Needless to say, corrupt officials have always had considerable latitude to manipulate the ration system.

Except for the highest-level officials, meat and even fish have always been luxury items, and by the 1990s virtually unobtainable. In better times the average North Korean might eat meat two or three times a year, when it was distributed to celebrate the birthday of Kim Il Sung or Kim Jong Il (or occasionally other national holidays), but after the famine of 1995 struck, meat and fish became even scarcer. The common people also have great difficulty obtaining their staple food of rice, making do instead with corn and other less desirable grains, and even then rarely receiving their allotted ration. Since 1995 the estimated daily ration is between 100 and 200 grams a day (one-half to one bowl of grain, rarely rice), with some Korean refugees in China claiming they received much less.[23] Many people resort to foraging in the fields and woods for edibles such as wild foods, grass, and tree bark. "Substitute foods" are made of a mixture of edible foods mixed with inedible foods to provide bulk, for example, bread made out of a small amount of corn mixed with crushed cornstalks. People in the large cities, especially the capital of Pyongyang, receive more regular rations than do people in smaller cities and villages, and farmers are better off than town dwellers, who have less opportunity to grow their own food. As food shortages worsened after 1995 the government became lenient in permitting people to travel around the country without travel permits in order to search for food.

The signs of malnutrition are evident throughout the country. Almost everyone is thin. Malnourished children exhibit stunted growth. Diseases such as tuberculosis are widespread. Digestive system problems result from eating indigestible foods. The energy level of workers is predictably low. And most tragically, the death rate from hunger and disease has risen dramatically since 1995, with estimates ranging from several hundred thousand to 3 million malnutrition-related deaths.[24]

The housing shortage in North Korea is a perennial problem but not a crisis. Almost all housing is owned by the state, and people are assigned living quarters according to workplace, occupation, occupational rank, and political considerations. Coworkers usually live in the same housing development, the better to keep an eye on each other. There are five types of housing:

Special, Number 4, 3, 2, and 1, in order of declining desirability.[25] Special housing, a detached single-family house of one or two stories with a small garden, flush toilet, hot and cold running water, and central heating, is for officials of the deputy minister rank in the KWP or the government's Administrative Council, and major general rank or above in the military.

KWP officials of director rank, director-general officials under the Administrative Council, important university professors, colonels in the military, factory managers, top cadres in the arts, and so on, are eligible for number 4 housing in Pyongyang's high-rise apartments. Each apartment has at least two rooms, a verandah, shower and flush toilet, and hot and cold running water (when electrical power is available).

Senior party officials, city officials, deputy factory managers, and similar officials live in number 3 housing: a medium-sized, single-family detached house or older apartment with two rooms and a kitchen. The working intelligentsia with no special skills or rank such as government and party clerks, live in number 2 housing, which is a one- or two-room apartment with kitchen.

At the number 1 level three types of housing exist. Multifamily houses or flats with one or two rooms and a space for cooking for each family are for low-rank officials and ordinary workers. Workers on collective farms get two rooms and a kitchen in multiunit housing; some farmers live in the traditional two- or three-room Korean farmhouses. The housing shortage presents a special problems for newlyweds, who must wait two to three years for their own home, in the meantime living with relatives or even with strangers.

Since the 1960s, the dream of the North Korean people—and the promise of the party—has been to "eat rice and meat soup, wear silk clothes and live in a house with a tiled roof."[26] The silk clothes would be the traditional Korean costume (hanbok) worn on festive occasions. In principle, every year two sets of working clothes and street clothes are provided. In actuality, the immediate concern of most North Koreans has been how to obtain such basics as shoes and socks. A North Korean pilot who defected to the ROK with his airplane in May 1996 was wearing foot wrappings instead of socks. He said the wrappings were standard issue for soldiers, but pilots such as himself received two pairs of wrappings and two pairs of socks every year (he did not explain in the interview why he was not wearing the socks).[27]

Anyone who has examined a picture of Kim Jong Il, however, will have noted that his clothes are tailor made. Close observation of North Korean delegates attending foreign conferences offers an interesting glimpse of the gradations in clothing worn by North Koreans of different ranks. For example, the head of a delegation is likely to be dressed in a top-quality double-breasted suit, wing-tip shoes, and a designer-quality tie. His second in command will wear a suit of lesser quality, good shoes, and a merely respectable tie. The junior member of the team will have a poor-quality suit, inexpensive tie, and shoes that seem to have been (poorly) made in North Korea or China.

Economic Problems

North Korea's economic officials see problems wherever they look. Ko Young-hwan, a North Korean embassy official who defected to South Korea in 1991, recounts an incident said to have taken place at a consultative meeting of the State Administrative Council in 1988 (before economic conditions turned from bad to worse in the 1990s):

> The meeting participants discussed the causes of economic difficulties and groped for ways of solving them. . . . Fountain pens, ones that university students use for writing, you know, were in short supply. The participants asked the director of a fountain pen plant why he had not produced fountain pens. He replied that he had not been supplied with metallurgical materials. They asked the director of a steel mill why he had failed to supply the fountain pen plant with materials. He said: Because I did not get any iron ore from the smelter. The director of the smelter said he had not gotten ore from the mine. The responsible official at the mine said: I produced some, but rail transportation was not available to the smelter. The railways minister was then summoned and asked: Why did you not transport the mineral ore? He said: Because we did not get any railroad ties from the Forestry Ministry. The Forestry Ministry replied that it did not have any gas to produce timber.[28]

The myriad problems plaguing the North Korean economy can be found at many levels—from the structural weaknesses of socialism as an economic model to the obvious shortages of consumer goods and services encountered by any visitor to Pyongyang.[29] For years Kim Il Sung promised his people they would see the day when the "problems of food, clothing, and housing" had been solved, but the fulfillment of that promise receded from view in the final years of his life.

The economy suffers from at least four debilitating weaknesses. First is the inability of central planners to coordinate economic activities in the absence of a market pricing mechanism. State enterprises engage in production without regard to profit or loss. Achieving state-assigned quotas is more important for one's career than making quality products. In one of his on-the-spot visits in 1998, Kim Jong Il, "showing a stern expression on his face and scolding the [factory manager], said that products that are consumed domestically deserve better quality than the goods that are exported."[30] Since the publication of that article, numerous follow-up articles have appealed for product quality, not for competitive or market-share reasons, but because improving quality is "a noble manifestation of patriotism," and "a long-range undertaking for the sake of posterity."[31] Neither motivation is likely to inspire workers to devote increased attention to quality.

Economic statistics are routinely manipulated or fabricated to enhance the reputation of the production unit and its manager. Competition between enterprises for scarce resources is based on political rather than economic considerations. The economy is not planned; rather, it is in large part irrational and anarchic—precisely the characteristics North Korea attributes to capitalist economies. Kim Jong Il makes matters worse by championing his pet projects, thus requiring industrial production plans to be changed to accommodate his desires, with a predictable ripple effect throughout the economy.[32]

As a work motive, socialist ideology is a poor substitute for individual material incentives. This is the economy's second weakness. The motivation problem has been addressed at many times in many ways: for example, by trying to root out bureaucratism (one of the tasks of the Three-Revolution Team Movement) and by staging mobilization drives in individual enterprises and sometimes throughout the entire North Korean work force. North Korean officials have an ambivalent view of the use of material incentives. Through introspection they must recognize their importance, because government and party officials are notorious for demanding bribes for performing their duties. Yet as Kim Jong Il has said in a major policy statement, "Trying to move a man by means of money contradicts the intrinsic nature of socialist society."[33] For years economic officials have been trying to find a way to finesse this problem. Consider this unhelpful advice from an article in North Korea's major economic quarterly: "The accurate utilization of economic levers to suit the transitional characteristics of socialism offers an important guarantee for actively pushing forward the development of science and technology and improving economic efficiencies. . . . The great leader Comrade Kim Chong-il pointed out as follows: 'Material incentives should be accurately applied as an economic means for better implementing the principle of collectivism on the basis of giving priority to political means.'"[34]

The autarkic nature of Juche as an economic principle is a third problem plaguing the DPRK, whose outmoded technology attests to the impracticality of developing modern technology without buying or borrowing from other economies. In the early days of the republic technology was imported from the Soviet Union and was in any case not up to date. Today, state-of-the-art technology is not only more complicated, but it also has a shorter life span. Not even the most advanced economies can afford to ignore technological innovations of other nations. North Korea tries to do without foreign technology as a matter of Juche principle and as a matter of necessity dictated by a lack of foreign exchange. The import-substitution approach to trade has prevented North Koreans from developing comparative advantage in products that could be sold on the international market for the foreign exchange necessary to buy foreign technology.

A fourth weakness is the tremendous drain that maintaining a million-strong army imposes on the economy, consuming 25 percent or more of GNP. Thus the irony: the very military capability that is supposed to preserve North Korea's national security has become one of the main threats to the country's long-term security.[35]

The most pressing economic problem is the food shortage. The apparent (but wrong) solution to the problem is to try to achieve agricultural self-sufficiency, in line with the Juche principle. The more farsighted solution would be to strengthen those export industries in which North Korea might have comparative advantage and trade its products for food grown by countries that have a more hospitable growing environment than does North Korea.

Solving the food problem has always been high on the government's agenda.[36] The cool climate and hilly terrain of North Korea are not well suited to growing rice, which is the food staple throughout Asia. Land reform was undertaken immediately after the war, followed by collectivization in the 1950s. In 1964 Kim Il Sung's "Theses on the Rural Question" called for a technological, cultural, and ideological revolution in the rural areas, with the goal of transforming agricultural collectives to state farms. To implement the theses, a "four-point rural movement" involving irrigation, farm mechanization, rural electrification, and development of agricultural chemicals was initiated. In 1976 a "five-point nature transformation policy" was instituted to bring more land under the plow. In 1981 a "four-point nature transformation program" set new goals for creating arable land, most notably by constructing the West Sea Barrage. While these programs did make more land available for crops, they often created natural hazards by overterracing and overcutting hillsides, rendering the land vulnerable to erosion during heavy rains.

The agricultural system suffers from at least four basic problems.[37] First, the deterioration of the general economy deprives the agricultural sector of needed support of energy and raw materials. A serious shortage of electricity prevents pumping stations from irrigating the fields. Oil and parts shortages have idled farm machinery. Fertilizer factories are shut down for lack of energy and raw materials. Second, the collective system does not impart sufficient motivation to workers, who are often paid according to how many days they work, not to how much work they do. A large but undetermined amount of crops are stolen by workers before they reach the warehouses.[38] Third, agricultural technology is lacking. The party's "scientific" policy of "planting the right crop in the right soil at the right time" in practice means that the party determines what to plant. Kim Il Sung was a strong advocate of growing corn to supplement the rice crop, so large expanses of land were planted with corn, which by definition was the "right crop." Kim Jong Il has decided potatoes are the right crop. Farmers have little say in the matter.

The agricultural sector has never been able to supply enough food to satisfy the domestic market. In the 1970s and 1980s Kim Il Sung put forth the goal of producing 10 million tons of grain a year, but it is unlikely that more than 8 million tons were produced. Grain production fell to 4 to 5 million tons in the 1990s, and after severe floods destroyed much of the crop and land in 1995, production fell to 2 to 3 million tons for the remainder of the decade, producing an annual grain shortfall of 2 to 3 million tons.[39] International food contributions—principally from China, the United States, South Korea, the European Union, and initially from Japan—totaled an estimated 900,000 tons in 1996, 1.2 million tons in 1997, and 1.3 million tons in 1998.[40] But by 1999 donor fatigue was setting in as the food shortage continued, the DPRK government interfered with the distribution and monitoring of food aid, and no significant economic reforms were initiated.

The North Korean response has been within the perimeter of its socialist economic policies. In a series of *Nodong Sinmun* articles on agriculture run in May and June 1999, ten policy goals were outlined, some more practical than others: adhere to the Juche farming method (self-reliance by farms and county agricultural organizations); implement the "potato revolution" (grow more potatoes); implement the "seed revolution" (develop better seed strains); level more farm land, especially to make it suitable for mechanized farming; expand double cropping; adhere more faithfully to the "right crop in the right soil at the right season" policy; increase agricultural mechanization; raise more grazing animals, especially rabbits and goats; increase the use of microbial (animal and human waste) fertilizer; and expand rice farming lands.[41] The tendency shown in most of these policies is to manage farming with less dependence on the general economy. That is, work harder, grow rice substitutes that are better suited to the terrain and climate, even if they do not appeal to the Korean palate, and raise small animals that do not need as much feed grain as pigs and cattle.

The country's economic infrastructure is seriously eroded. Of equal importance, but more difficult to measure and infinitely more tragic from a humanitarian standpoint, is the degradation of the nation's human capital. Visitors to the DPRK report seeing listless workers who do not consume sufficient calories to put in a day's work, even if they had the desire to do so. One former North Korean reports that parents teach their children in subtle ways not to work hard. A North Korean cornfield may look well cultivated from the outside, but penetrate into the center (where the farm manager is unlikely to muddy his feet) and wild grass is growing so thickly that "a tiger could deliver cubs without being disturbed."[42] The food shortages that struck the country in the latter half of the 1990s are weakening an entire generation of North Koreans, who will remain physically and, in some cases, mentally stunted for the rest of their lives.

The problems of North Korea's economy cannot be solved by economists, for the root of the problems lies in the political system. Kim Il Sung may not have realized that Juche socialism cannot work, but Kim Jong Il does understand socialism's limitations and has revealed this understanding in remarks secretly taped and smuggled out of the country.[43] At one point Kim is heard to say, "Socialism is fine, but there are many internal problems that need to be solved. Yes, I say people have no motivation to work." Unfortunately, Kim has inherited his position of leadership on the basis of filial loyalty and commitment to his father's ideology; the son is in no position to make significant changes to the system. Having created an ideologically based political economy touted as the most superior in the world, North Korea is now trapped in its own myths. Reducing the power of central planners and allowing individuals greater opportunities would weaken the political control that keeps Kim Jong Il in power and gives North Korea its rationale for a separate existence apart from capitalist South Korea. Opening North Korea's borders to trade and investment would allow outside information to penetrate the society, revealing the innumerable lies on which the Kim family cult is based, thereby destroying the legitimacy of the Kim regime.

Economic Adjustments

The Kim regime has not been oblivious to the need for changes in economic policy. Some foreign analysts have pointed to economic adjustments made since

1984 as an indication that North Korea is on the road to economic reform, but most believe these adjustments fall woefully short of what is needed to put the North Korean economy back on its feet.[44] A real danger is that the adoption of minor adjustments may fool North Korean leaders into believing they have responded adequately to changing situations and that the lack of substantial results from these changes is because of bad luck or hostile foreign pressures rather than the tentative nature of the reforms.

Nicholas Eberstadt, in a widely cited paper on North Korea's "muddling through" policies, has highlighted some of the shortcomings of North Korea's economic reforms: no reduction of military mobilization or conversion of military industries to domestic use; no move to provide a larger share of the national economy for personal consumption; virtually no acceptance of the principle of private property; no official acceptance of market mechanisms; no attempt to strengthen the inconvertible North Korean currency; no allowance for increased flows of information or increased scientific contacts with foreign specialists; no attempt to service or retire the national debt.[45]

Two kinds of modifications have been made to the socialist command structure: one, minor changes in the domestic economy (not unlike the overly cautious approach taken by the rulers of the Choson dynasty in its last days), and two, a limited opening to foreign investment. An early domestic reform was the institution of the Chongsan-ni management method, named after the Chongsan-ni Cooperative Farm to which Kim Il Sung in 1960 made one of his famous on-the-spot guidance visits. The ostensible goal of this method is to induce managers to become familiar with the workers and their problems. The means Kim offered to achieve this laudable goal was to put a party committee in charge of production (according to the party's "mass line," the people spoke through the party). Unfortunately, since the party's stock in trade was ideological indoctrination and political motivation, the response of the workers to the new system was predictably apathetic. The following year Kim visited the Taean Electrical Appliance Factory and formulated a similar management system for industry, called the Taean Work System.[46]

As its trade relations with socialist economies weakened, North Korea turned to the hated capitalists for capital and technology. A Foreign Joint Venture Law was promulgated in 1984, followed by three implementing laws on taxes in 1985. Kim Il Sung had visited China in 1982 and with Kim Jong Il in 1983, seeing for themselves the promising results of foreign investment that were beginning to accrue from China's Joint Venture Management Enterprise Law. North Korea's version of the law was not particularly successful in attracting investment. The law's contents were not detailed enough for serious foreign investors, North Korea's debt was worsening, and its infrastructure was weak. Most joint ventures were established with pro-DPRK Koreans living in Japan and China. The money invested is estimated to be only $150 million—until 1998 when South Korean President Kim Dae Jung relaxed restrictions on investment in North Korea and the founder of the Hyundai conglomerate, Jung Ju Young, began pouring hundreds of millions of dollars into North Korean investments to promote peaceful inter-Korean relations.

In December 1991 the DPRK set up its first foreign economic trade zone (FETZ), a 621-square-kilometer region in the Najin-Sonbong area in the northeast corner of the country bordering China and Russia along the Tumen River—as far from North Korea's major cities as possible (to limit foreign influence). The zone is within a larger area designated by the United Nations Development Program (UNDP) in 1990 as an international development area. In 1992 the DPRK proposed a three-stage infrastructure development plan for the zone, with a first-stage (1993–95) investment of $1.3 billion, a second stage (1996–2000) investment of $1 billion, and a third stage (2001–10) investment of another $1 billion. By the end of the 1990s only a few small (foreign) investments in highways, hotels, and telephone lines had been made, and the completion date for the first phase of development was postponed indefinitely. An article in the usually sympathetic ROK periodical *Hangyore 21* reported that the North Korean leadership seems to have at least temporarily pulled back from its support of Najin-Sonbong.[47] The "free" market operated in the zone has diminished in size, apparently because of stricter government control over vendors. Billboards have disappeared. Fewer foreign companies are showing interest in investment in the zone. Even before the downturn the zone was not a hospitable place to visit. The American journalist Andrew Pollack, who attended a business conference in the zone in September 1996, gave the following description: "This town and neighboring Sonbong are strangely lethargic, with none of the hustle and bustle found in other Asian countries. . . . People here cannot speak freely. Any foreigner leaving the conference site was followed by security agents."[48]

Private ownership of stores by Koreans is permitted in the zone, and the exchange rate of 200 won to the dollar is more realistic than the official rate of 2.1 won that prevails throughout the rest of the country. The North Koreans continue to solicit foreign investments in the zone, but the political climate is not favorable for serious investment as long as North Korea's relations with the major capitalist countries remain poor. The three countries bordering on the Tumen River—North Korea, China, and Russia—have made few efforts to coordinate development of the Tumen River area.

In 1984, the same year the Joint Venture Law was promulgated, two modest reforms in the domestic economy were instituted. The Independent Accounting System, first proposed in 1973, was more fully implemented. Under this system local production units were given more responsibility for developing procedures to meet quotas and were allowed to keep earnings from the sale of goods that overfilled quotas. Another reform, this one under the guidance of Kim Jong Il, was the August Third Consumer Goods Program. After conducting an on-the-site inspection of an exhibition of light industry products in Pyongyang on August 3, 1984, Kim urged workers to use locally available resources, including scrap materials, to make consumer goods for the local population, to be sold in direct sales stores rather than at the government-run distribution centers. In fact, the August Third program is similar to a campaign initiated in 1958, whose goal was to encourage small-scale enterprises to manufacture locally needed goods with local materials. The original program met with some success but seems to have been gradually brought under central planning and control and thereby stifled.

In a small but promising agricultural reform, the size of work teams on collective farms was reduced in the late 1990s. A cooperative farm might have ten work teams of 50 to 100 members each, subdivided into squads of 8 to 10 members. Teams specialize in field work, livestock tending, machinery repair, and so forth.[49] The new work squads often comprise members of a single family, who receive a plot of land to fill quotas specified by the management of the collective. The family may keep any surplus. The smaller work unit in principle lessens the problem of free riders and, especially when it is a family unit, increases work motivation. Any surplus, as well as other goods, can be sold in farmers' markets where private enterprise rules under the watchful eyes of state security personnel. Market prices are far higher than in the state stores, but a larger variety of goods is available. Whereas the Joint Venture Law could be considered a direct challenge to the autarkic economic philosophy of Juche, the August Third program and the agricultural work squad program challenge the principle of central control. All three reforms have given the North Korean people some experience in capitalist practices, and this experience, regardless of what the leadership in Pyongyang intends, may pave the way for more significant economic reforms.

Multiple Economies

One sign of contradictions in the communist economic system is the operation of several parallel economies in North Korea. The struggling primary economy, encompassing production in state factories and on state and collective farms, with payment to the workers in the form of a nominal wage and distributions through the official ration system, is complemented by several secondary economies: a "court economy" for the elite, a black market for the masses, and a separate military economy. On the fringes of the primary economy, but shading into the secondary economies, are illegal but widespread activities such as bribery, pilfering, and undocumented production.

Kim Jong Il and the top cadres have their own stores, foreign trade organizations, and bank accounts. Vasily Mikheev, who worked as the first secretary of the Soviet embassy in Pyongyang in the 1980s, describes how North Korea's top cadres have adapted to international market conditions to provide for their own needs.[50] The court economy obtains goods for the ruling elite (broadly defined, a class of almost a million citizens) through foreign market transactions. Structurally, this economy consists of financial, industrial, and trading companies able to secure state resources but unaccountable to the economic bureaucracy. The industrial companies manufacture goods for export, the trading companies market them, and the financial institutions bank the profits. Mikheev reports that the first of these organizations was established in the 1970s in connection with the Taisung and Bongwha-Kumkang foreign trading companies and their associated banks.[51] Kim Jong Il appears to have taken control of much of this court economic activity long before he succeeded his father in 1994, operating it from two or more KWP offices.[52] North Korean government and party officials also engage in many illicit activities such as counterfeiting, production of illicit drugs, and smuggling (especially conducted by the DPRK's foreign diplomatic corps).[53] Many of these activities are sanctioned or condoned by the party or government; others are free-lance operations intended to enrich individuals.

Kim Jong Il realizes the danger of permitting the members of the elite to enrich themselves, thereby making them independent of him. Presumably to gain greater control over foreign trade, a Ministry of Foreign Trade was established by the tenth SPA in 1998 and the number of foreign trade organizations was reduced from about 300 to 100.[54] Several of North Korea's top foreign trade specialists disappeared within a few months. Whether they were purged or removed as part of the reorganization of trade offices is unknown.[55] Their unexplained disappearance was disconcerting to their foreign business contacts.

Just as the elite population has its own means of circumventing the restrictions of the official economy, so too do the masses. Members of the elite use their economy to enrich themselves and maintain their ruling position by procuring the necessary resources to keep the government running sufficiently well to provide national and regime security. The masses turn to the black market to survive.

Every city and town has its farmers' markets where products can be bought and sold outside of the state distribution system. Originally these markets were meant to provide an outlet for the surplus produce of farming cooperatives and to enable workers on collective farms to market the produce grown in their garden plots. Since 1984 markets have expanded into permanent places of business complete with food and beverage stands, all overseen by local officials. Markets were originally operated on the eleventh and twenty-first days of the month, which are farmers' holidays, but by the late 1990s they were operating on a daily basis in many cities and towns. Besides produce from farmers' private plots (and pilfered goods from the fields), nonfarm products such as used furniture, clothing, and household goods are sold or bartered for food. Authorities often close their eyes to black market activities that have sprung up within the marketplaces, where people sell items such as cigarettes and liquor that are legally prohibited from sale.[56] Market prices are determined by supply and demand. In 1998, as part of Kim Jong Il's attempt to stem the tide of social and economic disorder and take greater control of the economy, people's markets were reportedly reined in. The (North) Korean Central News Agency (KCNA) rebutted a Japanese report that the government was closing its "free markets" by denying the existence of such markets: "This is a wholly unfounded fabrication and no more than a virulent anti-DPRK false propaganda which was made by the paid mass media of Japan on the basis of misinformation provided by the South Korean 'intelligence service' [this is boiler plate denial for North Korea]. . . . There are only farmers' markets. . . . Farmers sell at the markets some surplus agricultural products and live-stock products."[57]

The court economy and the emerging civilian off-plan economies are essentially capitalist economies and in that sense have already moved North Korea along the road to economic reform. These secondary economies, including the military economy, probably exceed the primary economy in size.[58] As long as these secondary economies meet the minimum needs of the North Korean people—who have low expectations—the leaders in Pyongyang need not fear public unrest.

Models of Reform

North Korea's Foreign Joint Venture Law and the foreign trade zone in Najin Sonbong are modeled after similar economic initiatives in China, yet for the most part the North Koreans have ignored the dramatic economic changes taking place in China, even though the Chinese have urged their fellow travelers in North Korea to reform their economy.

Economic reforms were introduced in 1979 under the stewardship of Deng Xiaoping, who sought to free the Chinese from some of the ideological economic constraints imposed by Mao Zedong.[59] The reforms were accepted to remedy serious deficiencies in the people's standard of living and to address the growing problem of unemployment. With the party's permission, in some of the poorer rural areas farmers on large collectives could elect to form small work teams according to a "group responsibility system." These groups functioned as quasi-independent economic units, paying a specified amount of their production to the state and keeping the rest. The farming of small privately held plots of land and the establishment of small privately owned retail establishments were also permitted.

The Chinese peasant did not have to be asked twice. As many as 80 percent of the Chinese population—primarily those living in the countryside—were not covered by the vaunted communist welfare system, so they had little to lose. As many as 200 million were essentially jobless, barely subsisting within communes, and this number of unemployed was growing by several million a year, posing a destabilizing threat to the Beijing regime, which had less political control in the country than in the cities. Given the opportunity to become independent, the peasants took the reins and instead of forming artificial work groups, proceeded to take their allotted plots of land and turn them into private family farms. Within four years, 97 percent of the Chinese collective farms were privatized.

The privatization movement spread to rural businesses, set up by many of those millions of rural unemployed who now became traders and entrepreneurs. When the authorities in Beijing realized that a wildfire of capitalism was spreading, they turned to Deng, who merely said, "Let us take a look at it." Presumably recognizing both the cost of privatization, which meant an erosion of state power and control, and the benefits, which were gainful employment for millions of Chinese whom the state could not care for, Deng adopted an unofficial policy of the "three no's": no official promotion of private enterprise, no propaganda for it, but also no crackdown on it. Thus Chinese agricultural reform, which gradually spread to urban settings, was a bottom-up movement in which the peasants, who had little commitment to communism and nowhere else to turn for sustenance, took advantage of an opportunity offered them by the party. For the Chinese peasant, privatization was not a vote against communist ideology; it was a pragmatic response to the need to survive.

Many Chinese Communist Party (CCP) cadres disapproved of this economic revisionism, but the party had limited resources to discourage the reform. The CCP had been turned upside down by the years of chaos surrounding Mao's ill-fated Great Proletarian Cultural Revolution. Most party members in the countryside were poor, lived thousands of miles from Beijing, and had a poor education (even in the mid-1980s, two-thirds of party members were illiterate or had only a grade-school education). In short, the party was not a strong controlling force.

At the top, Deng had given his tacit endorsement, and at the local level, administrators found that private enterprises could be made to pay taxes, which filled local coffers. The most astute of the local cadres also realized that they were well positioned to profit from capitalism. Officials requested bribes to ensure that enterprises operating at variance with regulations would not be shut down. Relatives of cadres and retired cadres became successful entrepreneurs by using their party and government connections.

This mass economic reform scenario is not one that the totalitarian Kim regime is likely to tolerate willingly. Nor for that matter is Chinese privatization a movement that can easily be replicated, for the Chinese differ in important respects from the North Koreans. From a historical perspective, the Chinese were probably in a better position to embrace private enterprise. Before the communists came to power, Chinese peasants arguably enjoyed more independence than most Korean peasants, who labored under the efficient security system of the Japanese.

The one Chinese economic initiative that did appeal to Kim Il Sung was the opening to foreign investment. Yet foreign investment was only a facilitator in China, and the amount of investment was small ($34 billion from 1979 to 1992) relative to the size of the Chinese economy. Most foreign-sourced investment, technology, and management skills came from overseas Chinese, who saw an opportunity to renew ties with the homeland while making a profit. Except in South Korea, few overseas Koreans were ready to make substantial investments in North Korea.

Twenty years after the beginning of economic reforms in China the CCP remains in control of national politics and major industries but has lost much of its influence over the local economy and certainly over the ideological beliefs of the Chinese people. Those state-owned industries that have not been privatized are still a drain on the national budget. An increasing number of Chinese live their lives as much as possible oblivious to the party and the government. Occasional crackdowns against economic and political freedoms such as Tiananmen may occur, but the CCP is weakened if not irrelevant. This is not a model the North Korean elite would wish to adopt, although in a watered-down form, it may be the least destabilizing of the available models.

When the North Korean press is looking for an object lesson on the perils of economic reform, it turns to the former Soviet Union and Eastern Europe, warning that if the North Korean people abandon socialism, they will face unemployment and chaos. It is true that the Soviet privatization experience has been far less successful than the Chinese one. Whereas Chinese reform began in the rural economy and was tolerated by the distant communist bureaucrats in Beijing, reform in the Soviet Union began in Moscow with Gorbachev's perestroika in 1986, a political decision intended to have economic side effects. Russia, like China, North Korea, and all other communist societies, had always had its second economy of black-market traders and garden farmers. According to Minxin Pei, in 1985 a quarter of the Soviet Union's agricultural output came from the 35 million private garden plots and herds, which accounted for only 3 percent of the farmland.[60] The first economic enabling legislation of perestroika was the 1986 Law on Individual Labor Activity, which permitted private employment in second jobs and for the "marginal" labor force of students and housewives but prohibited the formation of a primary independent labor market. Yet from the start this modest opening to capitalism was resisted by many officials, who strictly enforced regulations against private property. For example, in 1986 a government campaign against "unearned income" targeted many of those who had made money in the second economy.

Pei cites two important domestic factors explaining why capitalism never caught fire in the Soviet Union as it did in rural China. First, the government was of two minds about reform, sometimes complaining that the people were too slow to adopt new methods and other times punishing them for earning money. This reflected Gorbachev's ambivalence toward reform, which he saw as a way to save communism, not replace it. Gorbachev lamented that rural reform was being met "with caution by collective farmers and workers who have lost . . . the habit of working hard, and have become accustomed to steady incomes regardless of end results."[61] Yet he remained a committed communist working within the party, where he had to contend with a strong conservative coalition that eventually staged an unsuccessful 1991 coup, opening the way for Yeltsin, an avowed noncommunist. But by then the Soviet (now Russian) polity and economy had disintegrated. Rather than adopt a "three no's" policy, the Soviet government took a confusing yes-and-no position that jeopardized the fortunes of those who chose to strike out on their own.

Equally important for explaining the failure of economic reform in the Soviet Union is that the Soviet people were unexcited about capitalism. People were suspicious of the new cooperatives formed by the privatization of small- and medium-sized industries, especially in the service sector. They viewed, often accurately, the privatization of large businesses by public ownership vouchers as a scheme by which managers enriched themselves at the expense of their workers. Why the Soviet people failed to exhibit a spirit of capitalism is undoubtedly a complex question. As Pei points out, since almost everyone in the Soviet Union was covered by social security (such as it was), everyone was at least surviving before the reforms. A second reason Soviet citizens failed to embrace capitalism may be found in the long period they had lived under communism (since the 1917 revolution) and the mind-stunning oppression they had suffered during those years. General Dmitri Antonovich Volkogonov, who in 1991 wrote an official history of World War II, recounted the following to the American writer David Remnick:

> Totalitarian systems usually absorb people absolutely. As I have come to realize, very few people have been able to transcend such a system, to tear themselves away from it. Most people of my generation will die imprisoned in this system, even if they live another ten or twenty years. Of course, people who are twenty or thirty are free people. They can liberate themselves from the system quite easily. . . . I am now convinced that Stalinism created a new type of man: indifferent, without initiative or enterprise, a person waiting for a messiah, waiting for someone to come alive and solve all of life's problems.[62]

Soviet citizen-reformers were also at a disadvantage compared with the Chinese. The Chinese peasant entrepreneurs could work at what they already knew, which was farming—a small-scale, low-technology occupation. Russian farms had been collectivized for so long that people had forgotten how to do small-scale farming except in garden plots. An old grandmother told Remnick, "My grandchildren wouldn't know what to do with a piece of land. Even my own children have a hard time telling the difference between a horse and a cow. . . . [The] gigantic state farms killed the villages and put nothing in their place."[63]

In the cities, few Russians knew anything about building or managing a large business. Running small businesses was easier if one could avoid harassment from officials. The easiest business to get into was the protection racket, which required only muscle. Hence entrepreneurs came to be seen as capitalist crooks, living off the work of others. In the absence of an efficient state police system, the Russian crime syndicate became an extremely profitable enterprise.

It may be that the socialist principle of equality (rather than equity) became too ingrained in the Russian people. Many writers have commented on the strong jealousy that Russians show toward the newly wealthy. Another of Remnick's interviewees complained that older people "are so used to being equal in poverty that they assume if you have money, you are a crook."[64] Economic equality, after all, is incompatible with capitalism, which depends on the principle of equity to make it run. This principle seems to have survived in China but was lost in the Soviet Union, either during the long period of communism or even earlier.

Socialism Meets Capitalism

The quandary for North Korea's leaders is that no politically attractive model for economic reform exists. China is closer to North Korea geographically and culturally than are Russia and the Eastern European states, but unlike China, North Korea is primarily an industrial society, modeled after the Soviet economy. Following the Soviet or Eastern European model of economic reform would seem to invite economic chaos and would not augur well for the stability of the Kim regime. Kim Jong Il is looking for a third way: North Korea's "socialism in our own style." Reforms in the domestic economy and opening to foreign influences are being adopted gradually and with a strict limit that will permit the regime to keep the North Korean people permanently sealed off from the outside world. Within these limited confines of reform, the North Koreans are trying to adapt to changing conditions in the international economy.

Faced with the disappearance of fellow socialist economies to trade with, North Korea has been forced to study capitalism. In 1995 a course on capitalism began to be offered at Kim Il Sung University. Although few North Koreans have been exposed to any information about capitalism (apart from propaganda condemning it) the ruling elite, especially economic officials, are being introduced gradually to market principles. A perusal of articles published in the North Korean quarterly *Kyongje Yongu* [Economic Research] provides a clue to the understanding people have and the ideological strains that are evoked in a discussion of market principles.

A February 1997 article endeavors to describe the "Principal Economic Laws That Function in the Market Economy."[65] First is the law of values: everything has a price. Not just products "but also honor, offices, conscience, and even love." Money decides everything. The purpose of this valuation is to trade products in the market to obtain a profit, with the value determined by "the size of the labor undertaken . . . for production." Trading follows the law of supply and demand, with prices rising in a seller's market and falling in a buyer's market, although the author is prompted by his belief in the inherent value of a product to teach that prices (that is, market value) rise above or fall below the "true" value of a product.

Compared with the socialist economy with its central control and multiyear plans, the market economy is "spontaneous and anarchic." This is considered a major flaw, since, according to the author, for an economy to develop "appropriately," it must be planned so that the market is "rationally balanced." In the market economy, "not just the individual capitalists, but also the states are unable to single-handedly control or command the economy." The invisible hand of supply and demand does not count as a controlling agent. One of the "laws of motion" of this anarchic market is the law of competition, with the "stronger preying upon the weak aimed at capturing the market." An important method to drive out the competition is to lower prices, which requires a reduction in production cost if profits are to be maintained. Production cost can be reduced by increasing labor productivity through increased mechanization, seeking technological breakthroughs in production, or by reducing wages.

On the marketing side, advertising and improvements in service competition "rage fiercely" in the market. "The competition of the stronger preying upon the weak aimed at capturing the market is essentially a competition of exploitation and a competition of plunder," and the working masses bear the brunt of this exploitation. The disadvantage for the workers allegedly has to do with the difference between the value of a product and the price of a product, or in the author's words, between demand and "ability-to-pay" demand. As capitalist employers lower wages to improve their competitive position, their workers have diminished means to purchase products that they need, resulting in a chronic oversupply of products. The labor that went into the making of these unsold products is wasted. Thus the capitalist market is unbalanced. Yet this cannot be the end of the cycle if the law of supply and demand is in force. "The stronger-preying-upon-the-weak competition gives rise to prevalent bankruptcies and downfall, frauds and swindling, and speculation, fostering chaos and disorderliness in economic life." (Left unsaid is that the bankruptcies are visited upon the capitalists, who own the means of production, thus reducing supply and tending toward a balance of the market.) This picture of a market economy is essentially accurate, although the author fails to grasp the essence of market value and discounts the balancing power of supply and demand. The description also neglects to note that capitalist economies are not purely market driven but are regulated by an extensive web of laws and norms.

A companion piece in the following issue of the journal instructs cadres on how to trade with the capitalist economies, following Kim Jong Il's instructions that "we must make inroads into the [capitalist] foreign markets by hook or by crook to develop our trade" since "socialism can no longer form its own markets and the old trade policy based on the socialist market has become unrealistic, *a temporary phenomenon though.*"[66] North Korea's ideological preference has always been to trade first with Southeast Asian nations, since they are geographically close and presumably considered less detestable than the "imperialist" states (namely, Japan and the United States). A second line of trade would go out to the European states. The principal goal of trade is to obtain hard currency (for example, dollars) with which to purchase needed products on the international market.

The *Kyongje Yongu* article says the first step in international marketing is to assess the market, which, unlike a planned market, is a moving target: consumers' demands change, and buyers and sellers are forced to negotiate new types of deals. The marketing task is especially challenging because "the world capitalist markets are surplus commodity markets" in which commodities (undifferentiated goods) can only be sold by "pushing" them with advertising and publicity. "Market research, assessment, environmental analysis, consumer-behavior study, commodity development, price-setting, distribution route structuring, advertising and publicity, service—these are essential activities in developing overseas markets."

To succeed in the international capitalist market characterized by "anarchy and spontaneity," "one has to deny and topple others to survive the social chaos and disorder. With the capitalist economy, struggle for existence is a way of life." This is especially true when someone is selling the same goods as other producers in a commodity market in which the seller cannot influence the price. Thus the article recommends that North Korea avoid such markets, concentrating on those in which North Korean products have few competitors. Yet technology makes it difficult to keep a monopoly on a product for long (and North Korea is notoriously short of technology). Although the author does not state the obvious, North Korea seems to be faced with marketing commodity products and taking whatever price it can get. No suggestions are made on how to escape from this dilemma.

The remainder of the paper is largely devoted to wishful and contradictory thinking. North Korea is faced with a U.S.-led embargo. It must expand trade with other nations to break this embargo.

In the course of expanding and developing trade with many countries, we will see the ranks of supporters and sympathizers for our revolution expand further and the defense of our socialism grow firmer. . . . Socialization of production is expanding daily on a global scale. . . . The new trade policy set forth by our party is indeed a revolutionary policy making it possible to always defend the interests of our people and hold fast to our way of socialism to the last amid the changing international environment.[67]

Other articles from this same journal deal with business topics related to international marketing such as how to make international payments or set up joint ventures. They are written at the level of an introductory college textbook, and like articles on all topics treated in North Korean publications, they begin by quoting the wisdom of Kim Il Sung or Kim Jong Il, as in "Comrade Kim Jong Il has noted: To do a good job of international settlements is important in expanding and promoting economic and cultural relations with other countries" or "Today a beneficial environment is being created in our country for widely developing contractual and equity joint ventures . . . under the sagacious leadership of the great leader Comrade Kim Jong Il, upholding the behest of the great leader Comrade Kim Il Sung."[68]

Most articles written for the North Korean public and officials, even in this economic journal, espouse the traditional economic line, bothering very little with economic reality. Although by 1997 North Korea's civilian factories were operating at no more than 25 percent of capacity, the author of a *Kyongje Yongu* article boasts, "Our party, under the sagacious leadership of the respected and beloved Comrade Kim Il Sung and the great leader Comrade Kim Jong Il, has led the struggle of our people for socialism along the one road of victory for as long as a half century, without a single error or bias."[69] North Korea's problems in "normalizing production" are attributed to the U.S.-led economic embargo, the disappearance of other socialist economies, and bad weather. The only advice the article can give for overcoming economic problems is to "correctly define priorities." These priorities, set by Kim Jong Il and his father, are no priorities at all: "While focusing on the food problem on a priority basis, we [must] solve problems in the production of primary consumer goods, and problems with coal, electricity, railway transport and metals." After mentioning the need to solve multiple severe problems, the author boasts, "Comrade Kim Il Sung . . . built our type of economy. . . . the firmest in the world and most promising in its prospects for development. . . . Our mighty heavy industry . . . can produce anything it wants to . . . Our modern light industry can satisfy domestic demand for consumer goods with no limit. . . . All the people enjoy the highest level of state and social benefits in all spheres of life, materially and culturally."

It is difficult to believe that the relatively educated readers of *Kyongje Yongu* believe a word of this tract. How must they react? Perhaps with understanding, considering it the party's duty to put the best possible face on conditions. On the contrary, though, some readers may be repelled by such flagrant lies, distancing themselves psychologically from the party. The truth may be somewhere in the middle: those who do receive newspapers (which are narrowly distributed to conserve paper) generally ignore the featured propaganda articles unless required to study them in political discussion groups.[70]

Conclusions

The economic policies of Kim Jong Il and his late father are fanciful daydreams of leaders who are isolated from the outside world and to some extent even out of touch with the lives of the average North Korean.[71] They are also an appalling fraud on the North Korean people. After two decades of economic progress achieved by Stalinist methods, the economy in the 1970s began to stagnate and then decline as the limits of the socialist method were reached and the nature of the international economy changed. However, Kim Il Sung's economic policies failed to change; first, because he had claimed his policies were based on scientifically correct economic theory; and second, because his desire to maintain totalitarian control over the people necessitated a socialist command economy that would keep the people dependent on the party and the state. Beginning in the 1980s the gap between official descriptions and actual conditions of the economy widened, as did the gap between the promised future and the one that unfolded. Dire economic problems in the 1990s gave rise to the myth of a "turning point economy." Like the White Queen in Lewis Carroll's *Through the Looking Glass*, Kim Jong Il offers his people "twopence a week and jam every other day" (*but never today*). From one year to the next the New Year's message lauds the great success of the preceding year and promises an even better year to come, even though the preceding year was a failure and the following year will be as bad if not worse.[72]

In 1990: "Last year, the self-reliant foundation for our industry was further consolidated through the great construction struggle by all people and more favorable conditions were realized to vigorously accelerate the socialist construction." [73] In 1992: "1991 was a year of severe trials, a year of worthwhile struggle and a year of glorious victory for our people. . . . We should bring about a new upswing in socialist construction."[74] In 1994: "Last year. . . . our people brilliantly adorned the last year of the Third Seven-Year Plan by accelerating the construction of the socialist economy with great revolutionary enthusiasm. . . . The New Year 1994 is a year of revolutionary advance when the building of socialism in our country will enter a new stage of development."[75] In 1996 (after the devastatingly bad harvest of 1995 and the beginning of mass starvation): "Last year the internal and external situation of our revolution was very rigorous. . . . We must dynamically advance in high revolutionary spirit with confidence in certain victory and revolutionary optimism so that we can effect a revolutionary turn and win a great victory in the spirit of the red flag this year."[76] In 1997 (with hundreds of thousands dying of hunger and more factories closing their doors): "The past year of 1996 was one of severe trials, and a year of worthwhile struggle and victory. . . . Our people, with a conviction of sure victory and an undaunted spirit, will exert themselves to make 1997 a new turnaround for the DPRK revolution, a year of revival and of a promising victory."[77] In 1998, as the famine continued: "Having successfully weathered the strenuous moments of the arduous march, we have opened a breakthrough for a new advance and a leap ahead."[78] And in 1999 the New Year's editorial entitled "Let's Make This Year Mark a Turning Point in Building a Powerful Nation," opened with the now-familiar words, "Today, we greet the hopeful New Year 1999 with the great pride of socialist victors."[79]

Kim Jong Il cannot afford to substantially modify or open North Korea's economic system for fear of jeopardizing his political power. This judgment begs the question of whether Kim, his economic planners, or for that matter the North Korean people, recognize the basic flaws in their economic system. As for Kim, three sources of information shed light on his true beliefs: official propaganda, a few minutes of secret tapes made in the 1980s, and his lifestyle. The propaganda suggests a firm belief in the eventual victory of Juche socialism. The tapes suggest he has some reservations. His lifestyle indicates that while he may believe socialism is best for the people, it is not for him. Reports on all sides tell of his lavish lifestyle and fondness for imported goods (most famously, cognac and videos). Photographs of Kim depict a plump man attired in well-tailored clothes, not a man who has been eating two meals of gruel a day and wearing wrappings around his feet.

All but the most sophisticated North Korean economists probably view the economy as a simple, linear flowchart of inputs and outputs, where labor is just another input to be managed like coal or water, and consumers patiently wait for the system to crank out goods required to fill their basic needs. Of course such a model is grossly inadequate to deal with rapidly changing conditions or highly complex economies in which every change in the system requires adjustments throughout the rest of the system. The alternative to central control—allowing the system to maintain itself through individual enterprise and self-regulation and making the people the defining characteristic of the system—is probably not considered a viable economic policy even by those technocrats who are unconcerned about keeping Kim Jong Il in power. The hypothesis that order can arise from chaos is not self-evident.

Six years after the disappointing conclusion of the Third Seven-Year Plan, the proclamation of ideological slogans has replaced the promulgation of economic plans, a sure sign that the North Korean leaders are confused and desperate. Muddling through has given way to crisis management. It seems likely that incremental reforms will be made in the domestic economy, primarily in loosening domestic travel and marketing restrictions to enable the people to secure their own welfare outside the primary economy. As anomie has spread throughout the land, the government has warned the people that they must depend on their own efforts, not the assistance of the state or foreign governments. A *Nodong Sinmun* article appearing just before the planting season of 1999 warns farmers, "If people should sit back and do nothing but look to higher levels for help, they are bound to fail in farming 100 percent. . . . That is, if we quit depending on chemical fertilizer and vinyl sheet [to protect seedlings] we succeed in our farming; if not, we fail."[80]

Since the floods of 1995, food rations have been sporadic or nonexistent for much of the population, and the continuation of this crisis suggests that the government may adopt, by default, a form of "exceptionalist welfare," whereby people are largely responsible on the local level for their own well-being but may occasionally receive "gifts" from their benevolent leader in Pyongyang. Such a gift, the arrival of several truckloads of fruit (thanks to the benevolence of Kim Jong Il) to the privileged residents of Pyongyang was deemed worthy of a news story on Korean domestic television.[81]

It is difficult to believe that any changes made in the North Korean economy will approach those made in China.[82] In Beijing the overriding concern is to keep the party in power; in Pyongyang it is to keep Kim Jong Il in power. Strict limits will be placed on changes in order to keep the North Korean people isolated from foreign influences. Kim Jong Il seemingly will go to any lengths to preserve his regime, even accepting the deaths of millions of his people. He relies on tradition, ideology, and social control to keep a suffering and unhappy populace from revolting. Propaganda emphasizing that "paradise" for the North Korean people means an ideological paradise, not a material paradise, is designed to keep popular expectations low. In the late 1990s, rather than initiating the bold reforms needed to turn the economy around, Kim promoted economic initiatives that would turn the North Korean people into premodern farmers and hunters and gatherers. His endorsement of self-help campaigns to grow potatoes and raise rabbits and goats replaced the traditional promises of providing the people with rice and beef soup.[83]

In foreign economic policy Kim is keen to substitute capitalist foreign aid and investment for the lost aid from the former Soviet Union, while keeping the aid pipeline from China open. The success of this policy must surprise even him: from 1994 through 1998 North Korea received $250 million in aid from the United States—a country it characterizes as its sworn enemy—making it the largest recipient of American aid in East Asia.[84] Washington's listing of North Korea as one of its major national security threats, a listed terrorist and drug dealing nation, have not stopped this aid. Pyongyang solicits economic assistance by appealing to humanitarian values, coupled with the threat (as perceived by donor nations) that if such aid is not forthcoming, a North Korean collapse would require much larger foreign donations to address a much more serious humanitarian tragedy. Yet, an authoritative *Nodong Sinmun-Kulloja* joint article of September 1998 warns, "There has never been any foreign capital that contributed to national economy development ever before and no such incident should occur. Foreign capital is like opium."[85]

In August 1998 North Korea announced as its national goal *Kangsong Taeguk*, a "militarily and economically strong nation." The strategy, as it seems to be unfolding in Pyongyang's negotiations with Washington over nuclear and missile issues, is to demand aid from foreign governments in exchange for limiting North Korea's production and sale of weapons of mass destruction. The 1994 Agreed Framework with Washington has convinced Pyongyang that only military threats will bring foreign powers to the bargaining table. One corollary to this strategy is that North Korea does not expect to gain goodwill from other states but rather to get what it wants by threats. One domestic consequence will be a growing gap between the health of the civilian economy and the strength of the military economy as more money is devoted to weapons technology and production. If this is a fair description of North Korea's economic strategy, it is bad news for the North Korean people. Oh Kil-Nam, a South Korean economist who ill-advisedly emigrated to North Korea and only barely escaped a year later, compares the Kim regime to a Dracula that sucks the blood from its increasingly weak victims, the North Korean people.[86] The military-first policy also poses a challenge to foreign governments seeking to contain an implacably belligerent North Korea. Most tragically, relying increasingly on foreign aid and the manufacture of weapons of mass destruction will enable the Kim regime to avoid facing up to the inherent weaknesses of its economic system.

CHAPTER FOUR

The Leader,

His Party,

and His People

*Kim Jong Il Emerges as the Lodestar for
Sailing the 21st Century.*[1]

Kim Il Sung achieved the distinction of becoming the world's longest-ruling leader of his time, and by the turn of the century his son has been managing the day-to-day affairs of the republic for a quarter of a century. From the beginning, Juche ideology was formulated not only as the first principle of policymaking but also as a powerful weapon to preserve the Kim family dynasty. Juche was gradually transformed from a principle whereby North Korea could maintain its independence from stronger nations, including its cold war allies, to a theory of sociopolitical unity under the leadership of an omnipotent and omniscient leader.

"Great Leader" Kim Il Sung

The man known as Kim Il Sung was born Kim Song-ju on April 15, 1912, in the town of Mangyongdae near Pyongyang to an herbal pharmacist who had attended a school established by American missionaries.[2] The Kim family moved from Japanese-controlled Korea to Manchuria when Kim, the eldest of three sons, was seven. After several years of schooling in Badagou, he returned to Pyongyang for two years of middle school before returning to school in

Badagou at age thirteen. His father died the following year, and his mother would die seven years later. At age fifteen Kim enrolled in a middle school in Jilin, Manchuria, a city with about 400,000 ethnic Koreans. Kim joined the Korean Youth League and participated in activities against the Japanese, who were taking control of Manchuria. His name first appears in Japanese records on May 1929, when Kim (age seventeen) was arrested and jailed for a few months for helping to organize a Korean Communist Youth League. Kim's formal schooling ended at the eighth grade with his entry into politics. Out of jail within a few months, Kim became a member of the organizing committee for the Eastern County Korean People's League, a newly formed coalition group in the Jilin area. Around this time he may have spent several years earning his living by teaching school. Kim's military career began at the age of twenty or twenty-one when he joined a guerrilla band calling itself the Korean Revolutionary Army. The young Kim, who by now had taken the name of a famous Korean resistance soldier, Kim Il Sung, kept a low political profile, not supporting any of the contending Korean factions nor taking a leadership role in the guerrilla group. The guerrilla band was broken up by the Japanese and its leader jailed, but Kim managed to stay out of jail and, from 1932 on, fought the Japanese with various small bands of guerrillas attached to larger contingents of Chinese forces in Manchuria and occasionally crossing over into Korea. He eventually became the leader of his own small band of soldiers, but rarely had more than a hundred men under his command, and often far fewer.

The Chinese army and Korean resistance forces were no match for the well-trained and equipped Japanese forces that overran northern China, and Kim and his compatriots were forced to flee into the Russian Maritime Province in 1941. Kim was assigned to a camp near Khabarovsk, where he received further military training. At this time he also married Kim Jong-suk, who had joined Kim's band of soldiers in 1936. Their first son, Kim Jong Il, was born at the Khabarovsk camp on February 16, 1942. Although Kim Il Sung gained notoriety among the Japanese soldiers and fame among Korean patriots for his exploits, he was only one of a number of similarly brave Korean fighters. Kim's advantage over the other leaders was that he managed to evade capture by the Japanese, thus emerging "victorious" at the end of the war.

The Japanese surrendered to the allied armies on August 15, 1945, and by agreement the Americans moved into Korea from the south to accept the Japanese surrender while the Russians, who had declared war on Japan only a week before, moved in from the north. A month after the Japanese surrender, on September 19, Kim Il Sung arrived in Korea by boat, not as a conquering hero but as a captain in the Soviet army. His arrival was politically inconspicuous.

He was not a member of any of the political groups that immediately sprang into action in Korea, including the Korean communists who had survived underground during the Japanese occupation. His political advantages were that he had demonstrated his ability to survive under harsh wartime conditions, was respected for his military exploits (although many people refused to believe that a thirty-three-year-old could be the famous guerrilla fighter Kim Il Sung), and was a known quantity to the Soviet authorities. The Russians' first attempt at organizing a provisional government that would include both communist and noncommunist groups was unsuccessful. In any case, Kim Il Sung was not included in that government. The Russians, in line with the Yalta Agreement, were inclined to accept Washington's idea of a five-year trusteeship for Korea, but the Korean noncommunist groups were strongly opposed to this idea, and the provisional government came apart.

The Russians then formed a provisional people's committee on February 8, 1946, and appointed Kim Il Sung to lead it. Under the political guidance of a Colonel Alexandre Matcevich Ignatiev, Kim worked to bring the various active political groups into the people's committee: indigenous Korean communists and nationalists, Koreans who had returned from China, and those who, like him, had returned from Russia. In his own political organization, Kim could count on the loyalty of fewer than 200 partisans with whom he had fought, and he had no support from the indigenous Korean political groups. But Kim's political fortunes were enhanced because most of the prominent Korean politicians had gone to Seoul, which they assumed would become the political center of a unified Korea. Their departure left the field in Pyongyang relatively free for Kim and his Soviet advisers to maneuver in.

The Korean Workers' Party (KWP) was inaugurated during the last days of August 1946, but despite strong Russian support, Kim was not elected chairman. Instead, the more famous Korean politician Kim Tu-bong, a member of the China group, was elected, while Kim became one of two vice chairmen. Kim maneuvered to strengthen his political position, gaining the KWP chairmanship in 1949, a position he would hold until his death in 1994.

By 1949 it had become clear that Korea would remain divided for some time to come. A separate government in South Korea had been recognized by the United Nations as the only legitimate government on the peninsula, and with American backing the South Korean president, Syngman Rhee, prevented communist groups from gaining a foothold in the South. Kim decided that the only way to reunite Korea was through force.

Kim launched the Korean War on June 25, 1950, after obtaining the grudging support of Josef Stalin and Mao Zedong. Despite early military successes,

the North Korean forces, without the help they had expected from an uprising of sympathetic Koreans in the South, were pushed back across the 38th
Parallel dividing the two Koreas, and then back toward China by the U.S.-led
UN forces. The Kim regime was saved by the entry into the war of a million
Chinese forces who took over control of military strategy for the remainder
of the war. Kim blamed others, including some of his own partisans, for his
battlefield failure, and began to purge political opponents as soon as Chinese
forces had recaptured Pyongyang from UN troops. Trials and executions of
alleged traitors got under way as soon as the Korean War Armistice was signed
in 1953, and the purges continued throughout the 1950s until Kim had eliminated all political opponents and taken full control not only of the government,
but of North Korean history, recasting himself as the victorious general who
repulsed the American aggressors.

For the next forty years Kim oversaw the reconstruction of North Korea
while skillfully and ruthlessly enhancing his power. His leadership abilities were
prodigious. He was a tireless worker, going among the people dispensing advice
(much of it wrong) and focusing their energies on the construction of a socialist society, but never abandoning preparations to reunite the Korean Peninsula
by force. He also developed into an able statesman within the communist world,
frequently traveling to China and the Soviet Union (usually to ask for aid).
Except for visits to Algeria and to Indonesia, Kim never set foot in the noncommunist world, nor did he ever meet with a leader of a major Western
country. His world was bounded by communism. Kim Il Sung did not live
according to the title of his multivolume autobiography, *With the Century*. As
Adrian Buzo has argued, Kim never really advanced intellectually beyond the
experiences of his early days:

> [Kim Il Sung's] strengths were basic—self-discipline, resilience, mental
> toughness, and a strong work ethic—but the weaknesses were far more
> significant. They began with Kim's intellect, which was formed under
> the influence of limited schooling, extended military struggle, and polit-
> ical combat within the oligarchy. As a result, he could not frame effective
> policies to pursue economic development and modernization, nor was
> he able to seek the advice of those who could. Convinced of the univer-
> sality of Stalinism, he was not interested in any further refinements or
> revisions, and his concept of modernity increasingly became frozen in
> the past.[3]

Kim's political position had become unassailable by the end of the 1960s.
Under the 1972 constitution, Kim became president of the government (he

formerly ruled as premier), while continuing in his post as chairman of the KWP. At about the same time, he began to give serious thought to grooming a successor. His first wife, Kim Jong-suk, had died in 1949 while giving birth to Kim Jong Il's younger brother, who died in childhood. Kim Il Sung remarried in 1963, and by his second wife, Kim Song-ae, had another son, Kim Pyong Il. In the early 1970s, Kim chose his first son as his successor, in proper Confucian tradition, although the junior Kim was not publicly introduced as the future leader until 1980.

Kim Il Sung presided over a country beset with mounting economic problems and suffering from increasing political isolation throughout the cold war. During the 1970s Kim Jong Il gradually took over management of domestic affairs, leaving his father free to host foreign dignitaries and write his autobiography. Kim Il Sung continued to be active to the day of his death from a heart attack on July 8, 1994, at the age of 82. When he died, he was sincerely mourned by most of the North Korean people, who, although they were experiencing increasing hardships, remembered him as the man who had guided North Korea's recovery after the Korean War. The true facts of his life—his failure to liberate Korea from the Japanese, his responsibility for starting the Korean War, and his small stature on the international stage—had been replaced over the years by a fabricated history of an "ever-victorious" soldier and a leader of the progressive peoples of the world. This is the Kim whose death the North Korean people mourned.

"Dear Leader" Kim Jong Il

While his father was alive, Kim was called the "dear leader," but since then he has more frequently been referred to as the "respected and beloved general," an appellation more suitable to the father than to the son, who, after a rather wild youth, grew into an able manager but hardly a heroic military figure.

The Early Years

Born in a Russian military camp near Khabarovsk along the Amur River in Siberia, Kim Jong Il was given the Russian name of Yuri (nickname Yura), which he kept until high school.[4] Yura spent his first years in the camp nursery, along with other children of the guerrilla fighters. His personality in some ways imitated that of his father: a wild child who frequently got into trouble. In looks he took after his mother, being short in stature and rather homely. Kim's younger brother, Shura, was drowned at the age of five in a small pond in the family's yard while playing with Yura.

When Kim Il Sung returned to Pyongyang a month after liberation, Yura and his mother stayed in Russia for two more months, arriving in Korea on the northeast coast on November 25 at the town of Unggi (later renamed "Sonbong," meaning "leading torch"), a town that is now part of the Najin-Sonbong free trade zone. The family took up residence in Pyongyang, where Yura entered the privileged-class Namsan school at the age of seven. When his father remarried eighteen years later, it was to a more attractive and sophisticated woman, and Yura is said to have been intensely jealous of his stepmother and angry with his father for the remarriage. After Kim Il Sung's death in 1994, his second wife, Kim Song-ae, became a nonperson in North Korea, while his first wife, Kim Jong Il's true mother, was posthumously elevated to the status of hero.

When Pyongyang fell to UN forces in 1950, Yura and his mother fled to Jilin in Manchuria. After Chinese troops recaptured Pyongyang, Yura and his mother returned to the city, and the child attended a number of schools, finally graduating from Namsan Senior High School in 1960. Although he is listed in the high school yearbook as Yura, he began to use his Korean name, "Jong-il," which was originally written in Chinese characters as "Jong the first" [2973 0001] but changed to "Jong the sun" [2973 2480] when he made his political debut in 1980. The new "sun" name is the same character as the first one in his father's name, "Il Sung." Interestingly, his mother's name, Jong-suk, which was originally written with the Jong character meaning "virtue" [6297], was posthumously changed to the Jong character "righteousness" [2973], the same as her son's Jong character.[5] Thus Jong Il conveniently ended up with one name from his father and one from his mother, meant to indicate that he is truly in the "revolutionary bloodline." By the 1990s this nominal sleight of hand was meaningless to most North Koreans, since Juche principles forbid the teaching or use of Chinese characters.

Some sources believe Jong Il attended the Air Force Officers School in East Germany after high school, but if he did it was for only a few months, because he enrolled in the Political Economy Department of Kim Il Sung University the same year he graduated from high school. After graduating from the university in 1964 he was put in charge of his father's bodyguard, taking a position in the KWP Central Committee's Organization and Guidance Department. This department, the most important organization in the party or government bureaucracy, was headed by Kim Il Sung's younger brother, Kim Yong-ju, who seemed at the time to be a prime candidate to succeed Kim Il Sung. During his ten years with the department, Kim Jong Il apparently did not get along with his uncle (or for that matter with any other authority figure).

Succession

The long-term campaign to make Kim Jong Il his father's successor may have begun at the Sixth Meeting of the League of Socialist Working Youth (now called the Kim Il Sung Socialist Youth League) in June 1971, when the elder Kim is believed to have suggested that the older generation must let the postliberation generation carry the torch of revolution.[6] If this was intended as a political signal, it meant that a generation or two would be passed over in consideration for the top post. A clearer sign of Kim Jong Il's eventual succession may be found in reports of a closed session of the KWP's Central Committee at the Sixth Plenum of the Fifth Congress in December 1972, when Kim Jong Il's name was proposed by two of his father's partisan days' comrades-in-arms.[7] At the same time, the dubious question of whether a socialist state should condone hereditary succession was being addressed in official literature. The Academy of Social Sciences 1970 edition of the *Dictionary of Political Terminologies* denounced hereditary succession, calling it "a reactionary custom of exploitative societies" and "originally a product of slave societies . . . later adopted by feudal lords as a means to perpetuate dictatorial rule." This statement was deleted from the dictionary's 1972 edition.

In 1973 the thirty-one-year-old Kim (about the same age as his father when he had returned to Pyongyang after liberation) was appointed to the Politburo and named director of the Organization and Guidance Department, the most powerful bureaucratic position in the party or government. He was also publicly designated as "the leader of the party and the people." At the same time, for reasons that have never been made clear, the press began to refer to him not by name but as the "Party Center," a usage that continued to the end of the decade.[8] Unlike his father, the junior Kim avoided making public appearances.

To promote his role as the elaborator and implementer of his father's political philosophy, on April 14, 1974, Kim Jong Il announced the "Ten Principles," including injunctions that the entire society be dyed in Juche ideology and everyone be absolutely loyal and obedient to Kim Il Sung.[9] This became a sort of ruler's constitution designed to make the state and the leader a single conceptual entity. Officials from Kim's Organization and Guidance Department visited every corner of the country to explain these principles and announce that the younger Kim would be the next leader. As a newly emerging young and mysterious figure, Kim Jong Il caught the attention of party members, who discerned the wisdom of ingratiating themselves with the future leader, and who saw the junior Kim as a somewhat glamorous rising political star. When Kim began to wear his hair in a crew cut, many party members dubbed it "speed battle hair," after Kim's promotion of work-harder-and-faster campaigns, and began wearing their hair in the same style. When Kim changed over to the permed bouffant style, many party members did the same.

It was wise to take Kim seriously, because as soon as he was designated successor he began to consolidate his power by courting powerful figures who could be persuaded to support him and moving against those who might oppose his succession. Nam Il, one of Kim Il Sung's partisan comrades who is said to have been unenthusiastic about Kim Jong Il's succession, died in 1976 when his car was run over by a large truck in the middle of the night. Another partisan, Vice Premier Kim Dong-kyu, reportedly criticized Kim Jong Il in a party meeting in 1976 and was sent to a concentration camp, where he died in the 1980s.[10] These were just two of the high-level cadres who fell by the wayside as Kim Jong Il drove to power. In the 1970s Kim Jong Il replaced thousands of officials at all levels of the party with younger members who would be personally loyal to him in gratitude for their promotion.

Kim Jong Il is famous for lavishing gifts on his supporters, sometimes expensive gifts such as Mercedes Benz cars (with his special birth date license plate number of 2-16). One former North Korean official tells the story of Kim Jong Il's attending the opening of a foreign currency shop in Pyongyang (a shop selling foreign luxury goods that can only be purchased with foreign currency and is therefore off-limits to the common people). Kim told his subordinates to pick out whatever they wanted as a gift from him. At first, the shoppers were cautious, choosing items like ballpoint pens or mirrors. Kim told them to behave like real men by choosing something of value worthy of being a present from him; in less than an hour the officials emerged loaded with television sets, refrigerators, and the like.[11] Kim did not neglect the military. He is said to have been particularly solicitous of Oh Jin-u, one of his father's partisan comrades, who as defense minister was the third most powerful man in North Korea (he died of a serious illness in February 1995). Kim lavished praise and presents on Oh and is rumored to have overseen his recovery from a serious automobile accident.[12] Oh became a Kim supporter, often lending his august presence to Kim's visits to military bases and other sites.

Kim's Organization and Guidance Department played an important role in the succession process, and his position as head of the department placed him in the best position to control personnel matters in the DPRK. The department employed the brightest minds in the country to direct its propaganda and agitation. These individuals (most famously, Hwang Jang Yop, who defected to South Korea in 1997), created not only the substance of Juche philosophy and its many elaborations but also the myth of the two Kims. For example, when Kim Jong Il placed emphasis on the traditional "red flag" image of communism, the staff created an entire Red Banner Thought campaign. Presumably these people are responsible for most of the hundreds of articles said to be written by Kim Jong Il, who would hardly have time to write them, even if he had the inclination, given his role of managing the country.

Kim's public introduction as the designated successor occurred at the Sixth Congress of the KWP in October 1980 (as of late 1999, the congress still had not held another meeting). In the reports of the congress he was listed as second in the ten-member Party Secretariat, fourth in the five-member Politburo Presidium (or Standing Committee), and third in the ten-member Military Commission. The only other individual to serve on all three powerful committees was his father. The head of the government's Supreme People's Assembly, Hwang Jang Yop announced, "The leadership of the party and the chieftain should be handed over and completed without interruption: the question of succession is a fundamental and vital one that determines the fate of revolution and it was resolved for the first time in history by the chieftain."[13] Thanks to this smooth succession process, North Korea would not go through the same turmoil of finding a successor that China had experienced after Mao, and Kim Il Sung would presumably not suffer the same fate as Stalin, who was denounced by his successor Nikita Khrushchev.

After the public announcement of his succession, the North Korean press gradually discontinued the use of Party Center as his code name, and he more frequently accompanied his father on "on-the-spot inspections." But Kim worked mostly behind the scenes. Only in the final days of Kim Il Sung's reign did it become apparent that his son had been running much of the government throughout the 1980s, and—according to Hwang Jang Yop—even in the 1970s.

Kim Jong Il did not take his first government (as opposed to party) position until 1992, when he was awarded the title of "Marshal" and appointed Supreme Commander of the Korean People's Army. This was a politically awkward appointment on two counts. First, Kim had never served in the army, and second, the constitution stipulated that the president (Kim Il Sung) had supreme command of the army. The second matter was adjusted the following year when the constitution was duly amended. The matter of Kim's lack of military experience was taken up by the Propaganda and Agitation Department, which began to fabricate a suitable resume for him. To further consolidate his control over the military, Kim had himself named chairman of the National Defense Commission (NDC) in 1993.

Consistent with his custom of working without appropriate titles—and a strong indication that North Korea is a ruler-based rather than law-based government—Kim continued to rule North Korea after his father's death by controlling the government in his position as supreme commander. In October 1997 he was chosen "by acclamation" to fill his late father's position as chairman of the KWP, without the nuisance of convening a Party Congress. In 1998 a new Supreme People's Assembly was finally elected (the first since 1990), and pursuant to a revision of the constitution, the position of president was abolished so that the late Kim Il Sung could be the eternal president. Kim Jong Il was re-elected (that is, reappointed himself) to the chairmanship of the National Defense Commission, but he took no new titles. To nominally head the government and make public appearances, the former foreign minister, Kim Yong-Nam, was elected to the new post of chairman ("president" in news releases to foreign audiences) of the presidium (standing committee) of the Supreme People's Assembly. But to make no mistake about who was really in charge, Kim Yong-Nam announced, "The office of the [National Defense] commission chairman is a very important post; it is in charge of the whole of our political, military and economic powers and is the top post of the republic."[14] But no adjustment was made in the constitution to confirm the supreme position of the NDC, which by law directs only military affairs.

Since his father's death Kim has continued to keep a low public profile. Although hundreds of papers have been published under his name, his only known public utterance was made in 1992, when he shouted, "Glory to the heroic Korean People's Army" during a military parade.[15] The tradition of an annual New Year's Day speech by the leader ended with the death of Kim Il Sung. Since then, New Year's editorials have been published jointly by the major North Korean news media. On New Year's 1997, Kim Jong Il released a brief handwritten letter but made no speech. In 1998 the North Korean news media explained the absence of a New Year's message by saying that immediately after Kim Jong Il had paid his filial midnight New Year's visit to his father's grave, he had left for an army unit to give an on-the-spot inspection.[16]

Kim Jong Il has rarely made himself available to visiting dignitaries, nor has he traveled widely. As a young man he accompanied his father on trips to Moscow in 1957 and Eastern Europe in 1959, and perhaps spent a few months in East Germany at the Air Force Academy. In 1983 and 1984 he traveled to China. His father enjoyed meeting foreign dignitaries, but Kim Jong Il has always been ill at ease with people. The only Western figures he is known to have met are two Italians. In 1992 he entertained Carlo Baeri, an Italian businessman visiting North Korea, and a month after his father died he met Giancarlo Elia Valori, secretary general of the Italian Institute of International Relations.[17]

Personality

Some analysts have predicted that Kim Jong Il, unlike his father, will be forced to share power, but most of the limited evidence on North Korean politics suggests that Kim Jong Il was exercising almost total control over the government even before his father died. Hwang Jang Yop, the elite cadre and Juche theoretician who escaped to South Korea in 1997, has been very clear on this point:

> Who is in charge? No one has real power. You should know that clearly. Suppose a person comes to the fore in the diplomatic field. This does not mean he has real power. As for the chuche idea, I had given guidance to the overall work for the chuche idea for almost 20 years. However, I did not have real power. We should know the North Korean structure. Only Kim Chong-il has real power. . . . A person who gains some trust today may be gone tomorrow. Therefore, it is better not to pay attention to individuals but policy.[18]

Kim Jong Il is secretive by nature—a secrecy that also characterizes national policy in North Korea, and for that matter in most autocratic states. Back in 1960, before the public emergence of Kim Jong Il and the creation of a personality cult for himself and his mother, Japanese correspondent Ichiro Shimizu asked a North Korean journalist if President Kim Il Sung had any children. The journalist replied that he didn't know whether Kim Il Sung had a wife or not, adding that it was not an important question and that nobody was interested in such a matter.[19] When the journalist Ian Buruma visited North Korea in 1994, he asked his guide where Kim Jong Il lived and how many children he had. The guide replied, "We don't discuss such things with foreigners."[20] It is doubtful if the guide could have answered if he had wanted to: Kim Jong Il has many residences and reportedly many mistresses. Foreign analysts believe he has at least two daughters and two sons by one or more wives and mistresses.

Even though reclusive, Kim has had to deal with many people over the years, and some of these people have been persuaded to tell what they know. A number of North Korean defectors, most notably Ko Young-hwan and Kang Myung-do, have had occasion to speak with Kim and observe his behavior. The former North Korean party secretary Hwang Jang Yop has also added a little to our knowledge about Kim, although for the most part he is of the opinion that an understanding of Kim's personal life is irrelevant to an understanding of his political behavior.[21] Some idea of Kim at leisure is provided by Japanese women who visited Pyongyang to earn money and were invited to attend one of Kim's intimate parties (he drank heavily, scattered hundred dollar bills around, and sang a Japanese army ballad).[22] And Yi Nam-ok, the niece of Kim's second wife (or perhaps mistress), who was brought to one of Kim's residences to be a companion for Kim's son, Chong-nam, before moving to the West in 1992. She speaks well (and prudently) of Kim, saying he is industrious, intelligent, humorous, independent, lacking in self-interest, and an altogether charming "bon vivant" kind of person.[23]

The most extensive and reliable firsthand information on Kim is provided by Shin Sang-ok, a South Korean film director and his wife, the actress Choe Un-hui, who were abducted separately from Hong Kong and taken to North Korea on Kim Jong Il's orders in 1978.[24] After five years of detainment for reeducation, they began to make movies for Kim, who had abducted them in a typically bold move in order to give a boost to the North Korean film industry. They escaped to the West while on a trip to Austria in 1986. In several tape recordings they secretly made of a few of their conversations with Kim, and one with his father, Shin and Choe provide a documented view of Kim's thoughts.

From these multiple sources a tentative picture of Kim's personality can be pieced together. The traits most frequently mentioned are Kim's independence, arrogance, and lack of respect for seniors—a serious breach of social relations in Confucian society. Related character descriptions include "conceited," "displaying a superiority complex," "haughty," and "cold." Examples of behavior given in support of these characterizations include the young Kim's habit of talking to elders with his hands in his pockets or with his hands clasped behind him (a prerogative of superiors), and Kim's failure to acknowledge the presence of others (as in failing to offer greetings and salutations). Kim's impulsiveness is also a noted trait. Faced with few constraints on his behavior, he expects to be immediately obeyed. Related characterizations include decisiveness, boldness, recklessness. Kim is energetic; he works, thinks, and talks fast. He believes that if people work hard enough, they can accomplish any of his plans. Past failures of execution appear not to enter strongly into his calculations. Kim's daring plans often misfire: the 105-story Ryugyong Hotel in Pyongyang, built to be the tallest in Asia, has never been completed for lack of technology and economic resources. Terrorist campaigns against South Korea have served only to get North Korea blacklisted in the international community. Kim issues orders for changes in resource allocations in the command economy that serve only to worsen the balance of supply and demand. Not surprisingly, Kim's hobbies are consistent with his impulsive nature and his openness to experience: fast cars, fast horses, party girls, hunting and shooting, and watching action films.

Kim is said to be quick tempered and at times violent. He yells at subordinates, and besides directing terrorist acts, he is alleged to have ordered the killing of officials (including a former agriculture minister) with whom he was displeased; in one case, he allegedly carried out the execution on the spot himself.[25]

Kim is shy, uncomfortable among strangers and in front of the public, preferring to deal with a small circle of associates. He has never addressed a large crowd or given a major speech. Ko Young-hwan, who worked for the North Korean Ministry of Foreign Affairs, recalls Kim's visit to the ministry in 1986. Ministry personnel were told to put their offices in order and come to work the next day wearing their best clothes, but they were not told who would be visiting. At 10 the next morning the chief of Kim Jong Il's security unit arrived with his men and inspected the windows, hallways, and offices of the ministry. A security check was conducted to ensure that all employees were at their desks. Then the doors to the building were locked so no one could enter or leave. When Kim arrived, he spoke for about ten minutes with the foreign minister and three of his aides and then departed, concluding the on-site inspection.[26] Needless to say, such cursory visits, unlike those conducted by the gregarious Kim Il Sung, are unlikely to raise worker morale.

The contrast between Kim and his father is painfully obvious in a video documenting the festivities celebrating the DPRK's fortieth anniversary in 1988. Kim Il Sung is resplendent in a white Western-style suit; Kim Jong Il is wearing a gray Mao jacket. As the two Kims and other dignitaries review a mass demonstration and parade, young boys, presumably from the Young Pioneers, approach each dignitary to wrap a red neckerchief around his neck. The young man who approaches Kim Il Sung salutes him and skillfully wraps the scarf around the Great Leader's neck. Kim firmly grasps the boy's shoulders, speaks to him, gives him a bear hug, and then a handshake. Meanwhile, another Young Pioneer has loosely wrapped a red kerchief around Kim Jong Il's neck. Kim fusses with the scarf and then gives the boy a light pat, first on the left shoulder and then on the right, looking all the while distinctly uneasy. In this video and in many photographs taken at public ceremonies, Kim Jong Il appears to be wishing he were somewhere else.

The contrasts in physical structure between Kim Jong Il and his father are striking. The elder Kim looked every inch the statesman, 5 feet, 6 inches (170 cm), above average height for his generation, and weighing a heavy 183 pounds (83 kg). Standing straight with his hands clasped behind his back and torso thrust forward (in the traditional Korean style appropriate to superiors), he

projected authority. He tried to give the appearance of a down-to-earth com-
monsensical man, but he could not have attained or kept his position without
indulging in considerable intrigue and stage management. According to Mike
Chinoy, who visited Pyongyang as a CNN correspondent covering the visit of
former president Jimmy Carter in 1994, when Kim began to offer a toast at a
luncheon he was hosting, hidden lights in the room were faded up to make
the room brighter, and then faded back down after he had finished speaking.[27]
Most of the foreign guests who met Kim were charmed by his presence, leaving with the impression that he was a man they could deal with.

Kim Jong Il's awkwardness with people can probably be traced to a variety
of sources. First, he has never had to please people in order to get his way. Second, his reputation and accomplishments are inferior to those of his father.
Third, Kim Jong Il's physical stature is short and pudgy—5 feet, 2 inches (160
cm), and 176 pounds (80 kg). Kim wears his hair in a bouffant, presumably
to add an inch or two to his stature. He reportedly wears lifts in his shoes, inviting the unflattering nickname of "altitude." Like his father, Kim is overweight
in the midst of famine. His customary uniform is a gray or tan factory fore-
man's slacks and short jacket, beautifully tailored but far from distinguishing.
On formal occasions he sometimes abandons his factory attire for a gray Mao-
style jacket. This is not to say that looks determine a man's success. Khrushchev
was not unlike Kim Jong Il in appearance, but the roly-poly Soviet premier
radiated vitality, whereas Kim just seems ill at ease.

Kim Jong Il probably does not completely trust even his closest associates. Any dictator must expect the occasional assassination attempt, the
substitute for democratic politics in an authoritarian state. Rumors of such
assassination attempts on Kim and his father have surfaced from time to
time, although hard evidence is lacking.[28] Kim governs with the aid of a
small group of associates, including his sister and her husband as well as
other relatives, but he is suspicious of his stepmother and her handsome
and well-liked son, Kim Pyong-il, thus limiting the family circle from which
he can draw support.

Kim is an artistic man with a strong imagination. He loves action films and
is said to have a video library of thousands of films. He enjoys staging fights,
for example between soldiers or security agents, much like a Roman emperor.[29]
He is said to be an excellent amateur musician, playing the piano and violin,
and directing the chamber orchestra that plays at his parties. His publicists say
he is responsible for the layout of Pyongyang and the design of many of its
buildings and monuments. Kim appears to be a creative thinker, as one asso-
ciate put it, an "amazingly modern thinker." Employing his sharp mind, Kim

plays with a wide range of ideas, putting many of them into operation, often without adequate preparation.

As much as his responsibilities permit, Kim is said to enjoy life, and according to the niece who became the childhood companion of Kim's son, he was a loving father, although of course he did not have much time to spend at home.[30] The late-night parties of his younger days are legendary. He can be a charming and thoughtful host when he puts his mind to it, although he tends to be oblivious of the feelings of subordinates. Carlo Baeri, the first Western businessman to meet Kim Jong Il, spent a day fishing with Kim in 1992. Baeri said the Dear Leader was a perfect host. Baeri and three associates were met dockside by Kim, who escorted them onto a boat that took them out to sea. An elegant lunch of several soups, Korean dishes including shellfish and shrimp, wine, and liquors was served. During the meal Kim Jong Il opened an expensive bottle of brandy that Baeri had brought to Pyongyang on a previous business trip. Kim also ordered his crew to provide the businessman with a thick jacket when the wind came up.[31]

To complete Kim Jong Il's portrait, serious consideration should be given to long-standing rumors of ill health. At times Kim has been out of sight for extended periods of time, and in the 1990s, especially just before and after his father's death, he looked to be in ill health. Rumored ailments include epilepsy, diabetes, heart trouble (including a heart transplant), and brain damage (from a car accident or a fall from horseback). Whatever the truth of these rumors, any ailments he has must not be debilitating: Kim's (relatively few) foreign visitors report that he appears to be in good health.

Grasp of Reality

Is Kim aware of North Korea's problems and concerned about finding solutions? On the one hand, reports from former North Korean officials reveal that Kim's subordinates often lie to him about deteriorating economic and social conditions to avoid his criticism. But even a cursory examination of the main propaganda themes in the North Korean media suggests that Kim is well aware of the signs as well as the causes of many of North Korea's problems. Repeated calls for the elimination of self-interest as a motivating factor reveal his recognition of socialism's motivational weakness. Campaigns to eliminate bureaucratism (that is, self-interest on the part of socialist managers) are perennial.

Kim's own off-the-record remarks captured in the secret tape recordings of Shin and Choe also reveal his recognition of what he termed "flaws in socialism," although he acknowledges to his two abductees that if anyone but him were to make such criticisms that individual would be branded a capitalist flunky (and sent to a re-education camp or worse). Kim characterizes (in the mid-1980s) South Korea's technology as being at the "college level" while North Korea's is at the "kindergarten level." He complains to Shin and Choe that "Our people do not want to accept new ideas." He admits that while "socialism is fine . . . there are many internal problems that need to be solved." In a discussion with director Shin about the lack of motivation on the part of North Korea's actors and directors, Kim agrees when Shin suggests that the party needs to establish a competitive system where people are rewarded for good work. Kim laments that North Korean actors don't work as hard and improve their skills as much as South Korean actors, because the North Koreans are guaranteed a living as long as they engage in minimal effort. Directors waste film because they don't have to pay for it.

Kim sees the flaws in socialism, yet he has been unwilling to reform the system. Rather, he turns time and again to ideological indoctrination. Does he believe North Korea's problems can be solved with more propaganda? Quite possibly he does, given his immersion in the fantasy world of film and his confidence in his superior intelligence and ability to control others. What he lacks is the recognition that the commitment to socialism that he expects in others is totally absent in his own life. Either he is a great hypocrite or he believes that he is a superior being not subject to the same psychological factors as other human beings, or he fears the conservative military and the consequences of reforms for his own welfare. The truth is probably a combination of all these factors.

Governing Style

Governance in North Korea is a case of personalized rule. The Kims, father and son, have promoted top party cadres, government officials, and military officers on the basis of their personal loyalty. The most senior cadres of Kim Il Sung's regime came almost exclusively from a small group of partisan comrades who fought alongside Kim in China and Siberia during the Japanese occupation. The KWP was Kim's party, and the inner sanctum of the party, in particular the Central Committee, was where the real decisions of government were made.

During the last twenty years of his life, Kim Il Sung allowed his son to run the day-to-day affairs of the republic. During this period Kim Jong Il gradually took over more leadership roles, until by the time of his father's death he was the supreme leader in all but name. Kim Jong Il relies on a kitchen cabinet composed of a small group of friends and family members of approximately his own age, especially trusting a few close relatives and drinking buddies, including Kim Kyong-hui, his younger sister and her husband, Chang Song-taek. Members of the government's cabinet (formerly the Administrative Council) also wield considerable power, in most cases concurrently occupying top positions in the KWP, but they are unlikely to be in the central decisionmaking loop.

Kim Jong Il's reliance on informal consultation and decisionmaking is consistent with his dislike for large meetings. He obviously relishes his role as a behind-the-scenes operator, a kind of wizard of Oz. This is not an unusual role for powerful politicians and businessmen in Asian societies to take, especially when dealing with foreigners. Kim's love of secrecy is in part explained by his deep suspicion of foreigners (a trait he shared with his father and with many other communist and totalitarian leaders). He has said, "We must create an environment as if it is surrounded by fog so our enemies cannot see us directly and clearly."[32] North Korea has gone so far as to sacrifice many of its people to starvation rather than open the country widely to foreign media and food aid monitors.

While Kim Il Sung was alive, his son's behind-the-scenes governance was often assumed to reflect the junior Kim's filial desire not to upstage his father. But as Kim Jong Il has continued this mode of governance even after his father's death, this argument loses much of its persuasiveness.

Kim's style of governance is described in the official press as *kwangpok chongchi* and *induk chongchi,* meaning broad scale and benevolent governance. The junior Kim has initiated many of North Korea's grandiose architectural projects and special events whose primary purpose is to glorify the country and the Kim family. It was presumably his idea to spend some $4.3 billion to stage the Thirteenth World Festival of Youth and Students in 1989, North Korea's answer to the 1988 Seoul Olympics. During the famine years after Kim Il Sung's death, Kim Jong Il is reputed to have spent almost $900 million renovating the Kumsusan Palace to house his father's remains.[33] In 1999 the North Korean press proudly noted that "construction of monuments to revolutionary exploits of the three commanders [Kim Jong Il and his parents] is making brisk headway in Korea.... The last five years have witnessed the building of many monuments at more than a hundred units of different domains. ...The exquisitely carved large granite monuments have letters and poems praising their on-site guidance and immortal leadership exploits."[34] Kim's boldness is praised as "the grand envisioning power of aiming high at all times and making a bold operation, the skillful organization and extraordinary sweep of achieving a target with the mobilization of all forces, the staunch propelling power of attaining one target after another for leaping progress without marking time."[35]

To make good decisions, Kim needs full and accurate information about the state of the nation. Perhaps his greatest managerial achievement has been to establish a reporting system that funnels information directly to his office. Beginning with his stewardship of the Three Revolution Team Movement, in which young party members were sent to work sites throughout the country to direct the revolution and gather information for Kim, he has increasingly turned North Korea's elaborate intelligence system to his own use. According to the so-called Three Report System, reports are to be delivered to Kim within three days of preparation by officials from the party, the government, and the security services.[36] Urgent reports about disasters or instances of failure to carry out Kim's direct orders are to be telephoned to his office immediately.

Kim Jong Il likes to keep people guessing. He does not deliver New Year's messages. He has failed to attend important events, including his own birthday celebrations. Even when the SPA was finally convened in 1998, on the fiftieth anniversary of the founding of the DPRK, Kim did not give a speech; instead, the assembly listened to the tape of a speech delivered by his father at the convening of the 1990 assembly. Kim enjoys conducting surprise on-the-spot inspections, appearing for a few minutes to the officials of organizations, especially military organizations. The North Korean press depicts Kim both as a larger-than-life figure and as a man of the people. As an example of the latter image,

> One day in early August Juche 56 (1967) the great leader Kim Jong Il was on a local guidance mission for rural communities in Yonggwang Country, South Hamgyong Province. When he stopped near a dam of Generating Shop No. 5 of the Jangjingang Power Station, workers of the station ran toward him, greatly happy to see him. . . . Kim Jong Il shook hands with them each and praised them for hard work. . . . It was past lunch time, so officials told him it was time to leave. . . . He said he would share lunch with the workers lest they should feel sad after a pleasant time. He sat on the concrete floor, surrounded by workers. His lunch was bread, a few side-dishes and nothing else. He said he was sorry that the lunch with workers was quite simple. He asked them to help themselves [to]enough. The lunch with him was, however, more significant than any banquet.[37]

Official reports say Kim leads a simple life, worthy of a man who loves the people and understands the hardships they are undergoing. "The jacket comrade Kim Jong Il usually wears shows well his traits as the people's leader who has always led a plain and simple life. Several days before a New Year's Day, officials presented a new suit to him who had always worn plain clothes. He refused to wear it, telling them that if they wanted to do something for him, they had better work hard to solve the clothing problem of the people."[38] A close examination of any photograph of Kim shows that his workman's slacks and jacket are finely tailored. As for eating simple fare, it is unlikely he could have attained his ample girth on such a diet, but to hear the North Korean press tell of it, he must be wasting away:

> Keeping in mind President Kim Il Sung's lifelong desire to have the peo-ple "eat rice and meat soup and live in tile-roofed houses," General Kim Jong Il has undergone all sorts of hardships for the people for the past three years [1995-1997] without taking care of his own health. With a pain in his heart about the fact that the people cannot afford to eat their fill, the general said that "I do not care if I eat only soup," and that "Day and night, I always think about ways to have our people live more afflu-ently." In fact, he often ate merely a bowl of corn soup or a rice ball as a meal while giving on-the-spot guidance to the Army and people. Who is really on the "arduous march"?[39]

Kim's benevolence to his people is capricious. While condemning millions to illness and death from starvation by failing to adjust his economic policies and insisting on keeping North Korea a closed society, he is said to attend to the smallest things. For example, the press has described his concern for the female traffic police in Pyongyang (who appear to be chosen for their beauty rather than their traffic conducting ability, which is not important given the lack of vehicles on the streets).

> It was on December 21 last year [1996] when the great leader Comrade Kim Jong Il was coming back to Pyongyang after his visits to People's Army units. On his way back he came to have a glance at traffic control women on duty at intersections in the capital city. Hardly drawing back his eyes from those women, he told an official that he was sorry to see traffic control women performing their duty in skirts on such a cold day. And he said they should be provided with padded trousers. . . . Later he examined designs for uniforms and said trousers should be made tight to suit boots, a visor should be attached to the cap to shelter from snow and rain, and metal buttons should be fixed on the fur overcoat with a mark of shield on the arm. . . . On January 11 [1997] he said that the

streets have been further brightened with the changed dress of traffic control women and that they look taller and prettier than before. . . . Indeed, the traffic control women in Korea live in great happiness.[40]

The Kim Family Cult

The Kim cult has been created to provide much more than political legitimacy for Kim and his father—the cult makes them into figures of worship who can no more be held responsible for North Korea's woes than can the Judeo-Christian God be held responsible for natural disasters. In some cases the Kim cult images grossly exaggerate historical fact; in other cases, they are pure invention. The cult is Kim's greatest invention and his greatest weakness. If the people believe in him as a demigod, he can exercise almost unquestioned authority; but if the lies on which the cult is based are revealed, Kim will be forced to rule entirely by coercion.

The Kim Il Sung myth reaches back into history. Kim claims to come from a "revolutionary" family.[41] One of his great-grandfathers is said to be the Kim who led a successful attack in 1866 on an American merchant ship, the *General Sherman*, which entered the waters of the Hermit Kingdom to establish trade contacts. The ship was burned with the loss of all hands. There is no credible evidence that the Kim who led this attack was a direct ancestor of the Kim Il Sung family (according to Hwang Jang Yop, the ancestor would have been only ten years old at the time).[42] Kim Il Sung's father, the herbal pharmacist, is said to have founded an underground anti-Japanese group calling itself the Korean National Association. Kim Il Sung himself is depicted in the cult literature as an heroic militant from his boyhood days, forming the Korean People's Army as early as 1932, when he was only twenty years old.

Early on Kim Il Sung realized the importance of establishing his reputation as a revolutionary fighter. When he arrived in Korea as a captain in the Soviet army a full month after Japanese forces in the North had surrendered, he tried to convince the Soviet officials in North Korea to make it appear that he had entered with the vanguard units.[43] In the years immediately after liberation, Kim could not deny the crucial role that Chinese and allied forces had played in fighting the Japanese. But as the Kim cult grew, references to the Chinese role in Korea's liberation were downplayed. In his 1955 Juche speech, Kim remarks that his criticism of the lack of Juche in the party's ideological work is not meant to imply that "we have not made the revolution and that our revolutionary work was undertaken by outsiders."[44] Quite the contrary. Kim claimed to have single-handedly defeated the Japanese forces and liberated the Korean Peninsula.

According to the Kim legend, the Korean War began when North Korean troops resisted an attack by American and South Korean forces on June 25, 1950. According to the official North Korean history, North Korean soldiers under the leadership of Kim Il Sung utterly defeated the American forces. Despite the leading role that Chinese troops in fact played in pushing American-led forces back across the 38th Parallel, only two years after the armistice was signed Kim would say (in his Juche speech), "If we had not organized the People's Army with old revolutionary cadres as its core, what would have been the outcome of the last war? It would have been impossible for us to defeat the enemy and win a great victory under such difficult situations."[45] A North Korean defector speaks of the tremendous shock of discovering (after his defection) that it was North Korea that attacked South Korea in the Korean War.[46]

Until the 1970s, Kim Jong Il was a virtual unknown in North Korea, but after his father decided to promote him as the future ruler, North Korean propaganda began to create the Kim Jong Il cult image. Soon, rooms in every building (including homes) prominently displayed a picture of Kim Jong Il alongside that of his father, with a special kit to clean the pictures as if they were sacred icons. The propaganda effort to promote Kim Jong Il would prove to be a greater challenge than the promotion of Kim Il Sung because the younger Kim had made no heroic contributions to North Korea; in fact, the years of his rule coincided with a downturn in the country's economic fortunes. Thus the importance of promoting the legend of the revolutionary Kim family, providing an aura of legitimacy for the junior Kim, regardless of his personal contributions.

After his father's death, the North Korean press attributed to Kim virtually all of his father's alleged qualities, including world's greatest general, statesman, and philosopher. History was revised to make it appear that the young Kim, even before his teens, was assisting his father in military campaigns and managing foreign affairs (the two areas in which he had little or no experience). The media praised his long-range vision, capable of seeing hundreds of years into the future, and claimed that his every move was designed to achieve a distant but glorious goal.

The cult of the two Kims was crafted to provide the Kims with complementary leadership roles. To the father was attributed the higher-profile role of theory creator, economic czar, undefeated general, and foreign policy genius. While his father was still alive, Kim was depicted as the loyal son who helped his father by implementing his ideas and acting as a mediator between that exalted personage and the common people. To complement his father's image as the great general and stern but caring father of the country, Kim Jong Il was positioned as a softer leader, hence his title of Dear Leader alongside his father the Great Leader. Although Kim had no expertise in economics, he assumed the role of the promoter of the people's welfare, unsuccessfully championing light industry to provide the people with consumer goods. Consistent with this role as a servant of the people, Kim Jong Il was described as the personification of benevolence. Paradoxically, it was the father who loved to be among his people and who was in turn truly loved and respected by them. The son appears to care little for the people, and they care little for him, although out of respect for his father, and because the son is the only leader they have, or can even imagine having, they remain loyal to Kim Jong Il. Kim satisfied himself with the honorary title of *yongdoja* [leader], rather than appropriating the exalted title of his late father, *suryong* [top leader].[47]

Nothing New under the Son

The two pillars of the status quo in North Korea are ideology and social control. The two Kims have been so closely identified with ideology that only a change in leadership is likely to free North Korea from Juche's stifling teachings. No Mikhail Gorbachev or Deng Xiaoping is likely to emerge in Pyongyang. The succession of Kim Jong Il raised the possibility that changes might be forthcoming. Some foreign analysts even speculated that the younger Kim might turn out to be a closet reformer—after all, he is known for his boldness and unconventional ideas, and he has had many years of experience behind the scenes during which to contemplate changes.

Kim Il Sung overcame many hardships in his life to reach the pinnacle of power and remain there until his death. He ruled with an iron fist, employing both rewards and punishments to enforce his will, but underlying these levers of power the great leader had undeniable legitimacy by virtue of his long battle against the Japanese, and more important, his charismatic personality. A leader who relies on charisma to influence people has a difficult choice to make when he retires: find another charismatic leader with the same vision—an unlikely prospect—or institutionalize his rule so that a less charismatic individual can operate the levers of power already in place. Kim Il Sung devoted years to supplementing the personal identification that people had for him with social identification by which they might become committed to the political system he had created. This was the best he could do for his son.

Kim Jong Il succeeds his father with formidable handicaps as a leader, quite apart from the decline in the fortunes of his country. It is not simply a lack of charisma: he absolutely avoids the public. Among his small circle of colleagues, he must surely be considered a difficult, unpredictable, and even frightening person to work for. Yet the consensus among both foreign analysts and former North Korean residents is that Kim Jong Il has secured his position as the undisputed leader of the North Korean elite and masses by keeping a tight hold on the social control system and ruling in the name of his late father. To cast his power over the masses he has cloaked himself in his father's reputation. Shortly after Kim Il Sung's death, a new political slogan proclaimed that "Kim Il Sung is Kim Jong Il."[48] The younger Kim frequently reminds the masses that he is ruling according to his father's behest. The 1998 version of the DPRK constitution is called the "Kim Il Sung constitution." The DPRK is often referred to as the "Kim Il Sung nation," as if that were its formal name. It is difficult to deny the legitimacy of the son when he rules a nation named after his father.

To control the elite, including those in the military, Kim relies on "transactional leadership" in contrast to the charismatic "transformational leadership" of his father's regime. Whereas transformational leadership—resting on the power of a charismatic leader and the vision he communicates—works by transforming the people into loyal and motivated followers committed to the leader and his policies, transactional leadership strikes a deal with the followers: you follow me and I will see to it that you are rewarded—or in any case, not punished. The elite followers may not admire or respect Kim Jong Il, but if the rewards he offers and the threats he wields are strong enough, they will support him.

After the death of Kim Il Sung, the North Korean press quoted Kim Jong Il as saying, "Expect no change from me."[49] Kim has had a quarter of a century to secure his ruling position by eliminating those who were unenthusiastic about his succession. Nonetheless, Kim is unlikely to rule as long as his father, for he has violated a basic principle of leadership; that is, he has not established a genuinely reciprocal relationship with his followers, either the masses he seeks to indoctrinate or the elite he has attempted to bribe. He hopes to rule as another godlike Kim Il Sung, but even the elder Kim's power was beginning to ebb in his final years, as evidenced by the lack of enthusiasm exhibited by the North Korean people in pursuing socialism. Living in a time that is less accepting of totalitarian dictators than the past, Kim Jong Il can hardly expect to rule as long as his father did.

Kim and his father exhibit the classic characteristics of the "personalized power" leader: a desire to dominate followers by keeping them dependent.[50] The dominating ruler controls the flow of information and dispenses rewards and punishments to keep his followers loyal. If discipline slackens, an outside threat is created to trigger nationalistic feeling and rally people around the leader they know against the devils they don't know. The North Korean press repeatedly tells the people that without Kim Jong Il they are nothing. They may doubt this statement, but they have only a vague idea about what life might be like under a different regime. The elite have a much better idea, but they are more closely under Kim's surveillance and prefer to accept what rewards he has to offer rather than risk punishment by showing even a hint of disloyalty.

The weakness of Kim's leadership style is glaringly apparent: he has no one to correct him. Throughout his life he has cut himself off from direct contact with the foreign world, which he sees only through videos, briefing papers, and conversation with those loyal supporters who have been allowed to travel abroad, and who are unlikely to be brave enough to tell him anything that contradicts his beliefs. Nor is he constrained by public sentiment, for the people hardly count in his calculations: they simply supply the labor necessary to run the Kim Jong Il enterprise. Kim is essentially alone with his ideas, which are manifestly out of step with the trends of market capitalism and liberal democracy.

Kim is good at manipulating those around him to get what he wants, but his vision of what is best in the long term for him and for his country is deeply flawed. Just as Kim Il Sung looked to his guerrilla days' experience as a guide to running North Korea as its president, so Kim Jong Il looks to North Korea's policies of the 1960s as a guide to solving the country's problems in the new century. In domestic affairs, his energy is devoted to holding onto power through the crude means of social control and a cult ideology, and his unrealistic assumption must be that his people will never discover the lies on which the cult is based. The North Korean press touted Kim Il Sung as the greatest statesman of the twentieth century. In a headline from a full-page advertisement in the *New York Times* taken out to celebrate Kim Jong Il's ascension to the post of general secretary of the KWP in December 1997, the younger Kim is proclaimed "The Lodestar of the 21st Century," with a subhead reading, "The North Korean leader Kim Jong Il is a man of great leadership, remarkable wisdom and noble virtues. He is always with the popular masses sharing the ups and downs of life with them. Indeed, he is equipped with all the qualities a great leader needs. Kim Jong Il, a new leader of the twenty-first century, will surely break fresh ground in the political, economic, military, and diplomatic fields of Korea, succeeding excellently to the cause of the late President Kim Il Sung."[51]

CHAPTER FIVE

The Military:
Pillar of Society

The People's Army is the pillar and main force of the revolution and of the military, the party, the state and the people. This is the core of the great general's idea on attaching importance to the army.[1]

The military is an overwhelming power and presence in North Korea. The Korean People's Army (KPA), which includes naval, air force, and special forces contingents, is estimated to number 1.2 million, compared with South Korea's 700,000. Reserve forces total at least 5 million. Since 1996 Armed Forces Day has been celebrated as a national holiday, having been moved (in 1978) from February 8 (the day the KPA was founded in 1948) to April 25 (the day in 1932 on which Kim Il Sung allegedly founded the Korean army while in exile in China). In 1997, the day marking the signing of the Korean War armistice, July 27, was also declared a national holiday and named Victory Day. Foreign estimates have put the military budget at 25 percent of the country's shrinking GNP, but by the mid-1990s reports coming out of North Korea indicated that virtually the only factories still operating near capacity were military factories, suggesting that the military budget might be swallowing up the civilian budget. Despite chronic shortages of supplies and an arsenal of technologically obsolete weapons, the KPA remains a formidable fighting force. The North Korean attack that launched the Korean War on June 25, 1950, demonstrated Pyongyang's willingness to use force to achieve its political goals. Repeated military incursions and terrorist operations since the Korean War are testimony to North Korea's continued reliance on the military option. To keep its reputed enemies at bay, and to rally its citizens, the North Korean press routinely threatens violence against the United States, Japan, and South Korea.

Under Kim Il Sung the military enjoyed an honored but subordinate position in North Korean society. Kim was a military leader with (greatly exaggerated) credentials as a guerrilla fighter and as the commander of North Korean troops during the Korean War. Despite Kim's folly of launching the Korean War, those North Korean generals who survived Kim's postwar Korea purges presumably respected him as a brave and ruthless fighter, although not as a brilliant wartime strategist. He in turn gave the military preferential treatment in social status and standard of living. Kim Jong Il received no military training beyond the required short college training course and has no combat experience. He is a general in name only. Given this fact, which is widely known among the North Korean elite, one wonders how highly the North Korean generals regard their "supreme commander" and his growing cult of generalship.

Judging by the published rankings of top political figures, the military has increased its political stature. After Kim Il Sung's death, top generals were listed ahead of some full Politburo members, reversing the traditional ranking. In December 1998, five of the top ten political ranks were held by military figures (including Kim Jong Il), and fifteen of the top thirty-five ranks were from the military. In 1997 Kim proclaimed the army the "pillar" of socialism and a model for the party and the people. In 1998 the chairmanship of the National Defense Commission (NDC), with Kim Jong Il as its newly re-elected chairman, was declared "the highest post of the state."[2] Kim was also credited with formulating a revolutionary military-first policy.[3] Is Kim boosting members of the military because they are his most loyal supporters or is he soliciting their loyalty? Little is known about the attitudes of top military leaders, for they rarely leave the country or meet visiting delegations from the West. Consequently, it is difficult to determine how influential the generals are in policymaking, how satisfied they are with the Kim Jong Il regime, and whether they have any ideas about how to revive North Korea's moribund economy. Given the degree to which the party penetrates the military, it seems likely that the military, while it is potentially the most powerful institution in North Korea, remains firmly under the control of Kim Jong Il and the Korean Workers' Party.[4]

The military plays three important roles in North Korean society. First, it provides for national security. Second, it supports the Kim regime and maintains social control. Third, it is held up as a model for the rest of North Korean society.

National Security Role

North Korea's well-founded concerns about guaranteeing its national security are a major reason for keeping one out of every twenty-three North Korean citizens in the regular army. Korea has always been a shrimp among whales in Northeast Asia. Its neighbor, China, has at times been a protecting presence and at other times a military threat. Chinese forces periodically invaded Korea since Korean states emerged almost 2,500 years ago. The Japanese mounted major attacks on Korea in the sixteenth century, and the Manchus (initiating China's Ch'ing dynasty) invaded from the North in the seventeenth century. After defeating the Chinese (in 1895) and the Russians (in 1905), Japan annexed the helpless Korean state in 1910. Foreigners again trod Korean soil when Soviet and American troops accepted Japan's surrender on the Korean Peninsula in 1945 and sponsored separate governments in the North and South. After Kim Il Sung's ill-advised attack on South Korea in 1950, American-led UN forces overran North Korea, only to be pushed back by 1 million Chinese troops. Many Chinese troops remained in North Korea after the signing of the armistice in 1953 to help with reconstruction before departing in 1958. Approximately 40,000 American troops have remained in the South at the request of the ROK government. In light of Korea's history as a victim of subjugation and foreign conquest, it is hardly surprising that North Korea today strives to make itself an "impregnable fortress," self-sufficient in military equipment and unitary in ideology.

Throughout the cold war, North Korea was sheltered under the strategic protection of its communist neighbors China and the Soviet Union, facing American troops in South Korea and an economically resurgent Japan across the straits. In the 1990s the Soviet Union and its successor state, Russia, distanced themselves from North Korea. Russia notified Pyongyang in August 1995 that it would no longer extend its Treaty on Friendship, Cooperation, . and Mutual Assistance signed in 1961. A new treaty, initialed in February 2000, reportedly deleted the provision promising Russian military assistance to the DPRK in the event of an attack.[5] China has remained North Korea's loyal and unenthusiastic supporter but seems highly unlikely to back up a North Korean military adventure as it did in 1950.

In the post–cold war era North Korea's security environment has become more rather than less hostile. Pyongyang perceives a clear threat from the United States. According to the North Korean press, the United States desires to wipe out the last pockets of socialism in the international community. In fact, the threat is based primarily on the American concern over North Korea as a threat to international nonproliferation regimes, with American revulsion over Pyongyang's human rights policies in the background. U.S.-led attacks against Iraq and Serbia have alarmed the North Koreans, who fear similar treatment.

Defense Strategy

Pyongyang has adopted a porcupine defense suitable for a medium-size peninsular state. According to North Korean thinking, if foreigners are given an inch, they can easily overrun the entire country. Kim Jong Il's (secretly recorded) objection to tourism as a national industry rests exactly on this point: "The entire coastline is dotted with military fortresses.... In this case, the opening up is no different from the withdrawal of a country's troops, is it not? ... If we open Pyongyang, it will eventually be the same as pulling out troops from the borderline to Pyongyang. ... It would be naturally tantamount to disarmament. Do we have to do this for a meal?"[6]

In line with Juche theory, Kim Il Sung in 1962 adopted a "people's defense" strategy to replace the conventional "big-forces" military doctrine inherited from the Soviet Union. Kim's "four military lines," set forth in article 60 of the constitution, call for arming the entire population; fortifying the entire country; converting the members of the armed forces into politically reliable cadres; and modernizing the army. The first and second lines provide for a "deep" defense of North Korean territory to counter the threat that hostile forces could penetrate North Korea's borders and quickly overrun the country. A quarter of the population is enlisted in the military reserves, and all able-bodied children and adults periodically receive military training. The country is laced with military checkpoints, and critical factories and military installations are built underground. The South Korean government believes that North Korea has more than 8,000 such underground installations, including 500 kilometers of tunnels.[7] The third military line, making soldiers into loyal cadres, is an extension of the strategy of arming the entire population with a militant, xenophobic Juche spirit that will motivate people to defend their soil, after the manner of Churchill's wartime pledge, "We shall fight on the beaches, we shall fight on the landing grounds, we shall fight in the fields and in the streets, we shall fight in the hills." Indeed, North Korea has many hills and mountains, making a guerrilla defense eminently practical. Not only is the entire army and population urged to become "bullets and bombs" to protect their country, their party, and their leader, but they are put in constant fear of an invasion. Throughout the 1990s the North Korean press warned that fighting a defensive war against South

Korea and the United States was inevitable, the only question being one of timing. War fever reached a pitch in December 1998 when, in response to public disclosure in the United States and ROK of an updated contingency plan (operation plan 5027) for dealing with conflict on the Korean Peninsula, the KPA General Staff released a belligerent statement that claimed that the United States had already embarked on the first of five stages of "waging the second Korean war."[8]

North Korea's military strategy and weapons procurement policies are grounded in the Juche doctrine of self-reliance and adaptation to Korean conditions. Most North Korean arms, including missiles but excluding aircraft are copies of Soviet and Eastern European designs manufactured domestically. An example of Kim Il Sung's Juche approach to national defense is the instruction: "Remember! Our fatherland has many mountains, rivers and valleys, unlike China and the Soviet Union with their vast flat lands. Because of these mountains and long coast line, a 60 mm gun will work better than a supersonic jet that can fly over our land so quickly. I am not against obtaining supersonic jets if we need them, but we must promote a system proper to our natural terrain."[9]

A second political principle applied to military affairs is the development of a political ideology and strategy to defeat an enemy that may be superior in manpower and technology. Ideology and strategy are said to flow from the mind of the leader, the source of national strength. Kim Il Sung's fictionalized biography boasts that his guerrilla victories against the Japanese during the colonial period and his alleged victory against the Americans in the Korean War were because of his superior strategy and ideology.

A third political principle is the unity of the people. Like Mao, Kim Jong Il has constantly stressed the importance of cooperation between the army and the people, although the constant reminder of its importance suggests that it cannot be taken for granted.

The disposition of KWP military forces, not to mention the character of North Korean rhetoric, is offensive in nature, standing as a warning that "if [the enemy] violate[s] an inch of land, a blade of grass and a tree in Korea" he will be "punished mercilessly."[10] An offensive strategy would be particularly effective against South Korea, with its relatively flat land, its capital city within thirty miles of the North Korean border, and the relaxed security posture of its citizens. Between 60 and 70 percent of North Korean forces are positioned between Pyongyang and the demilitarized zone (DMZ). As well as being consistent with North Korea's offensive military strategy, this disposition of troops is a logical defensive strategy since troops stationed far from the border would have little frontline defensive value given the North's poor road and rail network.

North Korean military strategy calls for the use of deterrence to discourage an enemy attack. The North's formidable military, its offensive position, hostile rhetoric, and its demonstrated willingness (in the Korean War and since) to launch attacks against South Korea are in themselves deterrents. Pyongyang's "complete denial but no verification" policy in regard to nuclear, biological, and chemical weapons (NBC) also provides a powerful deterrent. The North Korean missile program, which is less of a threat in terms of accuracy than in terms of reach (the largest multistage missiles can hit any point in Japan and perhaps reach Alaska), also acts as a deterrent, especially with Pyongyang's suspected NBC capability. Moreover, the North Korean leaders have cultivated an image of irrationality that provides its own deterrent effect.[11] In the United States and South Korea the opinion prevails that North Korea would pose a real military threat under at least three circumstances: if the ROK-DPRK military balance were to tip decisively in North Korea's favor, if economic or social conditions in the DPRK should deteriorate to the point that the integrity of the state were in danger; or if a foreign government were to launch an air strike against North Korean targets.

If North Korea's strategy for attacking South Korean and U.S. forces were likened to a chess game, it could be said that the North Korean military has opening and endgame strategies but lacks a middle game strategy. The North Koreans might favor a preemptive attack under circumstances in which they perceive that either side is militarily vulnerable. In December 1998, as Washington applied pressure to inspect a North Korean underground site near the Yongbyon nuclear complex, the KCNA warned, "Pyongyang is filled with conviction that the option for a preemptive strike is not a monopoly of the United States. . . . Invincible is the KPA that has increased strike capacity and unlimited and practiced protean tactics. . . . Sooner or later, the U.S. will be aware of what the Korean War method is like."[12] If North Korea were to launch a preemptive attack, it would employ surprise, overwhelming firepower, blitzkrieg speed, night-time operations, and special forces. The North Koreans characterize this battle strategy as *tangi kyoljon* [quick and decisive victory].[13] With the majority of its troops stationed close to the South Korean border, an attack could be launched with relatively little warning, especially if preceded by heightened troop activity misinterpreted by the enemy as a North Korean bluff or brinkmanship or training activities. To break through the natural and man-made barriers along the DMZ, North Korean troops would probably concentrate on a few southward corridors, with the main attack directed at Seoul.

A heavy artillery bombardment along the front line and into Seoul would be followed by a massive infantry and mechanized assault. Besides diversionary attacks along the DMZ, North Korea would send down special forces troops by sea, air, and through tunnels dug under the DMZ. These troops, many of them dressed in South Korean uniforms, would create a second front behind enemy lines in an attempt to divert South Korean troops, disrupt ROK-U.S. command, control, communication, computer, and intelligence (C⁴I) operations, and prevent U.S. reinforcements from landing in South Korea.

For this battle strategy to succeed, Seoul must be captured before U.S. reinforcements reach Korea and U.S. aerial counterattacks degrade North Korean military capabilities. The North Koreans would have only a few days to capture or surround Seoul and hold the city hostage in a bid for a cease-fire and truce negotiations. It is highly unlikely that the North Korean army, with its relatively weak logistical and C⁴I capabilities, could overrun the entire peninsula. The capture of Seoul would complete the DPRK's opening game.

If a blitzkrieg attack on Seoul were to fail, or if the ROK refused to call a truce to save Seoul, the DPRK would expose itself to a middle game of enemy aerial bombardment of troops and territory. In this event, the DPRK would quickly move to an endgame strategy by destroying Seoul and retreating to hardened positions in the North, using all available means in a last-ditch attempt to survive. As called for in the four military lines, many of North Korea's industrial and military facilities are located underground, and the North Korean people are trained to take up arms to mount a strong defense of their homeland. Although much of the North Korean economy and military forces would be destroyed by a counterattack, it is not clear that the country itself could be brought to its knees. This would be the strength of the DPRK's endgame.

North Korea hardly lives up to the traditional Korean sobriquet of "Land of Morning Calm." The leadership and the people are on edge. They fear giving the appearance of conciliation or compromise. They worry that even small changes to their system or culture may prove to be the thin end of the wedge that will destabilize the entire system. They believe there is no room for misjudgment or misstep, since their capitalist enemies are just waiting for a chance to "crush" (*apsal*) the last bastion of socialism.

Military Capability

A strong military, including weapons of mass destruction, is the backbone of North Korean foreign policy.[14] To keep its military strong the government has had to deprive the civilian economy of valuable resources, creating chronic hardships for the people. North Korea claims its active military totals only

400,000, but foreign analysts unanimously place the number at just over 1 million.[15] Two demographers, Nicholas Eberstadt and Judith Banister, analyzed population data submitted by North Korea to the United Nations Population Fund in 1989 as a condition for receiving UN assistance in conducting a nationwide census.[16] Their demographic model suggested that 1.2 million persons were "missing" from the data. Since most of the estimated missing persons were males between the ages of seventeen and fifty-four, the demographers speculated that they were in the military (after 1975 North Korea excluded military personnel from its population statistics). North Korean officials have disputed this estimate. Perhaps the difference in figures reflects the North Korean government's failure to count as active military the tens of thousands of soldiers who at any given time are assigned to farm or construction work. Or perhaps North Korean officials are trying to convince outsiders that they are more peace loving than South Korea, which has approximately 700,000 people under arms. Possibly the culture of secrecy is the determining factor: North Koreans treat almost all information about their country as a secret.

An estimated 900,000 active duty military are in the KPA ground forces, and most of these soldiers are light infantry. The infantry is supported by mechanized divisions and a large arsenal of artillery and rocket launchers. Not only is it cheaper to equip foot soldiers than to outfit mechanized divisions, but North Korea's rough terrain is ill-suited to mechanized equipment. Transportation is a serious problem because of a limited road system and a chronic shortage of fuel. North Korea's C^4I technology is fairly primitive. In 1996 a squad leader from a North Korean reconnaissance battalion who defected to the South reported that Kim Jong Il had ordered that Russian-made telephone pagers be supplied to battalion and company commanders to provide communication with headquarters from the field. Most communication in the military (as in the rest of society) is vertical—to and from Kim Jong Il, who is said to require his personal authorization for military exercises down to the battalion level. The vertical command structure results in a communication system that is efficient in implementing orders from headquarters (as long as communication channels remain open) but deficient in coordination and information sharing among military units.

The North Korean navy is estimated to have approximately 50,000 personnel, manning small boats and submarines designed for coastal defense and special forces operations. The air force, with an estimated 100,000 personnel, relies mostly on old aircraft purchased from the Soviet Union. Judging by the loose screws and bolts on MiG-19 aircraft flown to South Korea by a North Korean defector, it appears that maintenance of military equipment may also

Top: A bronze statue of Kim Il Sung on Mansudae (Mansu Hill) in Pyongyang, erected in 1972 on Kim's 60th birthday. Behind the statue is a mural of Mt. Paektu. *Bottom:* Bowing to the statue of Kim Il Sung at Mansudae, with one of two flanking sculptures depicting the North Korean people's revolutionary struggle, accompanied by the words "Hail to General Kim Il Sung."

All photographs, except as noted, by Frank Hoffmann. Reprinted by permission.

The Tower of the Juche Idea, across from central Pyongyang, along the banks of the Taedong River. Like most monuments built since 1980, its conception and design are attributed to Kim Jong Il. The tower was completed for Kim Il Sung's 70th birthday in 1982.

Photographs above and on facing page, Chosun-ui Yonggwang *(Pyongyang)*

Above: Kim Jong Il escorts his father to the Tower of the Juche Idea on April 1, 1982. *Inset:* A photograph of Kim Jong Il that accompanies the publication of his discourse, "Let Us Exalt the Brilliance of Comrade Kim Il Sung's Idea on the Youth Movement and the Achievements Made under His Leadership," *The People's Korea,* no. 1757 (September 7, 1996), p. 2.

Top: View of Pyongyang from the 45-story twin-towered Koryo Hotel, the principal abode of foreign visitors. *Bottom:* Vista of central Pyongyang from the Grand People's Study House along the Taedong River, with a portrait of Kim Il Sung in the foreground and the May Day Stadium in the distance.

The 105-story Ryugyong Hotel in Pyongyang, built for the 1989 World Festival of Youth and Students, but never completed or opened, apparently because of structural flaws.

Top: A Pyongyang traffic policewoman. The women are said to be chosen, in part, for their good looks. *Bottom:* The American spy ship *Pueblo*, captured in 1968 (in international waters, according to the Americans). The *Pueblo's* 83 crew members were released eleven months later. Since this photograph was taken in Wonsan harbor, the *Pueblo* has been moved, by unknown means, to the other side of the Korean Peninsula. It is now berthed on the Taedong River in Pyongyang, where it is said to be a popular tourist attraction and the focus of Korean hatred toward the Americans.

Top: A poster mounted on a pedestrian overpass in downtown Pyongyang, proclaiming "Hail to the great Juche idea!" *Bottom:* A sculpture of plenty in Pyongyang. The building in the background bears the word "solidarity."

Young women, probably on summer military training, visiting Mt. Paektu, the sacred peak along North Korea's northeastern border with China.

Top: One of many "slogan trees" displayed and appropriately protected near Kim Jong Il's purported birthplace on the slopes of Mt. Paektu. The carvings, said to have been made when Kim Il Sung and his soldiers were fighting the Japanese, foretell the coming of another "great general," Kim Jong Il. *Bottom:* Chon Lake (Lake of Heaven), the crystal-clear crater lake at the top of Mt. Paektu.

Top: A tourist group contemplating a poem written by Kim Il Sung and dedicated (in very un-Confucian fashion) to his son. In the background, Jong Il Peak (with the name carved into the rock) stands over the site of the log cabin where the young Kim is said to have been born on Mt. Paektu. *Bottom:* An outdoor painting of the "three generals" of Mt. Paektu and their soldiers during the war against Japan. The young Kim Jong Il is seated on the horse held by his mother, Kim Jong-Suk, who stands beside Kim Il Sung.

Top: Paramilitary visitors to the statue of the young Kim Il Sung in the plaza of the Grand Monument at Lake Samji in the Mt. Paektu area, erected in 1979 to commemorate a battle between Kim's guerrilla troops and the Japanese. *Bottom:* The Palace of Culture in Kaesong, overlooking traditional tiled-roof houses. Kaesong is the DPRK's third-largest city, a traditional city of culture and commerce, only 78 kilometers north of Seoul.

Top: A private truck garden in Kaesong. *Bottom:* A broad street in a new section of Kaesong.

Top: The late Kim Il Sung's presence on a street in Kaesong. The caption reads, "The respected father-comrade Kim Il Sung will live forever in the hearts of the people." *Bottom:* A memorial painting of Kim Il Sung at the entrance to the Kumgangsan (Kumgang Mountain) Hotel, a famous tourist site in the southeastern corner of North Korea. One of the children wears Kim's fedora.

Top: Two women (with an oxcart in the distance), on a path in the scenic Samilpo area along the eastern coast between Kumgang and Wonsan. *Bottom:* A tractor running on "substitute fuel." In the face of a chronic gasoline shortage, many buses and trucks as well have been converted to wood-burning steam engines, a conversion that drastically slows their pace.

Top: Country houses almost smothered by private gardens, which provide an important part of rural North Koreans' food needs. *Bottom:* Supplementary inter-city transportation. Travelers offer a small payment in exchange for the unauthorized ride.

People walking on the roads in the outskirts of Pyongyang.

be a problem, because of shortage of supplies and because military personnel are poorly motivated.

Since the establishment of the DPRK's Second Economic Commission (in charge of the military industry) in the early 1970s, North Korea has produced a wide range of relatively sophisticated weapons. Starting with reverse-engineered Soviet-style Scud missiles believed to have been imported from Egypt in the late 1970s, North Korea has developed the capability since the mid-1990s to produce 100 Scud-B and Scud-C missiles annually, with a range of 300 to 500 kilometers.[17] The ROK government believes that by 1999 some 450 of these missiles had been sold to Iran (200), Iraq (100), and Syria (150). The Nodong 1 rocket with a range of 1,300 kilometers was first test fired in 1993, and by 1999 between five and ten were believed to have been deployed in North Korea. A Nodong 2 with slightly greater range may be under development. In 1998 the 2,000-kilometer Taepodong 1 was test fired, and a 4,000–6,000 kilometer Taepodong 2 is believed to be under development.

North Korea is suspected of possessing biological and chemical weapons.[18] The question of nuclear weapons has been widely debated, with speculation converging on no more than one or two weapons, if that. As a deterrent, however, suspected possession counts almost as heavily as known possession.

Domestic Roles

The KPA is too large a manpower resource to be devoted solely to defense. The KPA performs several missions besides national defense, including domestic security and intelligence, foreign infiltration and espionage, border security, supplementary labor for construction, industry, and agriculture, munitions manufacture, and foreign trade.

The Army of the Party and the Leader

According to article 59 of the constitution, "The mission of the Armed Forces in the Democratic People's Republic of Korea is to defend the interests of the working people, defend the socialist system and the gains of the revolution from external invasion, and protect the freedom, independence, and peace of the fatherland." Thus, the military's first task is not to protect the country from external threats but to defend the interests of the working people, that is, defend the party, which leads the working people. The 1980 charter of the KWP is clear on this point: "The Korean People's Army is the revolutionary armed forces of the KWP in the glorious tradition of the anti-Japanese armed struggle" (article 46). As the position of the leader has been elevated, the KPA has become not so much the army of the party as the army of the leader. By the mid-1990s appeals to protect the person of Kim Jong Il became common-place—and increasingly strident: "To annihilate those who dare to thrust their claws to the headquarters of the Korean revolution and become lifeguards of the supreme commander is the first mission and great honor of our army."[19] Even more desperately, "The revolutionary spirit of suicidal explosion is the spirit of dedicating one's life for the party and the leader by becoming a self-detonating bomb. . . . Included in this spirit is a resolute and affecting determination to dedicate [one's life] without hesitation to defending and protecting the respected and beloved general."[20] To illustrate the importance of protecting the leader, this news article describes how two North Korean sailors risked their lives to protect the shipboard portraits of the two Kims even as their boat sank.

According to North Korean logic, protecting the leader is a priority because the security of North Korea and the strength of the army as an institution are an extension of the will of the leader. In North Korean doublespeak, the distinction between the party, the leader, and the people is blurred: "For communists, the leader himself is the fatherland and the revolution. . . . The faithfulness to the revolution is, in itself, the faithfulness to the leader; the faithfulness to the leader is, in itself, the devotion to the fatherland and the people."[21]

Domestic Security and Intelligence

North Korea's domestic security apparatus, consisting of the quasi-military Ministry of People's Security (MPS) and the military-directed State Security Department (Secret Service) is highly effective.[22] As is true in any totalitarian society, maintaining internal security is a vital task since the leadership cannot count on democratic legitimacy to remain in power. Domestic security was increased in the mid-1980s when the North Korean economy began to show obvious signs of a slowdown, and the people's standard of living deteriorated. Security was heightened during and after the Thirteenth World Festival of Youth and Students in 1989, which brought thousands of foreign visitors to Pyongyang.

The domestic security apparatus has limited the communication and social congregation that would be necessary to spawn a civilian uprising. Security activities also seem to have prevented counterregime groups from forming within the military and other branches of the government, although reports of military purges suggest that dissident elements do exist. One potential weakness of the security apparatus is that it is fragmented, within and between security agencies. While this fragmentation prevents the emergence of a monolithic security force that could overthrow the regime, it also makes coordination of intelligence gathering difficult and creates the possibility of competition and conflict among the security services.

North Korea's northern borders with China and Russia are tightly controlled but can be crossed with relative ease by anyone willing to offer a bribe to border guards. The southern border with South Korea, with its fences, walls, and minefields, is virtually impenetrable. Most North Koreans who defect use overseas assignments or travel in China as a springboard. The North Korean government is concerned that as the economy deteriorates, more starving peasants and disgruntled members of the elite may flee the country. Presumably in response to this concern, the border garrisons along the China border were incorporated into the Ministry of People's Armed Forces (MPAF) in 1994. In October 1995 the entire Border Guard General Bureau, which had been under the authority of the State Security Department, was transferred to the MPAF, a further consolidation of the military's powers.

Public Works, Industry, and Agriculture

The KPA runs its own economic enterprises and provides labor for the nonmilitary sector. Soldiers assigned to construction projects, farming, factory work, and mining demonstrate "army-people unity" and help make up for a chronic labor shortage (even though most factories are closed, the economy is increasingly dependent on manual labor in agriculture and construction to replace inoperable machines). As part of Kim Jong Il's military-first policy, military officers have reportedly been put in charge of many civilian agricultural and industrial sites.[23] Soldiers are also engaged in farming, fishing, and foraging on their own behalf, and military organizations run their own foreign trade enterprises. The North Korean munitions industry is operated by the military under the direction of the National Defense Commission. The KPA, which is the only organization with enough operating vehicles and fuel to transport large quantities of goods, has also taken charge of distributing the foreign food aid.

While the employment of soldiers in the economic sector reduces the drag on the North Korean economy of maintaining a million-member army, the use of soldiers in construction, agriculture, and farming is not an optimal allocation of manpower, since these workers are not as efficient as experienced full-time workers in those industries. Temporary allocation of labor also complicates long-range planning. Military-run industries have first call on the nation's economic resources and are believed to run at a higher capacity than civilian industries, but their operation separately from the rest of the national economy prevents economic planners, who presumably are ignorant of the specifics of the military's economic activities, from coordinating national economic plans.

Political Role Model

Kim Jong Il is credited with the theoretical insight that the military is the "pillar and main force of the revolution," a slogan popularized in 1997.[24] What does this phrase mean? First, it is a recognition of the national security role of the military ("peace and victory of socialism exist on the bayonets of the People's Army"). Second, it can be interpreted as an acknowledgment that the military is first in line for economic resources. Third, it means that the military is an institution supporting the Kim Jong Il regime, just as the party was the main support of the Kim Il Sung regime. Fourth, the military is the main pillar in the sense that it displays the characteristics that Kim Jong Il would like to see in all North Koreans. If every North Korean citizen were a soldier, General Kim would have his hands firmly on the levers of power. A militarized citizenry would be well organized and inured to the hardship of a Spartan life, even taking pride in displaying its tough character. The obvious problem with turning the entire society into an army is that an army of followers is no better than its leader. If Kim Jong Il were truly "the only socialist political leader in the present world who is exercising skillful leadership over not only political, economic and cultural, but also military affairs," then the people as well as the army could do no better than to follow his orders.[25] But if the leader is bereft of ideas, or pursues the wrong ideas, the entire society founders. This is one of the great paradoxes of North Korean society. The first duty of a citizen is to obey Kim Jong Il, but Kim has turned his back on the people by asking them to look out for themselves according to the Juche tradition of self-reliance.

Military Leadership

Like all organizations in North Korea, the military has a dual command structure, receiving orders from the military chain of command and from the Korean Workers' Party, which is the highest authority. Figure 5-1 outlines the organizational lines of military authority after the 1998 revision of the constitution. The KWP's Central Military Committee is reputed to be the core decisionmaking group for the military and one of the most powerful party organizations, alongside the Organization and Guidance Department, which is in charge of personnel matters. It is not known if Kim Jong Il chairs the Mil-

Figure 5-1. *Military and Security Command Structure*

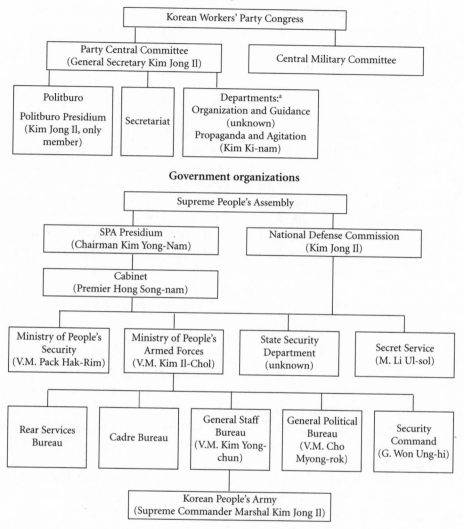

Party organizations

Korean Workers' Party Congress

Party Central Committee
(General Secretary Kim Jong Il)

Central Military Committee

Politburo

Politburo Presidium
(Kim Jong Il, only member)

Secretariat

Departments:[a]
Organization and Guidance
(unknown)
Propaganda and Agitation
(Kim Ki-nam)

Government organizations

Supreme People's Assembly

SPA Presidium
(Chairman Kim Yong-Nam)

National Defense Commission
(Kim Jong Il)

Cabinet
(Premier Hong Song-nam)

Ministry of People's Security
(V.M. Pack Hak-Rim)

Ministry of People's Armed Forces
(V.M. Kim Il-Chol)

State Security Department
(unknown)

Secret Service
(M. Li Ul-sol)

Rear Services Bureau

Cadre Bureau

General Staff Bureau
(V.M. Kim Yong-chun)

General Political Bureau
(V.M. Cho Myong-rok)

Security Command
(G. Won Ung-hi)

Korean People's Army
(Supreme Commander Marshal Kim Jong Il)

Sources: Chong Suk-hong, *Nam-Pukhan Pigyoron* [A comparative study of North-South Korea] (Seoul: Saramgwa Saram, 1997), p. 55; Yoo Young-ku, "Pukhanui Chongch'i-Kunsa Kwan'gyeui Pyunch'on'gwa Kunnaeui Chongch'jojik Unyounge Kwanhan Yon'gu" [A study of the evolution of the political-military relationship in North Korea and the management of political organizations within the armed forces] *Chollyak Yon'gu* [Strategy Studies], vol. 4 (Fall 1997), p. 102; and "Data 1998," *Vantage Point,* vol. 21 (December 1998), pp. 53–57.

Note: V.M., Vice Marshal; M., Marshal; G, General. The two marshals and the vice marshals listed in the figure were members of the Central Military Committee and the National Defense Commission as of December 1998.

a. These are two of many departments.

itary Committee (as did his late father). The Military Committee sets policy and oversees its implementation by other military organizations, working through the military's General Political Bureau. With political officers down to the company level, the General Political Bureau can exercise extensive control over the military.

On the government side the newly enhanced National Defense Commission (NDC), chaired by Kim, is the supreme state military organization and in fact the supreme governing organization. While the Central Military Committee and the NDC are in principle accountable to their respective elected bodies, the KWP Congress and the Supreme People's Assembly, both of which are infrequently convened rubber stamp assemblies. The NDC controls the MPAF, consisting of a number of bureaus. The General Staff Bureau directly oversees the operations of the KPA, headed by Supreme Commander Kim Jong Il, but in fact the General Political Bureau, with its connections to the Central Military Committee, is the most powerful of the MPAF bureaus. In reality, the official organizational chart depicts the *communication* structure of the military rather than its command structure, since Kim Jong Il, on his *personal* authority, can issue orders to any organization in North Korea, military or civilian, and expect to be obeyed.

Promotions and Purges

Since early in his career, Kim Jong Il's most important tool of power has been his control over personnel matters in the party, the government, and the military, through control of the party's Organization and Guidance Department. Like his father, the junior Kim controls by putting his people in positions of power and removing them when they displease him. Nowhere is this more evident than in the military.

Until 1991 Kim held no military position, nor was he known to have concerned himself with military affairs other than personnel matters. At the beginning of the 1990s Kim's father—or it might have been Kim himself—began to make final preparations for the succession. The first step was to get the military firmly behind the junior Kim. Kim had been appointed to the KWP's Central Military Committee in 1980, the same year he was publicly presented as his father's successor. In 1990 Kim was appointed first vice chairman of the NDC, his first government position. The following year he was named supreme commander of the Korean People's Army. Kim became one of only two marshals of the KPA (the other was Marshal Li Ul-sol, the elderly head of the Secret Service), ranking above all the generals but just below his father, who took the title of "grand marshal." In 1993 Kim succeeded his father as chairman of the

NDC, securing his leadership over the military. The press typically refers to Kim as the "respected and beloved general," but he has never appeared in uniform (nor did his father, who never employed his military titles, preferring instead the title of president). Kim has tried mightily to fabricate a reputation as a military man. In the 1998 SPA elections he was nominated as a delegate by a military constituency in Pyongyang, and he chose to rule the country not as president of the republic but as the re-elected chairman of the NDC.

During the early 1990s when he was collecting his military titles, Kim began to make mass promotions in the higher echelons of the military to install a new generation of military leaders who would be personally indebted to him. When Kim became chairman of the NDC, 660 officers, including many generals, were promoted; in 1993, 99 more promotions were announced; in 1995, 11 generals received promotions on the occasion of his (late) father's birthday. Although these promotions were made under the authority of the Central Military Committee and the NDC, unquestionably they were Kim Jong Il's personal choices. In 1997 he promoted 6 generals in February and 123 generals on the occasion of his father's birthday in April; in 1998 another 22 generals received birthday promotions; and in 1999 yet another 79 generals received birthday promotions, by which time the majority of the 1,200-strong general officers corps had received their promotions under Kim's sponsorship. Those who were promoted on Kim Il Sung's birthday were doubly indebted to the Kim regime: to the memory of Kim Il Sung as well as to Kim Jong Il. By the late 1990s, only a handful of the top generals were holdovers from Kim Il Sung's generation, and they no longer exercised real power. Top military men have also been purged, presumably under the personal orders of Kim Jong Il, but purges in North Korea are secretive in nature, so cause is a matter of speculation. Neither promotions nor purges seem directly related to an officer's performance of his or her military duties. Rather, the deciding factor is loyalty to the two Kims.

Over the years rumors of several military coup attempts have surfaced. In the 1950s and 1960s, when the Kim Il Sung regime was still consolidating its power, show trials were held to convict allegedly traitorous generals and politicians, most notably during the Korean War (when the tide of battle turned against North Korea) and in the periods of 1956–58 (when Kim Il Sung completed his major purges of political rivals) and 1969–70 (when officers opposed to the 1960s "people's military strategy" were purged). There are no indications that any coup attempts have come close to succeeding. The most frequently cited coup story relates to an incident in 1992 (some sources say in April, others say near the end of the year) when it is rumored that a group of officers who had received training in the Soviet Union plotted to kill an assemblage of North Korean officials by turning their tanks on them. It is said that the plot was discovered, the coup participants arrested and punished (presumably executed), and virtually all officers who had received training in the Soviet Union in the 1980s (approximately 600) purged.[26]

Supreme Commander Kim Jong Il

The North Korean press has created a military reputation for the junior Kim as "the most distinguished of all military geniuses heaven has ever produced" and "a great general of steel who has won 100 victories in 100 battles." So far as is known, the only military training Kim received was an obligatory two-month military training course in college. Yet on his birthday in February 1996, a North Korean television documentary showed a picture of Kim in his younger days sitting in the cockpit of a military fighter aircraft, with the accompanying text saying that he had been assuming military leadership since his early days.[27]

Kim Jong Il is presented to the people as the proper choice to lead the military not only because he received his father's blessing but more important because he was *born* to the position, just as he was born to rule North Korea. His alleged birthplace on the "sacred" Mount Paektu provides the illusion that he is a gift to the Korean people from heaven. The young Kim is thus one of the "three generals of Mt. Paektu"—the other two being his father and his mother. A North Korean press story says that during the Korean War (when he was ten years old), "Sometimes he sat up all night together with Comrade Kim Il Sung at the table for mapping out a plan of operation, asking about the situation of the front, thinking of how to frustrate the intention of the enemy and learning Comrade Kim Il Sung's outstanding commanding art."[28]

Kim is credited with making the North Korean soldier the most *ideologically* powerful in the world by arming him with the principles of Juche: self-sacrifice and total obedience and loyalty to Kim. "The power of the army can be determined by the spiritual strength of those soldiers who hold guns. . . . Today, the world's numerous war historians and militarists unanimously agree there is no army in the world that can catch up with our People's Army."[29] "It is not the guns but the soldiers holding the guns that fight the war. So all the military strategies must be centered on them and so designed as to raise the class awareness and revolutionary spirit in them.[30] Besides inculcating Juche principles in his soldiers, thereby making them "one-is-a-match-for-a-hundred" fighters, Kim is credited with recognizing the importance of army-people unity (Mao's idea), promoting the army as a model for North Korean society, and advocating that North Korea can have a powerful military and a successful economy if the soldiers lend a hand with civilian projects and if civilians "tighten [their] belts and simultaneously push economic and defense construction at any cost."[31] This is a return to his father's Equal Emphasis Policy of 1962.[32]

Yet in the final analysis the populace confers honor and respect on the battle-hardened veteran, not the shrewd manager. Kim needs military experience to bolster his claim to be a worthy successor to the great general Kim Il Sung, who, according to legend, defeated the Japanese and the Americans against tremendous odds. So Kim Jong Il's propagandists set about to create a military reputation for him.

Kim's brilliantly directed battles are imaginary. The North Korean press points to the valor and self-sacrifice of his on-the-spot guidance and inspections of military installations. Since the death of his father, Kim Jong Il has dramatically increased the frequency of his on-the-spot inspections to military installations, where he shows his face, briefly meets with a few ranking officials and—according to press reports—asks after the welfare of the common soldiers. Kim's heroism is counted in the number of these visits and in his fearlessness in visiting frontline troops (who of course are not in battle). Sometimes these accounts become surreal, as in this description that, by collapsing time, puts Kim Jong Il at the front line during the Korean War: "During the fatherland liberation war [that is, the Korean War], Chol Ridge served as an important military place . . . Whenever Marshal Kim Jong Il, another brilliant commander produced by Korea in the 20th century and son of guerrillas, passes the ridge, the idea and grit of the Korean People's Army has been further hardened. . . . Not escorted by tanks or armored cars, he has passed the ridge and crossed the rivers for forefronts without eating or sleeping. By doing so, he has devotedly tided over the crisis of the country and the revolution, winning one victory after another in the war without gun-report."[33] Out of seventy-one guidance visits in 1998, almost half were made to military installations.[34] During these visits Kim is said to give detailed instructions to the troops on an amazing variety of military activities. His biography recounts how, when he was told that flight training was conducted primarily on the ground (obviously because of a drastic shortage of fuel), Kim, after personally flying in the cockpit with the flight commander, instructed that "it was wrong to think lightly of training in the cockpit . . . even a motor car driver could sometimes become confused if he had not driven a car for several days."

Aboard a torpedo boat, "the Leader guided the crewmen and trained them in torpedo tactics."[35] Kim is reputedly on firmer ground when offering tips on marksmanship, which he has pursued as a sport, although probably not as successfully as his biography narrates: "The following happened in a certain year when he visited the rifle range of members of the Red Youth Lifeguards. Seeing the Red Youth Lifeguards practicing line firing, the Leader explained how to be a good marksman and showed an example. He quickly shot down five of the 10 bottles hung from a tree branch about 50 meters ahead in a quick running fire without aiming very carefully, and smashed the remaining bottles with the same speed after changing his rifle to a revolver and holding it in his left hand. . . . The Leader said one's right hand might be wounded in battle and that therefore it was necessary to train oneself in the use of both hands."[36]

The most outrageously fabricated evidence is Kim's leadership "in battle." Propagandists claim that no matter how well prepared soldiers are mentally and physically, "In modern warfare, a battle is a fight between commanders, and the fight between commanders is immediately a battle between brains."[37] Kim's "battles" consist of the occasional special forces operation against South Korea (which North Korea always denies), isolated attacks against U.S. forces along North Korea's borders, and imaginary confrontations with U.S.-South Korean forces. Kim is now taking credit for the capture of the U.S. spy ship *Pueblo* in 1968 (twelve years before he was even mentioned in the press as the successor to Kim Il Sung).[38] None of these operations, even if they were directed by Kim Jong Il, truly display the sublime traits of generalship ascribed to him. More recently, Kim is said to have achieved a great victory for North Korea by putting the entire country on a "semi-war" footing when the United States was threatening to seek a UN embargo of North Korea over the issue of nuclear inspections in 1993.[39] Kim is also said to be engaged in mortal combat whenever U.S. and South Korean troops stage joint military exercises, although of course no military engagement takes place.[40]

In Orwell's fictional *1984*, the party declares that "war is peace." In North Korea, peace is war. It appears that the majority of the North Korean people, like the indoctrinated and confused citizens of Orwell's Oceania—who could never be sure whom their country was fighting at any given time—believe they are on the brink of war with the United States, and that without Kim Jong Il's generalship, they would have been invaded long ago.

As a military commander, Kim is described in the North Korean press as brilliant, bold, and unflappable. He is famous for "clearly grasping the prevailing situation," and he "never becomes disoriented or confused."[41] Moreover, he has "uncommon farsightedness capable of foreseeing the situation that [is] to take place dozens of years and hundreds of years later."[42]

Above all, Kim Jong Il is audacious. "In a showdown with an enemy, one can wait for the situation to develop in favor of one and then strike at it or outflank it rather than mount a frontal attack. However, such methods are definitely conservative and passive. The most aggressive method capable of inflicting an ignominious defeat on the enemy is an offensive, and such a bold strategy can be executed only by a great military commander. The disposition of the respected and beloved general, the general of Mt. Paektu, is such that he, unmoved in the face of a formidable enemy, boldly confronts the enemy and strikes at it mercilessly. . . . overwhelming the enemy at one stroke."[43]

The Military and Change

Military organizations typically act as a force for stability and national security rather than as an instrument of change. The KPA is no exception. Military personnel appear to be more nationalistic than civilians. Especially at the higher ranks, soldiers are kept under close surveillance by Kim Jong Il's security people. Except for the few who are posted abroad, military personnel have less contact with foreign ideas and people than do civilians.

Soldiers enjoy a better standard of living than civilians (even though soldiers too must endure severe hardships from food and medical shortages). Thus they are more likely to support the status quo. Enlistment is an important qualification for party membership, which is the path to a comfortable life in North Korean society: soldiers may gain admittance to the party in three to five years, whereas civilians may have to wait seven or eight years.[44]

It is difficult to imagine that the military, or at least any large segment of it, would revolt against the Kim Jong Il regime, yet the military cannot be counted on to unequivocally support Kim, and probably considerable discontent exists. At the lower ranks, living conditions markedly deteriorated in the 1990s, and military life, with its ten or more years of service, including tough physical labor in civilian tasks such as construction, mining, and farming, is not easy.[45] The common soldier is also likely to sympathize with the impoverished civilians, starting with his own starving family, whom he cannot even visit, and grow impatient over Kim Jong Il's inability to improve the economy. Yet soldiers have no radical political ideas on which to act. They could stage a revolt, which would be isolated and promptly quelled (occasional reports of such incidents appear in the foreign press), or they could take individual initiative to break the rules and seek their own fortune by deserting and striking out on their own, as a few do. Calls in the press for law and order and reports of marauding soldiers seeking food suggest that discipline does occasionally break down in the military.

A greater threat to the Kim regime is dissatisfaction among high-ranking officers. One wonders how the better-educated officers view the worsening economic situation. As the economy weakens, so does the military, even though it receives first priority in the economic realm. Thus a patriotic officer might, in the service of national security, seek to terminate Kim Jong Il's career by independent and violent action. It is also difficult to imagine that professional military men accept Kim Jong Il as a brilliant commander. Resentment toward his military amateurism could well trigger a violent response based on the pride of a professional soldier. But if Kim should be deposed, it is difficult to believe that even the top generals would have the faintest idea of how to improve the economy or run a modern country.

In the final analysis, the military's inclination to support or replace the Kim regime comes down to the power dynamics between Kim and his generals— a topic about which little is known. A good guess is that the military dislikes Kim but is committed to him for at least three reasons. First, as individuals, they and their extended families face certain punishment if even the mildest complaint about his policies reaches Kim Jong Il's ears. Second, they fear losing their privileged place in society. Third, even if they should be successful in staging a coup, they see no alternative to Kim, for none of them has solutions to North Korea's myriad problems.

North Korea's soldiers live under constant threat of attack from foreign forces (or so they are told). Their mission is defense, not reform. If broad-scale reforms were introduced in North Korea, and if these reforms turned out as they did in Eastern Europe and the Soviet Union, North Korea would be absorbed by South Korea. North Korean soldiers may well fear that under those circumstances they would have no place in a unified Korean army, and those in the higher ranks who are most responsible for human rights violations would fear retribution.

Conclusion

In 1998 North Korea formally became a military-dominated state. Kim Jong Il was re-elected chairman of the NDC and in that position was proclaimed the supreme leader of the state, making the NDC the top government organization, consistent with the emphasis in the preceding year on the military as the pillar of society. Early in 1999 Kim's military-first policy was proclaimed the guiding policy in all domestic fields, including the economy, with the goal of creating a *Kangsong Taeguk* or militarily and economically strong state, "For a socialist political leader to successfully conduct the affairs of state, he must have his own leadership method. . . . The Military First Revolutionary Leadership of the respected and beloved general is, in short, a leadership placing emphasis on the army to foster the revolutionary armed forces into the pillar of the revolution."[46] The domestic and national security roles played by the North Korean military are inextricably intertwined. Kim Jong Il *is* the state, so the military must protect the Kim regime as diligently as it protects the state.

North Korea faces real as well as imagined security threats. By an accident of history, Korea was divided in the early days of the cold war. By the time the cold war had ended, North Korea had been transformed from a communist state into the "Kim Il Sung nation." Thus the end of the cold war is irrelevant to the political situation on the Korean Peninsula; the German model of reunification does not easily apply. North Korea must remain a separate and independent state in order to support the Kim regime.

As a premodern kingdom existing in the late twentieth century, a kingdom containing one-third of the Korean people, North Korea's political position is untenable and made even more so by its abysmal economic condition. That is clearly recognized by the ruling elite in Pyongyang, who see threats to their national security from all sides, especially from the United States, which seeks to promote a "new world order" in which "rogue" states such as North Korea—with their nondemocratic governments, human rights violations, and failure to abide by the international nonproliferation conventions imposed by the big powers—have no place. Indeed, the United States has promoted its values with military force on numerous occasions and has made veiled threats to do so in North Korea. It is no wonder that North Koreans believe that the maintenance of a strong military force is an absolute necessity.

The continued militarization of North Korea is self-defeating in two respects. First, it creates a hostility spiral whereby other regional powers build up their forces and stage military games to counter North Korea's military buildup. North Korea may manage to create a credible deterrent force, but it can never win the arms race. Second, creating a strong militarized state is incompatible with economic recovery and growth. North Korea simply does not have the resources to maintain one of the world's largest armies while properly feeding its people. Other North Korean foreign policy goals, such as inducing foreign investment and establishing better relations with the West, are also checked by this militarization. Kim Jong Il's military-first policy dooms North Korea to international ostracism and poverty.

CHAPTER SIX

Social

Control

Establishing the revolutionary law-abiding spirit is a demand to firmly consolidate the socialist foundation. This is to smash maneuvers by all class enemies; to defend and adhere to socialism of our own style; and to establish sound lifestyle habits throughout the whole society.[1]

To the extent that ideological indoctrination fails to bind the people to the party and the leader, social control measures must be employed. The character of North Korean society has been shaped by the desire of the Kims to subordinate people to their will. At least on the surface, the Kims have succeeded.

Pyongyang is a city of buildings, not of people; a gigantic version of the village that Field Marshal Grigori Aleksandrovich Potemkin built to dupe Catherine the Great. Visiting Western journalists have tried to capture the city's essence. Mike Chinoy observed that "Pyongyang seemed like a giant set for George Orwell's famous novel *1984*."[2] To Ian Buruma, "Pyongyang *is* like a huge stage set. It is the closest thing to Germania, Hitler's grandiose and happily unrealized vision of the future Berlin."[3] Don Oberdorfer reflected, "Pyongyang struck me as a city designed by Russian-trained architects with some nods to Mao at the height of the allegiance to the Little Red Book. It appeared well suited for gigantic displays but not very convenient for people."[4]

Pyongyang illustrates an essential truth about North Korea, where people are said to be the masters of society. Seen from a distance, as in a picture postcard, Pyongyang (meaning "level ground") presents itself as a model city of the future: gleaming high-rise apartment and office buildings set amid spacious lawns, well-cultivated parks, and broad boulevards. Two rivers, the Taedong and Potong, wind through the city, which is overlooked by the verdant Mansu Hill (Mansudae). The ugliness, noise, and congestion typical of most large cities have been banished from Pyongyang. Yet Pyongyang's serenity, cleanliness, and orderliness are not a testament to modern urban technology but to social control. Technology is in pitifully short supply in Pyongyang. On closer inspection, the high-rise apartment buildings appear poorly constructed. For want of repair and reliable power, buildings lack elevators and running water. Urban planners have not been challenged by traffic congestion because only the elite have cars, and in any case a chronic gasoline shortage keeps most vehicles off the road. At major intersections vehicles are directed by female traffic police chosen for their looks rather than their ability to move traffic.

The city comes alive on two occasions. When a grand demonstration or march has been ordered by Kim Jong Il, tens or hundreds of thousands of Pyongyangites are drafted to participate, often practicing for weeks or months to prepare for the event. And when an important group of dignitaries hits town, a Potemkin "street show" is staged for their benefit. A former North Korean government official recounts how almost the entire staff of his ministry—as many as a thousand people—would be mobilized to play the role of shoppers, drivers, and pedestrians to parade around the city. The only people who looked forward to these performances were the military personnel, who enjoyed the opportunity to wear civilian clothes.[5]

Pyongyang was largely destroyed by American bombing during the Korean War (visitors are informed that the Americans dropped 428,748 bombs on the capital).[6] The city's reconstruction was supervised by the two Kims, with the younger Kim taking a particular interest in city planning and architecture. The Kims put into the city what they wanted and kept out what they did not want. It is said that Kim Jong Il would look out over the city and order that some buildings be put up at a certain location because the view was incomplete.

Kim Jong Il favors the grand scale in buildings and monuments. The giant pyramid of the Ryukyong Hotel building, originally scheduled for completion in time for the Thirteenth Festival of Youth and Students in 1989, is 105 stories tall. Work on the structure stopped in the early 1990s, and foreign sources say that structural defects will prevent the building from ever being completed, but this difficulty has not prevented the North Koreans from trying to rent out the building's lower floors to gullible foreign companies.[7] The many monuments to Kim Il Sung need not be made habitable: they need only look grand. A twenty-meter bronze statue of Kim Il Sung, arm outstretched to encompass his city, sits atop Mansu Hill. The Arch of Triumph, an imitation of the Champs Elysees structure but several meters taller, commemorates Kim's seventieth birthday. The Tower of the Juche Idea with its red electric torch, surpassing by just a few feet the height of the Washington Monument, was also built for Kim's seventieth birthday to commemorate the Great Leader's ideological gift to mankind. Although North Korea suffered severe economic hardships in the 1990s, Kim Jong Il had his late father's Kumsusan Palace extensively renovated to house the Great Leader's remains, hiring Russian specialists to embalm the corpse for permanent display.

Kim Jong Il and his father did not plan the city for people. For the senior Kim, who seemed to truly like people, this design failure was an inevitable consequence of chasing after the dream of a totally planned society. For his son, the design is a reflection of his disregard for people. Although Pyongyang's population is said to number 2 million, the city's broad streets are largely empty of vehicles, and most of the day the sidewalks are empty of pedestrians except during commuting hours. There are few bicycles in Pyongyang, or stores, restaurants, or markets. No commercial advertisements but plenty of political banners and portraits of the two Kims. No churches to be seen downtown, although in the 1990s three small churches were built in the outlying suburbs of the city—which was a Christian stronghold in precommunist days—to demonstrate that the North Korean constitutional guarantee of freedom of religion is being honored.[8] The authorities periodically winnow the city's residents to weed out those who are politically and physically unqualified for residence in the capital. These individuals are banished to the countryside. Consequently, visitors report that Pyongyang has none of the street vendors, beggars, or prostitutes that are routinely encountered in other big cities around the world. As the food situation worsened in the 1990s, the government began moving people out of the privileged precincts of Pyongyang into the relatively primitive countryside where they could be gainfully employed in farming, a forced relocation that is glamorized and personalized in the North Korean press: for example in 1995 Korean Central Television reported in a brief story that a Pyongyang worker had decided to relocate to the Yongyang Mine because she was deeply moved by the movie "Mt. Paektu" and went to the mine to visit the miners on her vacation. She subsequently decided to show her loyalty to Kim Il Sung and to Kim Jong Il by working in the mine "like the agitator in the movie." In a companion story, a reporter and an editor of the party newspaper, *Nodong Sinmun*, decide to move with their families to a farm "to give happiness and satisfaction to the respected and beloved general [Kim Jong Il] with bumper crops."[9]

The Kim regime has dropped its own political version of a neutron bomb on Pyongyang; they have created a city for the Kims, not for the people. The city's 2 million residents travel from their apartments to nearby workplaces by foot or, when gasoline and electric power are available, by bus, tram, or subway. After the day's work, people attend evening political study sessions. They have little time for a casual walk through the parks until late in the evening or on Sundays. Stores for the nondiplomatic community carry a limited supply of goods. The informal people's markets are where the action is, but these markets, operated outside the state plan, are tolerated only as a stopgap measure until the command economy can get back on its feet. Dismal as their life may seem, Pyongyangites are the country's elite. At least they receive fairly regular, if meager, food rations.

A North Korean medical professional who formerly lived in Pyongyang describes a typical day during the mid-1990s, as the food situation worsened even in Pyongyang.[10] He rose early and ate a simple breakfast of porridge. He signed in at his hospital in time for the 7:30 bell calling everyone into the square for morning exercises. After the hospital director had made daily announcements, the staff adjourned to the auditorium for party instruction and a reading of articles from *Nodong Sinmun*, the party newspaper. The staff would then break into small groups to receive the day's assignment: herb gardening, visiting village clinics, and so forth. A village visit was a privileged assignment because in the countryside it was possible to obtain vegetables, meat, or homemade wine from grateful farmers as a gratuity for medical treatment (provided free of charge by the state). If the day's work was in the city, a lunch of boiled corn on the cob or corn porridge was eaten from 1:00 to 2:00. Following the afternoon work period of 2:00 to 6:00, medical and political classes met until 7:00, sometimes lasting until 8:00. Dinner at home consisted of vegetable dishes. Before the lean times, his family owned a television set, which they would watch for a while in the evening (they were forced to sell the television to raise cash). With no television, the family would generally retire at 9:00. On festive occasions, such as a birthday, a special dish of meat or fish with fresh fruit and a bottle of wine (if any of these items were available) was served, but such delicacies were becoming increasingly difficult to obtain in the 1990s.

The few foreigners who are invited to Pyongyang on business are restricted in what they can see of the city. Most foreigners stay in the twin-towered Koryo Hotel. Leaving the hotel without one's guide is prohibited, although savvy visitors occasionally risk the displeasure of their hosts by eluding their security escorts for an hour before breakfast or during the after-lunch siesta time. But a foreigner cannot walk far before being picked up by the security police and firmly but courteously escorted back to the hotel. Pyongyang citizens who are approached by tourists, escorted or unescorted, are wary and even afraid of conversing, because they will be subsequently interrogated by the police. North Korean guides appear to be genuinely puzzled by the curiosity of their foreign guests. In their opinion, what goes on in their country is their own business, and foreigners should play the role of honored guests by observing protocol and dutifully marveling at the city's architecture.

For the most part, foreign guests are driven around in a Mercedes-Benz or a Volvo, making no intermediate stops on the way to their destinations except to negotiate military checkpoints. During Kim Il Sung's lifetime it was virtually mandatory upon arriving in Pyongyang to pay a respectful visit to his log cabin birthplace at Manyongdae on the outskirts of the city; since his death the required stop is the Kumsusan Memorial, to present flowers at his bier. The North Korean press duly note that the visiting foreigners pay their respects to the memory of the Great Leader. The few visitors who received an audience with Kim Il Sung were expected to present him with a gift. More than 60,000 of these gifts, along with those sent to Kim Jong Il (who rarely met with visitors), are housed in the International Friendship Exhibition north of Pyongyang.[11]

The grand buildings and monuments of Pyongyang were built at great cost, both financial and human. Kim Jong Il spent an estimated $4.5 billion to prepare for the Thirteenth World Festival of Youth and Students in 1989, Pyongyang's answer to Seoul's 1988 Summer Olympics. Besides athletic facilities, large apartment buildings to house the foreign guests were constructed along Pyongyang's Kwangbok Street. The recollections of a former North Korean construction battalion commander reveal how the Kim regime's desire to impress foreigners overrides concern for its own people. The battalion commander oversaw the work of 600 of the estimated 180,000 people (100,000 civilians and 80,000 soldiers) who worked in Pyongyang from 1985 to 1989.[12] The construction crews were called "shock brigades" to give their work all the urgency and motivation that is supposed to characterize the military in combat. The workers, drawn from the entire country, were for the most part unskilled in construction work, and the men were away from their families most of the time, often not getting home leave for two or three years. Yet according to battalion commander Kim, working on a shock brigade was generally considered a privilege because it was a means of becoming a KWP member and guaranteed food, clothing, and shelter as long as the job lasted. Being away from their home towns, the men experienced freedom from neighborhood surveillance. The progress of construction was slow in the absence of modern labor-saving devices; moreover, ample loafing was tolerated, since both workers and supervisors received their socialist benefits regardless of how fast the work went. Flag-waving and drum-beating propaganda and agitation troupes visited the construction site to motivate the men but with little effect.

According to the commander, few safety precautions were taken on the job; an average of one worker a day died in the Kwangbok Street construction project over a three-year period. Scaffolding, handrails, and safety nets were rarely erected. The workers' thin plastic safety hats were more useful for wash basins and soup bowls than protection, although party officials who visited the site wore Japanese-made industrial-quality hard hats. No construction elevators were installed on high-rise projects, so the men would have to climb as much as thirty floors up stairways or scaffolding to get to their work (one can only imagine the hardships involved in building the 105-story Ryukyong Hotel building). By the time the men reached the upper floors, they were exhausted. The commander recalls that he would climb up his building every second day to supervise workers. Once on top, he would rest with his men. Even after they were ordered to work, some of the men would loaf unless a political officer came by. Construction materials were hauled up with cranes and winches designed for mine work.

Construction teams that overfulfilled their quotas received prizes: television sets for the commanders and clothing or foodstuffs for the workers. Pilfering of construction materials was a constant problem. Workers would sell pilfered items or exchange them for food. Upon returning to their families after several years of work, the men would take a few items of food and such sundries as toothpaste and bar soap, luxuries to most Koreans outside of Pyongyang.

According to the commander, by festival time many of the buildings were finished only on the outside. The shacks in which workers had been living were torn down and the men moved into the lower floors of the unfinished buildings, which had running water for only a few hours in the morning and evening, and no toilet facilities. Once the festivities began, workers were banned from entering the festival grounds, although some of them, including the commander, sneaked in, marveling at the soft drinks, souvenirs, postcards, and books being sold at the counters, and the noodles and beef and fresh fruits available in the food stalls run by overseas Koreans. Commander Kim purchased a cold drink at one of the stalls, but his domestic currency was not accepted; taking pity on him, the vendor waived payment. Kim felt frustrated and embarrassed that the workers who had labored for years to build the festival facilities could not even afford to buy a soft drink. In short, the festival, like the entire city of Pyongyang, was a showplace for foreigners and a residence for their upper-class North Korean hosts, not a place for the North Korean masses.

The Political Classification System

Kim Jong Il can call on a formidable arsenal of tools to control the North Korean people, ranging from physical coercion to thought control. Everyone, presumably except for Kim himself, is investigated, classified, and watched. In a report he delivered to the Fifth Korean Workers' Party Congress in 1970, Kim Il Sung outlined a classification system consisting of three loyalty groups and fifty-one subgroups, with its roots going back to 1958.[13] Of course China had a loyalty system during Mao's time, and the Soviet and Eastern European governments kept files on their citizens. The South Korean government, most notably during the military regimes of Park Chung-hee and Chun Doo-hwan, kept files on its citizens. North Korea's control system is exceptionally thorough. People are classified according to their loyalty to the Kim regime, and that classification depends heavily on family background, reaching back for several generations(in South Korea the political basis of surveillance was anti-communism).[14]

The three loyalty groups are the core class (*haeksim kyechung*), the wavering class (*tong'yo kyechung*), and the hostile class (*joktae kyechung*). Among the twelve subgroups of the core class, who constituted an estimated 28 percent of the population in the 1983–84 classification, are those who in the preliberation period (before 1945) were workers, poor farmers, office clerks, and soldiers. Examples include subgroup 1: laborers; subgroup 6: members of revolutionary (anti-Japanese) families; subgroup 9: families whose members were killed during the Korean War. Current members of the KWP (most of whom have such a family background) are also included in this category. Members of the core group, whatever their occupation, receive priority in obtaining promotions, housing, food, and medical services, as well as the many little favors in socialist life that can be obtained only through the goodwill of bureaucrats.

The wavering class (who can potentially be won over by political education) constituted 45 to 50 percent of the population in 1984. They come from families who in preliberation days were merchants, farmers, or service workers. Included in this category are families who immigrated from South Korea, China, or Japan, as well as those whose relatives left North Korea to go to South Korea. The wavering class is further divided into eighteen subgroups. Examples of the subclasses include subgroup 13: street vendors; subgroup 15: craftsmen; subgroup 19: those who stayed behind when family members (not guilty of criminal or political offenses) fled to South Korea. These politically middle-class North Koreans can live an ordinary life. They have some hope of advancement in their assigned occupation but rarely gain admission to the better schools or rise high in the party or government hierarchy.

Members of the twenty-one subgroups of the hostile class, which in 1984 constituted 20 to 25 percent of the population, have little opportunity for social or political advancement. They live and work under the close scrutiny of the Ministry of People's Security (MPS). This class includes those who have—by word or by deed—expressed dissatisfaction with the Kim regime or those whose families in preliberation Korea were wealthy landlords, merchants, or prominent members of religious organizations. Subgroups include subgroup 27: bureaucrats who worked for the Japanese colonial administration; subgroups 34, 35, 36, and 37: Protestants, Buddhists, Catholics, and Confucian scholars, respectively. Members of the hostile class lead difficult lives. They are assigned to the least desirable jobs and live in the poorest housing, often in remote rural areas where they receive few government rations. They are not permitted to live in Pyongyang. They have little chance of entering good schools, joining the KWP, or gaining promotions or leadership positions in their occupations. At the bottom of the ladder are the estimated 200,000 Koreans who live in concentration camps.[15] According to North Korean defectors, these people live an almost animal-like existence.[16] The North Korean government denies the existence of such camps:

> As is well known, there is no "human rights problem" in our Republic either from the institutional or from the legal point of view. So there is no "camp" in our Republic. In Sungho-ri, the place where the south Korean authorities allege there is a "camp of political prisoners" there are industrial establishments and cooperative farms animated with creative labor and rows of modern apartment houses and rural houses overflowing with the happiness of the people.[17]

It is not known exactly how thoroughly the MPS documents the three classes and fifty-one subclasses. Given the strict regimentation of North Korean society, it can be assumed that reasonably detailed records are kept of personal history and family backgrounds. In most cases the individuals themselves do not know what their exact classification is, but they can generally tell which of the three ideological classes they have been assigned to by the treatment they receive from officials.

A former officer in the KPA relates how, by surreptitiously gaining access to his security file, he discovered that the reason he was unable to gain further promotions was that one of his father's cousins, who was a government official in South Korea during the Korean War, was subsequently arrested and killed by the communists.[18] This fact was known to his parents, who had kept the knowledge from him to protect him. In his file he was classified as a member of the hostile class, even though he had risen to a fairly responsible position in the military and considered himself a loyal North Korean.

Security Organizations

People are monitored by overlapping military and quasi-military security organizations (see figure 5-1 in chapter 5). In matters of intelligence and counterintelligence, the Korean Workers' Party (KWP) sets policy for the government and oversees every aspect of its implementation. In the Central Committee, nine departments share some responsibility for intelligence operations in the broadest sense: Organization and Guidance, Propaganda and Agitation, Cadre, International Affairs, Unification Front, Operations, Foreign Intelligence, Social and Cultural, and South Korean Affairs. Of these, the Organization and Guidance Department is the most important, for decisions made in this department control the activities of all other departments and organizations in the party, government, and military.

The two principal domestic intelligence organizations are the Ministry of People's Security (MPS) and the State Security Department (SSD). The MPS, under the direction of the cabinet, functions as a police and public safety organization as well as an intelligence and counterintelligence bureau.[19] The MPS operates twenty-seven sub-bureaus employing an estimated 144,000 officers and agents operating in all geographical areas and in all civilian organizations. MPS personnel hold quasi-military status and wear military-style uniforms. Public safety functions include routine police work and fire protection. The MPS protects state property, provides security for railways, airports, and seaports, and runs the air traffic control system. The MPS conducts criminal investigations and manages the nation's prison system, except for political prisons. It also provides protection for high-ranking cadres, except for Kim Jong Il, who has his own secret service.

In the course of its police duties the MPS unearths suspicious cases that can be referred to the SSD. Through its informers, the MPS is on the lookout for any words or actions that could even remotely be construed as criticism of the Kim regime, including remarks made among family members. Surveillance of the citizenry is conducted by MPS operatives assigned to every workplace, and in the home and neighborhood through a household organization system whereby a small group of households (originally the *Ohoje*, or "five families" system, a legacy of ancient China, but now typically fifteen to twenty families) are placed under the responsibility of a neighborhood chief appointed by the local party chapter. The chief is charged with keeping track of everything that occurs in the neighborhood and reporting unusual, suspicious, illegal, or anti-regime behavior to the MPS. The neighborhood chief also sees to it that everyone attends required political study sessions.

The MPS investigates the background of North Korean citizens as a means of classifying them according to their loyalty to the regime. The background and behavior of visitors to the DPRK are also thoroughly investigated. Permission must be obtained from the MPS to change one's residence or job or to travel within the country. Needless to say, travel abroad is impossible for the ordinary citizen. The MPS controls the ration system, which—until the famine years of the mid-1990s—was the primary source of food for the population.

The SSD is comparable to the U.S. Central Intelligence Agency or to the South Korean National Intelligence Service. When the National Defense Commission (chaired by Kim Jong Il) was removed from the authority of the president and given virtually autonomous authority in 1992, the SSD was placed under its authority, parallel to the MPS and the Ministry of People's Armed Forces (MPAF). The SSD is believed to have sixteen bureaus, four agencies, and supporting research units. Like the MPS, the SSD has branch offices at all levels of society. The counterintelligence functions of the SSD overlap to some extent with those of the MPS: MPS personnel are likely to be the first to discover suspicious activities, whereupon the case is handed over to the SSD for further investigation. The SSD investigates political dissident suspects and manages political prisons. The SSD is also in charge of examining the backgrounds of important party and government officials and military officers, and monitoring their behavior. Electronic communication channels are monitored by the SSD. People with engineering or communication skills are said to receive special surveillance from the SSD.[20] A former MPS officer reports that considerable competition and often ill-will exists between members of these two security organizations.[21]

The military has its own intelligence, counterintelligence, and espionage organizations.[22] Military activities at all levels are jointly controlled by the party (under the direction of its Central Military Committee) and the government (under the direction of the NDC). The MPAF consists of five bureaus, including the General Political Bureau and the Security Command (formerly the

Political Security Bureau). The General Political Bureau operates under the authority of the Central Military Committee, and the Security Command is under the authority of the SSD. The importance of the General Political Bureau, which oversees all other bureaus in the MPAF, is indicated by the fact that its commanding general, Cho Myong-nok, outranks the head of the General Staff Bureau in the political (as opposed to military) ranking system. Cho ranked third in the national power hierarchy (following Kim Jong Il and chairman-president of the SPA presidium Kim Yong-nam) in late 1999.[23] At each level of the military, a political officer, who takes his orders from the party rather than the military chain of command, monitors all activities and exercises veto power over the military commander's orders. Besides monitoring behavior, the political officer is charged with conducting political study sessions. Top cadres in North Korea, especially those in the military, are subjected to intense scrutiny. KPA generals spend fifteen days a year at a study and self-criticism retreat operated by the General Political Bureau.

The MPAF's Security Command appears to duplicate many of the responsibilities of the General Political Bureau and the MPS, but it is more secretive in nature.[24] The command operates the Reconnaissance Bureau, which infiltrates agents into South Korea, and conducts counterespionage in North Korea. It monitors telephone conversations of top military officers and investigates draft dodgers. It also trains security agents, runs a broad informant network, and has been given responsibility for three border guard brigades along the Chinese border. According to Hwang Jang Yop, former party secretary, Kim Jong Il has been dissatisfied with the corruption-busting efforts of the MPS and SSD and has turned to the Security Command to conduct investigations in the civilian as well as military sectors.[25]

Crimes and Punishments

The goal of the security organizations is to permeate every sector of society and to monitor the private and public life of North Korean citizens and foreign visitors. People suspected of crimes often disappear during the night, never to be heard from again. Top cadres who fall from favor similarly disappear from public view. In a major campaign to stamp out illegal foreign currency earnings, Kim Jong Il replaced many of his foreign trade officials in 1998. What became of them is not known.[26] Needless to say, their disappearance disrupted North Korea's limited trade ties with other countries and sowed seeds of suspicion about the transparency of its economic policies. Public executions as a deterrent to crime and corruption have become more frequent in the 1990s.

Numerous reports indicate that even top cadres, including a party secretary in charge of agriculture, have been executed.[27]

The greatest threat to the security of the Kim regime would come from a palace coup by top cadres or by the security people. It may be recalled that in South Korea, President Park Chung Hee, himself something of a dictator, was assassinated by the head of his own Central Intelligence Agency. To forestall such a coup in North Korea, Kim Jong Il puts his top people under multiple sources of surveillance. Every government delegation traveling overseas includes at least two intelligence agents who report on the activities of their colleagues (and one another). The intelligence apparatus is compartmentalized so that different intelligence organizations have limited contact with one another.

The most serious crime a North Korean can commit is disloyalty to the leader. Acts of disloyalty are defined in ways that are unimaginable in liberal democracies. In every building at least one set of portraits of Kim Il Sung and Kim Jong Il is displayed on a prominent wall, away from any other pictures. Anyone caught treating pictures of the Kims with disrespect, such as letting them collect dust, is subject to disciplinary action. Pictures of the Kims in newspapers and magazines are not to be folded or torn. In October 1997 South Korean workers at a KEDO construction site in North Korea were confined to their dormitory when a crumpled copy of *Nodong Sinmun* was found in a wastebasket. A photograph of Kim Jong Il in the newspaper had been torn in two—a crime by North Korean standards. After the South Korean government protested that no insult was intended, and that in any case the workers were covered by diplomatic immunity, the North Koreans released the workers from house arrest.[28]

Another view of what counts as a crime in North Korea is illustrated by the predicament of an unsuspecting South Korean tourist. In June 1999, during a period of high tension between the two Koreas, a housewife on the Hyundai-sponsored group tour to North Korea's Kumgang Mountain was detained for six days by North Korean authorities. According to her report, backed up by South Korean witnesses, she told a North Korean security guard on the tour trail, in the context of a brief conversation, that she hoped he would come and live in South Korea after unification.[29] According to the North Koreans, "the South Korean authorities sent [her] as a tourist to Mt. Kumgang for the purpose of inducing persons in the north to defect to the south." Before being released, she was induced to sign a confession admitting to "all the grave political crimes committed by her and entreating for lenient pardon."[30]

The key to effective deterrence and punishment in North Korea is the use of the traditional custom of *yongoje* (family purge), whereby punishment for an individual's crime is visited as well on the extended family and often on friends and colleagues. A father who incurs the wrath of the authorities can expect not only his immediate family, but also his parents, uncles, and cousins, to suffer for his crime if not by imprisonment or banishment, at least by having the crime entered into their personal records. This form of punishment has proved extremely effective in deterring all but the most brave, selfish, or reckless individuals from going against the Kim regime. Even those with little to lose personally (such as those who may be dying of starvation) will endure injustice and hardship even to the point of death rather than escape or publicly protest. The families of North Korean officials who travel abroad are usually kept in Korea. The strong consensus among defectors from North Korea is that this instrument of terror has proved highly effective in keeping people in line. Those who defect live with feelings of guilt about the fate of those they left behind.

North Koreans are also deterred from defecting to South Korea (by way of China or Russia) by North Korean propaganda, which teaches that any North Korean who falls into the hands of the South Korean authorities will be tortured to extract information and then executed.[31] When North Korean commandos are stranded in South Korea, they usually commit suicide in order to die a hero's death, with the assurance that their loved ones will earn the special kind of treatment accorded to the families of fallen heroes. For those in North Korea who are detained by the security police or thrown into prison, there is one way out. The North Korean bureaucracy is so corrupt that money changing hands or a visit to the right official will often effect a release.[32]

Besides the threat of punishment, the government controls peoples' lives by controlling their livelihood. Until the breakdown of government services in the 1990s, most people depended on the government for food, clothing, and housing. Even travel between towns required special travel permits (although freedom of travel and residence is newly guaranteed in the 1998 constitution, that guarantee is probably as meaningless as other constitutional guarantees of human rights). Those who can get a travel permit must check in with the police at their destination to have their ration card validated to obtain food. Those banished from their homes for crimes and sent into the remote hills must forage for themselves, living like primitive hunting and gathering peoples.

North Koreans are expected to inform on one another, even children on their parents, because if they do not report a crime and it is discovered, they are implicated. A basic principle in North Korea is that two people who trust each other may discuss sensitive issues, but when a third joins them, nothing can be said. Between two people, if one accuses the other of disloyalty, it is one person's word against the other. With three people, each must fear that the other two may report the incident and thus each is motivated to report on his own behalf—an example of the prisoner's dilemma. Hence the near impossibility of organizing any kind of resistance movement against the Kim regime.[33]

Thought Control

Building on Confucian tradition, the Kims have taught that loyalty is the touchstone of all human virtues. They have promised that with unbounded loyalty and correct thoughts, people can accomplish anything; conversely, everything that generations of North Koreans have worked for will be lost if people abandon their leader. Political study sessions based on the teachings of the Kims begin at the kindergarten level and continue throughout life.

Korean children attend school for eleven years: one year of preschool, four of primary school, and six of senior middle school. An estimated 14 percent of students go on to specialized technical and professional schools or to Kim Il Sung University, the only university in the country.[34] The principal qualifications for admission to institutions of higher learning are political reliability and personal connections.[35] Schooling at all levels emphasizes political studies.

Kim Il Sung's 1977 Thesis on Socialist Education set forth four guiding principles: inculcation of party and working-class consciousness; establishment of Juche in education; combination of education and revolutionary practice; and the government's responsibility for education.[36] Kim stipulated that the educational curriculum consist of political education in Juche and communism, as well as general education and physical education.

Emphasis on political education begins early. In primary school, the following subjects are taught: history of Kim Il Sung's childhood days (one hour per week); special lecture on a political topic (one hour); communism and moral education (one hour); Korean language (seven to eight hours); math (five to six hours); natural studies (from third grade: three hours); health education (from fourth grade: one hour); physical education (two hours); music (two hours); and arts and crafts (two hours).[37]

This list of subjects may not seem overly laden with political studies, but political themes are an integral part of other studies. By one estimate, 35 percent of elementary schooling is devoted to political education, rising to more than 40 percent for university students.[38] For example, in Korean language training, only 15 percent of class time is spent on grammar, vocabulary, and comprehension. Readings about the two Kims take up 64 percent of class time, and lessons on the importance of manual labor, the collective life, and developing a fighting spirit against the enemies of communism account for 21 percent of class time. Wherever the names of the two Kims appear, they are set in boldface type and preceded by such honorifics as *Wonsunim* (Honorable Top Person) and *Chidoja Sonsaengnim* (Guiding Teacher). Of course this is standard practice in all North Korean publications. Words attributed to the two Kims or to Kim Il Sung's first wife are always presented in quotation marks and frequently introduce a paragraph or reading section, as if all wisdom originates with them.

School readings are filled with episodes illustrating how much the Kims love children; a strong theme of optimism about the future of Juche socialism is constantly present; stories about the evil deeds of North Korea's enemies (primarily the United States and Japan) are commonplace.[39] Students are taught arithmetic by counting how many American soldiers were killed and how many of their tanks were destroyed by the brave North Koreans during the Korean War.[40] In music class, students sing songs such as "Thank you Marshal Kim Il Sung for bringing us up as future pillars of society."[41]

Political education extends beyond the school room. Kim Il Sung taught that "Home education, social education and school education cannot be separated; they must go hand in hand. The real education to transform a human being begins at home, then schools strengthen their education, which has to be continued and consolidated by social education."[42] People of all ages are expected to become members of party-supervised groups in order to keep them under surveillance and further educate them in the party line. Besides regular school classes, students participate in twelve to twenty hours of social work a week, including participation in loyalty marches for the two Kims, cultural events, recycling activities, tree-planting activities, searches for edibles in the countryside, and harvesting activities.[43]

The prescribed regimen of eight hours of work, eight hours of study, and eight hours of sleep may not be strictly followed by the average North Korean, but political study sessions in which the Kims' works are read and discussed are an almost daily requirement for children and adults alike. One former North Korean jokingly predicted that North Korean children could easily win a world title for memorization because school students must memorize the major speeches made by the Kims. Committing one such speech to memory may take several weeks.[44]

It is difficult to determine just how effective North Korean propaganda is. Defectors almost unanimously claim that the cumulative effect of this indoctrination is very strong, given the absence of alternative channels of information. Just as Western television commercials influence the capitalist consumer, so too must a lifetime of political indoctrination come to shape the thinking of North Koreans.

The North Korean people are constantly tested in their beliefs. To determine if information has been memorized and understood, people are quizzed in political study sessions; those who fail to demonstrate understanding and commitment receive black marks on their political record. To translate learning into commitment and action, people undergo criticisms and self-criticisms. In group sessions they are required to confess their political failings, no matter how small, and tell how they will improve themselves. All North Koreans, even the top cadres, must regularly attend such study sessions. More intensive "re-education" is sometimes ordered. Those convicted of crimes, including political crimes, are sentenced to hard work, intensive study, and self-criticism (death or banishment for the most serious crimes). North Koreans who come into contact with foreigners (for example, returning North Korean diplomats) must undergo months of re-education in the countryside accompanied by manual labor, to remind them of the so-called classless nature of communism. One former North Korean claims that workers at joint venture factories run by South Koreans must spend one month in anti-imperialist re-education classes for every two months of work at the plant.[45] North Korean workers are rotated in and out of such assignments to prevent them from becoming too influenced by their foreign contacts.

Information Control

North Koreans live in the most closed society on earth. The masses receive no foreign newspapers, radio, or television broadcasts, and meet few foreign visitors. One former North Korean said he got rid of his radio because of the nuisance of public security officials making unannounced visits to his house to determine that the radio dial, permanently set to receive only the official radio station, had not been tampered with.[46]

As in the world of Orwell's *1984* (and to a lesser extent, in Stalin's Soviet Union, and to an even lesser extent, in South Korea in the 1970s), North Korean apartments, houses, and public buildings have a public address speaker wired to a local transmitter. Through this "third broadcast system" Koreans are provided with local news to complement the national news they receive from the state-owned radio and television. Sound trucks ply the streets broadcasting local announcements. For example, one North Korean tells how a sound truck would make the rounds announcing the imminent arrival of a group of foreigners, instructing people to stay indoors if at all possible, or else wear their best clothes in public. The lack of information from foreign sources prevents people from judging the validity of the Kim regime's negative propaganda about the outside world. For example, if people believe (as they are told) that the entire world is in the grip of a severe food shortage and that their fellow Koreans in the South are starving, they are unlikely to attempt to escape because of their own food shortage.

Inevitably, some information seeps in. Clandestine radio broadcasts are heard on imported or rewired radios. Government-sponsored broadcasts sometimes inadvertently reveal uncensored news of the outside world. When North Korean television ran coverage of the uprising of residents in the South Korean city of Kwangju, North Korean viewers were amazed to see the excellent quality of clothing the protesters were wearing.[47] And when a film about the lives of North Koreans living in Japan was shown on the government channel, viewers eagerly studied the background scenes to learn about Japanese life.[48] People can also glean news of the world from North Korean traders who travel to China, and from Chinese-Korean traders who cross into North Korea. Even those few North Koreans who travel abroad are subject to restrictions. A former North Korean diplomat serving at an overseas post recounts how he was criticized by a security agent attached to his embassy for reading *Paris Match.*[49] The diplomat, who was serving in Africa, explained to the agent that it was necessary for him to be familiar with France and to study the language, but he later heard that his reading had been reported to headquarters and that he might be investigated for harboring antisocialist ideas.

The Kim regime's response to the inevitable seepage of information into the country is twofold. One, people are warned that such "imperialistic pollution" is designed by North Korea's enemies to undermine socialist beliefs. According to this argument, those who believe what they hear from outside and act on it will end up becoming slaves of the imperialists. Two, those who share it with others are punished.

The Cultural Foundation of Totalitarian Control

The severe restrictions imposed on the people do not rest as heavily upon their shoulders as they would upon people from Western liberal democracies because the Kim regime is built on a strong Confucian tradition. North Koreans have never experienced democracy. Until the twentieth century most Koreans, in North and South, were peasants in a premodern social system headed by local *yangban* lords and a king and his court in the capital. The arrival of the Japanese changed little in the social order, for the Japanese became the new ruling elite and treated the Korean people even more harshly than their former rulers. When Kim Il Sung imposed a Stalinist system on North Korea, the fiction of people being masters of their own destiny was quickly dispelled by the totalitarian control exercised by the KWP under the direction of their leader, who, as he grew older, increasingly played the role of a modern-day king.

The Kim regime's use of groups to control the people is built on a collectivist tradition shared with other Asian cultures and borrows from the social control methods of Stalin and Mao. Koreans feel comfortable living and working in groups. The communists simply substituted their party-controlled groups for traditional family and village groups. As communist parties go, the KWP is not an exclusive party, even though only a minority of North Koreans are privileged to join. At Kim Il Sung's direction party membership was opened to all those who could prove their loyalty to the regime. At the last party congress, held in 1980, an estimated 12 percent of the population were party members.[50]

The parallels between social control in North Korea and in China during the Mao period are informative. In his study of Chinese communist work units, Victor Shaw discusses the ways that work organizations controlled their members.[51] Official ideology was taught in political study groups. People's home life was closely watched, a surveillance made easier because people lived close to their assigned workplace. A lifelong confidential dossier was kept by the local communist party office. Neighborhood watch committees and a neighborhood chief who reported to the local party committee kept tabs on people. On a broader level, the desire to be included in the group and avoid ostracism served to make people conform to group norms. All of these control mechanisms operate today in North Korean society, as they did in China before the economic reform and opening initiated in the 1980s by Deng Xiaoping loosened political control in China.

The Kim regime teaches a kind of Confucian morality. People are taught to do what is right (by party standards), not what works. Juche ideology as it has been developed in the 1990s exalts the virtue of dying for socialism and the leader rather than changing the leader's system. According to defectors, even as their economy crumbles and social infrastructure decays, most North Korean people remain loyal to their country and the memory of Kim Il Sung, the leader who got them into trouble in the first place. Of course loyalty to Kim Jong Il has never been as great, hence the redoubled propaganda campaigns to teach the virtue of absolute loyalty to him, regardless of what may come. Another virtue that has been reinforced by the communist tradition is sharing. Despite the hard times, North Koreans share with one another. This virtue, they are told, is totally lacking in the capitalist system, which is run on the principle of every person for himself.

The Limits of Social Control

Arguably, no government in the twentieth century has succeeded in exercising as much control over its people as has the Kim government. A half-century of propaganda and social control has shaped the attitudes, values, and behavior of the masses and the elite. The goal of this ideological and behavioral shaping is to transform the North Korean people into selfless socialists who unquestioningly obey their leaders. The Kims' attempt at total control, with multiple layers of control mechanisms reinforcing a corpus of lies, has created a society that on the surface is remarkably stable and resistant to change, considering the dire economic straits into which the people have fallen. But underneath this facade is a society riddled with corruption and plagued by dissatisfaction.

Social control mechanisms have functioned better in some respects than in others. Kim Jong Il's control of top government, party, and military leaders appears to be successful: they are closely watched, amply rewarded, and occasionally severely punished as an example to others. The ability of the MPS and the SSD to prevent the formation of unauthorized organizations and gatherings seems effective. Voices of dissent are not raised in public; even in private people are extremely careful about criticizing the Kim regime.

Social control seems to be slipping in regard to keeping the population from moving around the country. The security police often take pity on hungry people who are searching for food; in any case, the police will generally accept bribes to look the other way, even when people go back and forth across the Chinese border. Beginning in 1998 several sources reported that many North Korean children had left home or been abandoned by their parents, who were unable to feed them. These children roamed the countryside and cities as beggars, sometimes joining together in small bands. On September 27, 1997, Kim Jong Il ordered that these vagabonds, called *kotchebi* (flower swallows), be detained in special "9-27" camps.[52] Living conditions in the makeshift camps are said to be miserable, and children often escape to roam again.

The Kim regime has also been unable to prevent the formation of farmers' markets. These markets have existed in one form or another since the founding of the republic; they have been periodically suppressed by the authorities but always return.[53] To the masses, the markets gained increasing importance in the 1980s as the state food rationing system began to break down. For the privileged classes, the markets provide a means of disposing of surplus goods at a handsome profit.

The regime's social control mechanism is also failing to halt a rise in crime. Defectors from North Korea report that robbery and prostitution are widespread. Crime helps poor people cope with a worsening economy (although sometimes crimes are committed for personal gain, especially by the children of the elite). Criminal activity is made possible by the willingness of security personnel to accept bribes. Often security and military personnel engage in crimes; according to one report, hungry soldiers have even crossed the border into China to commit robbery.[54]

The Kim regime's social control efforts have been unable to stamp out corruption among officials and bureaucrats. On many occasions Kim Jong Il has publicly complained about the unsocialistic behavior of bureaucrats, and in a few cases he has made an example of high-level party or government officials who accepted bribes or conducted private business on the side. But Kim can hardly lead by example, for his corrupt practices put him in a class by himself, and the elite know this. Throughout the bureaucracy—especially as the primary economy has collapsed, taking the value of government salaries with it—corruption has become the primary means of livelihood for many officials and bureaucrats. To get anything done, such as receiving a job promotion or a travel document, one must *koyora* ("pile up the goods").[55] A former North Korean truck driver explains why so few of the goods he transported to Pyongyang from the Chinese border reached their destination: police as well as bandits would set up roadblocks on major trading routes. At each stop the driver would be forced to pay an unofficial toll. By the time the truck reached its destination, it would be carrying only 50 percent of its original cargo.[56] Left unsaid is the likelihood that many truck drivers sell some of the cargo for cash before reaching their final destination. Even though corruption is widespread, most of the North Korean people, including many bureaucrats and officials, are said by defectors to be honest. Many former North Koreans have recounted how neighbors, in a true communist spirit, share with one another. The tragedy is that the Kim regime has left the masses very little to share.

The Kims have tried to create a society in which everyone but themselves is subservient to the party. But rather than become productive workers eager to fulfill their assigned tasks, the people have become disillusioned. The government admits as much in its repeated calls for people to work harder and find their own solutions to problems. Since the death of Kim Il Sung, the ruling elite have lost much of their legitimacy and most of the reservoir of trust and hope that kept the people at their work. Kim Jong Il can remain in power only by giving his political and military associates rewards, of which there is a dwindling supply, and threatening to deliver punishments. No government can survive for long by relying solely on rewards and coercion, and the Kim Jong Il regime is unlikely to be an exception.

CHAPTER SEVEN

The Foreign Relations
of a Hermit Kingdom

*Our foreign policy is the most righteous and principled one for
the causes of socialism, which is also aimed at achieving independence for all humankind. We will further strengthen unity
with the progressive people of the world desirous of socialism
and with anti-imperialist, independent force[s] in the idea of
independence, peace and friendship, and will smash the
aggression and war moves of the imperialists and build a new
world, peaceful and independent.*[1]

North Korea, like the Choson dynasty "Hermit Kingdom,"
has throughout its fifty-year history kept its distance from other nations, showing little enthusiasm for diplomacy or people-to-people contact. Even during
the cold war, North Korea was a close ally of neither China nor the Soviet Union.
After the demise of European communism and the economic reformation of
China, North Korea became even more isolated.

North Korea's foreign policy is crafted against the backdrop of Korean history, especially the memory of recurring invasions from neighboring powers
and years of political subjugation. Given this history, it is unreasonable to characterize North Korean attitudes toward the international community as
paranoid. After the liberation of Korea from Japan, North Korea's struggle for
political independence continued in the context of its seeking to maintain political autonomy from its two larger communist allies—China and the Soviet
Union—while seeking to liberate the southern half of the peninsula (which
the North considers part of its territory). The achievement of this second goal
required not only that the North Koreans expel the Americans in South Korea,
but that the North Koreans compete and win in a zero-sum game of political
legitimacy with the South Korean government.

A Legacy of Insecurity

What John K. Fairbank, Edwin O. Reischauer, and Albert M. Craig said of the Korean kings of the eighteenth century is true of the leaders of North Korea today: "They maintained a rigid policy of seclusion until it was almost too late to learn the art of diplomacy."[2] The Choson dynasty lasted from 1392 to 1910, making it the longest-lived dynasty in East Asian history. During this period, Korea witnessed the change of power from China's Ming dynasty ruled by Han Chinese to the Ch'ing dynasty ruled by the Manchus. Japan, meanwhile, made the transition from the Ashikaga era to the Tokugawa Shogunate, before entering the modern world with the advent of the Meiji Restoration in 1868. The durability of the Choson dynasty conferred legitimacy on Korean monarchs, but Korean pride and overconfidence sowed the seeds of the dynasty's downfall, as Korea resisted the political, economic, social, and military changes that had transformed and strengthened the Western world and brought it to Korea's doorstep.

As citizens of a smaller power squeezed between large powers, Koreans have rarely been free to practice domestic politics undisturbed. In the late nineteenth century the Chinese, Japanese, and Russians sought to extend their influence over Korea.[3] The Chinese had traditionally held a suzerain relationship with Korea, but the Chinese themselves had for too long resisted political and economic reforms, and as a consequence had become weak. The Korean Peninsula was an attractive land to control: it had year-round warm-water ports, a long border with China, and extensive mineral deposits (in the North) and fertile rice fields (in the South). Korea's neighbors also recognized the geostrategic value of the peninsula as a bridge connecting the Eurasian land mass to Japan and the Pacific rim countries.

Nineteenth-century Koreans were of two minds about how to respond to foreign overtures. The conservative school, which counted the ruling class among its members, favored maintaining Korea's traditional political relationship with China. The pro-reform school, consisting of the young educated segment of Korean society, as well as some of the more enlightened ruling elite, saw a desperate need for Korea to modernize in order to hold its own in the new world order dominated by the industrial powers. These reformers took Japan as their model, for the Japanese, after a similar debate, had chosen the road to reform in the 1860s and were already beginning to mimic their Western imperialistic mentors. While the Koreans were debating, the surrounding powers were acting. The Korean government was forced to sign treaties opening the Korean economy and society to the Japanese in 1876, the United States in 1882, Britain and Germany in 1883, Russia and Italy in 1884, France in 1886, and Austria-Hungary in 1889. But Korea's strongest ties remained with the Ch'ing government of China. As the outside world pressed against traditional Korea, the reformers mounted a coup against the Choson court, demanding that the government sever its tributary ties with China and adopt a republican form of government. The coup failed and its leaders were captured and executed, leaving Korea at the mercy of whichever neighbor was strong enough to take advantage of its weakness.

The invasion of Korea was triggered by the actions of yet a third political force, the Tonghak (Eastern Learning) movement. Consisting largely of nationalistic peasants and led by the charismatic peasant leader Chun Bong-jun, this group mounted an insurrection against the government in February 1894, seeking a change in corrupt government policies and the expulsion of foreigners. Ironically, these innocent nationalists by their actions gave foreign forces an excuse to enter Korea. In June 1894 the weak Korean government appealed to the Chinese to send troops to quell the rebellion. China sent 3,000 soldiers. After a confrontation in 1884, China and Japan had agreed to withdraw their troops from Korea. With Chinese troops now back in the country, Japan sent in 8,000 soldiers, under the excuse of protecting its economic investments. The Chinese and Japanese were once again in direct contention for influence, and when Japanese troops seized the royal palace in Seoul on July 23, they triggered the 1894–95 Sino-Japanese War, which they won.

China's influence in Korea and throughout the region weakened as Japan's grew. Korea became the battleground for another regional conflict when economic and political rivalry on the Korean Peninsula between Russia and Japan exploded into the 1904–05 Russo-Japanese War, with the Japanese once again demonstrating how efficiently they had modernized their military. The Japanese were now recognized as full-fledged members of the imperialists' club, and in the Taft-Katsura memorandum of 1905, the United States agreed to respect Japan's preeminent interests on the Korean Peninsula (in exchange for Japanese recognition of American interests in the Philippines). Korea became an unwilling protectorate of Japan in 1905 and a colony in 1910. The Korean Peninsula was liberated from the Japanese in 1945 by American and Russian troops, and North Korea fell back on its ancient pattern of dependence on larger neighbors, in this case relying on China and the Soviet Union, with the Soviets having the larger influence on political and economic affairs until the collapse of the Soviet Union in 1991.

"High" Foreign Relations

To understand the constraints that totalitarianism places on North Korea's foreign policy, it is helpful to draw a distinction between "high" foreign relations
between governments (diplomacy) and "low" foreign relations between people (contacts and exchanges).[4] The policy goals formulated by governments
typically include national security, international prestige, protecting and promoting national values and ideology, strengthening the economy, and ensuring
the welfare of the people. Especially in a totalitarian or one-party state, an additional goal is to preserve and strengthen the regime in power. These goals are
pursued by diplomats, generally with little advice or consent of the public.

Relations with the Soviet Union and Russia

Meeting in private at the Yalta conference in February 1945, Franklin D.
Roosevelt and Stalin agreed on the timing of the Soviet Union's declaration of
war on Japan and on the entry of Soviet troops into Korea. On August 10 the
first contingent of Soviet forces landed on North Korea's northeast coast.[5] In
Tokyo, the Japanese government announced its surrender to the Allies on
August 15, 1945. On August 21 more Soviet forces landed in Korea, reaching
Pyongyang by August 24. Pursuant to the agreement with the United States,
Soviet troops stopped above the 38th Parallel, even though American forces
did not arrive from Okinawa to accept the Japanese surrender south of the
parallel until September 8. Soviet leaders in Moscow seemed to have no immediate plan to turn Korea into a Soviet satellite state: the evidence made public
to date suggests that Stalin was thinking in global geopolitical terms about the
Soviet Union's emerging competition with the United States, and his primary
interest was in Europe.[6] Roosevelt had suggested to Stalin that Korea be made
an international protectorate under the administration of the major powers,
but while Stalin apparently did not turn down the suggestion, he was not
enthusiastic. In any event the Korean people were vehemently opposed to the
trusteeship idea, which was never implemented.

In the northern half of the peninsula, the Russians worked behind the
scenes to shape Korean politics by employing existing Korean groups. The
most widely recognized, loosely knit group was the nationalists, headed by
Cho Man-sik, whose support was enlisted by asking him to chair a welcom-
ing rally for "General" Kim Il Sung, who arrived with a small band of unarmed
Korean guerrillas of the 88th Brigade of the Soviet army on September 19,
1945. But since Cho was not a communist, he was apparently not considered
a trustworthy instrument of Soviet political designs. The domestic Korean

communist groups that had survived underground were also not a viable choice for the Soviets, since their headquarters was in the capital of Seoul, in the American zone. Members of the so-called Yenan communist faction were beginning to return to Korea from China, but they owed little loyalty to the Soviet Union.

This left a communist group of soldiers who had been fighting throughout the war in Soviet territory, and a smaller "Kapsan group" under the leadership of the youthful Kim Il Sung, who had arrived in the Soviet Union from China in the early 1940s. Kim Il Sung must have been a skillful politician even then, because the Soviets put his group in charge of directing police and military functions, and from this position Kim and his close-knit band of followers merged and purged until they finally gained political control of the northern half of the peninsula.

Under Kim Il Sung, North Korea developed typical communist institutions. A major item on Kim's agenda was to bring South Korea under his control. Bruce Cumings has documented the contest between the two Koreas in the years preceding the Korean War, noting that both sides desired reunification, and both sides initiated border incidents.[7] While some scholars, most notably Bruce Cumings, have suggested that the causes of the Korean War, and even the events triggering the outbreak of the war, are too complex to enable blame to be assigned to one side or the other, official Soviet documents released in the 1990s indicate that Kim Il Sung actively worked and planned for war.[8] When Kim pitched an invasion plan to Stalin in a Moscow meeting in March 1949, Stalin opposed the idea on the grounds that the North Korean military was not strong enough to win. Stalin was also concerned that an attack on South Korea might trigger a global conflict for which the Soviet Union was not ready. But during his next round of meetings in Moscow with Stalin in April 1950, Kim was more persuasive, and Stalin gave his tentative endorsement on the condition that Kim receive the approval of Mao Zedong as well, suggesting that Stalin considered that a Korean war would be primarily an Asian conflict from which he might benefit without incurring high costs. Stalin's tacit approval came in light of what he termed a "changed international situation" (since the 1949 meeting). The changes he was thinking of may have included a consolidation of the anticommunist government in South Korea under the Syngman Rhee government, the continued strengthening of North Korea, Washington's apparent lack of interest in the security of South Korea, American recognition that the Soviet Union was a more formidable enemy now that it had an atomic bomb, and the strengthening of the North Atlantic Treaty Organization (NATO), which seemed to limit prospects for communist expansion in Europe.

In any case, Kim apparently received Mao's support when he traveled to Beijing in May 1950, and North Korea launched an all-out attack across the 38th Parallel on June 25, 1950.

The Soviet Union influenced the course of the war in two significant ways. First, because of its boycott of the United Nations Security Council to protest the council's refusal to seat the People's Republic of China, the Soviet delegation was unable to use its veto to block the U.S. resolution to send troops to Korea under the UN flag. And second, when the North Korean invasion had been repelled and North Korean troops were fleeing toward the Chinese border, Stalin urgently appealed to Mao to come to Kim Il Sung's aid. Neither of these actions necessarily changed the course of the war, because the United States would likely have fought whether or not under UN sanctions, and the Chinese would probably have sent in troops to keep the Americans away from their border without being asked. But beyond this influence, the Soviet Union was not a very active participant in the Korean War, either as an instigator or as a combatant.

After the 1953 truce ending the Korean War, Kim Il Sung, presumably disappointed with the lack of war support he had received from the Soviet Union, and suspicious of Moscow's hegemonic designs after witnessing the Soviet takeover of Eastern Europe, maintained a political distance from Moscow. In the 1960s, when relations between China and the Soviet Union became strained, North Korea tilted toward China. During the Great Proletarian Cultural Revolution, when Kim Il Sung was criticized by the Chinese Red Guards, North Korea tilted back toward the Soviet Union. Soviet leaders do not seem to have had great respect for Kim Il Sung—Khrushchev's attack on Stalin, delivered at the Twentieth Party Congress in 1956, could easily be interpreted in North Korea as an indirect attack on Kim, who had his own personality cult and was also guilty of directing political purges. Kim disagreed with Khrushchev's policy of peaceful coexistence with the capitalists, a policy that smacked of backsliding on the Marxist-Leninist revolutionary principle, and which implied that the Soviet Union would not support Kim in his long-term campaign to reunify the peninsula. In 1960 the Soviet government stated its official position. "It is impossible not to take into consideration that on the Korean peninsula there emerged actually two states with different political and economic bases.... When two states with different social systems do exist, unification of the country could not be achieved by imposing the will of one state [on] the other, or even more, by enforced annexation of one part of the country by the other."[9] This statement is almost identical to the official position of the DPRK government in the mid-1990s, but in the 1960s, when Pyongyang still hoped to unite the peninsula under its government, Moscow's "two-Korea" policy was viewed as heresy.

The last of the Chinese troops were withdrawn from North Korea in 1958. American troops remained in South Korea, backing up the U.S.-ROK security treaty that had been signed in 1953. On July 6, 1961, the Soviet Union and North Korea signed a Treaty of Friendship, Cooperation and Mutual Assistance, which stated (in article 1), "Should either of the Contracting Parties suffer armed attack by any State or coalition of States and thus find itself in a state of war, the other Contracting Party shall immediately extend military and other assistance with all the means at its disposal."[10] This guarantee was qualified in article 5 by the stipulation, "The two Contracting Parties consider that the unification of Korea should be brought about on a peaceful and democratic basis," presumably disqualifying a second North Korean invasion of South Korea from the article 1 guarantee. When North Korea's capture of the *Pueblo* threatened to spark a serious conflict with the United States, the Soviet Union, wishing to distance itself from such a conflict, provided an updated interpretation of the defense pact that included the provision that the pact would only be honored in the event that North Korea was the victim of large-scale *unprovoked* aggression.[11]

Even before the Soviet Union set its feet on the road to economic reform and democracy, relations between Moscow and Pyongyang could hardly be called close. Kim Il Sung let twenty-two years pass between his visits to Moscow in 1962 and 1984. On his second visit, hosted by Premier Konstantin Chernenko, the two leaders apparently had serious differences of opinion. No joint communiqué was issued, and Chernenko was quoted as saying, "The opportunities for our cooperation are far from being utilized."[12] No leader of the Soviet Union or its successor state, Russia, has ever visited North Korea while in office. The Russians thought Kim Il Sung strange and grew tired of the annual losses incurred by trade with North Korea.[13]

Relations between the two governments began to deteriorate when Mikhail Gorbachev took power in 1985 and introduced the principles of glasnost and perestroika. Yet through most of the 1980s economic and military assistance flowed from Moscow to Pyongyang. Relations between Moscow and Pyongyang were badly damaged when the Soviet Union established diplomatic relations with South Korea in September 1990, prompting North Korea's party newspaper, *Nodong Sinmun,* to say, "The Soviet Union sold off the dignity and honor of a socialist power and the interests and faith of an ally for 2.3 billion dollars," referring to Seoul's promise to provide Moscow with loans and trade credits.[14] South Korea-Soviet relations quickly blossomed. Presidents Roh and

Gorbachev met three times in one year, and Yeltsin visited South Korea in November 1992.

To add injury to insult, the Soviet Union announced in November 1990 that trade with North Korea would henceforth be conducted on a hard currency basis at world market prices. North Korea could no longer afford to pay for the million tons of oil a year it was receiving from Russia; Soviet-built factories, which provided 40 percent of North Korea's industrial products, could no longer be kept running.[15] Moscow also applied political pressure on North Korea to end its nuclear weapons program, prompting a *Nodong Sinmun* editorial to charge, "We cannot regard Russia otherwise than an ally of the United States in the attempts to stifle the DPRK."[16] For example, in 1993, when North Korea resisted nuclear inspections from the International Atomic Energy Agency (IAEA) President Boris Yeltsin joined with President Bill Clinton in calling on Pyongyang to abide by its nuclear treaty obligations. In 1995 the Russians allowed their Treaty of Friendship with the DPRK to lapse.

Russian-DPRK relations reached a low point in 1994 and 1995. Trade was at a standstill, Russia saw no prospect of recovering its North Korean debt, valued at between 3 billion and 5 billion dollars, and negotiations on the future security of the Korean Peninsula in the context of the four-party talks excluded Russia. Realizing they had lost all leverage over events on the Korean Peninsula by dealing only with the ROK, in 1996 the Russians began sending signals to Pyongyang that they would like to improve relations. Deputy Foreign Minister Alexsandr Panov visited Pyongyang in September 1994, returning with Deputy Premier Vitaly Ignatenko in April 1996, and a delegation from the Duma (the lower house of the Russian legislature) visited in May 1996. A revised Treaty of Friendship, shorn of its ideological ties and security guarantees, was initialed in February 2000. But the Russian economy remained in the doldrums, providing little prospect of a return to the earlier trading relations between the two countries.[17]

Relations with China

The other pillar of North Korea's foreign relations is China. China is Asian rather than European, agrarian rather than industrial, and nationalistic rather than imperialistic. Although for political and ideological reasons North Korea maintained cordial relations with both China and the Soviet Union, its cultural affinity with China was always stronger than its more utilitarian political and economic relationship with the Soviet Union. North Korea's relations with China began when the two countries established diplomatic relations in October 1949. Kim Il Sung consulted with Mao Zedong before launching his

Korean War assault. It seems unlikely that the Chinese welcomed the prospect of a war on their doorstep just as they were recovering from their own civil war and before having the opportunity to drive the nationalists out of Taiwan, but when UN troops pushed the North Koreans back to the Chinese border, Mao heeded Kim's pleas for assistance and sent 1 million Chinese soldiers to repel the UN forces. During the war an estimated 180,000 Chinese died, giving rise to the oft-repeated assertion that Chinese-North Korean relations are "sealed in blood." After the war Chinese volunteers provided 5 million workdays' worth of labor to help rebuild the North's devastated economy. On July 11, 1961, the two governments signed a Treaty of Friendship, Cooperation, and Mutual Assistance modeled on the treaty that the Russians had signed with North Korea five days earlier, although like the treaty with Russia, this document no longer seems to be fully in force: a Chinese Foreign Ministry spokesman visiting Seoul in 1995 said that the treaty should not be interpreted as a promise to dispatch troops in time of war.[18]

Relations between Beijing and Pyongyang remained cordial throughout most of the cold war. During the Sino-Soviet dispute in the early 1960s, North Korea sided with China against what Pyongyang considered the imperialistic tendencies of the Soviet Union. During the Chinese cultural revolution in the late 1960s, when Kim Il Sung was characterized by the Red Guards as a revisionist and the "Khrushchev of Korea," relations with China cooled, leading Kim Il Sung to elaborate his line of independent diplomacy and seek a role in the Non-Aligned Movement. Relations also cooled somewhat when Richard M. Nixon was invited to Beijing in February 1972, but China sought to assure the North Koreans of its continued friendship by boosting its aid donations. After China was admitted to the United Nations, it consistently lent its support in the Security Council to North Korean positions until 1991, when it refused to block the ROK's bid to join the United Nations as a separate state, thereby forcing the DPRK to reverse its long-standing objection to the admission of two separate Korean governments and join as well.

Through the early 1990s the Chinese and North Korean leaders met fairly frequently. Looking only at visits since 1980, Kim Il Sung visited China almost every other year, although his only two state visits took place in September 1982 and May 1987. Kim Jong Il made a "state" visit in June 1983 (although he held no official government position), providing much-needed legitimacy for his role as designated successor, although it is unlikely that the Chinese approved of the concept of dynastic succession. Both Kims thus had ample opportunity to view the results of China's open door economic policy. High-level Chinese visits to North Korea were also fairly frequent through the early

1990s. Premier Zhou Enlai visited in 1970 and Vice Premier Deng Xiaoping visited in 1978. Zhao Ziyang traveled to North Korea in 1981 and 1989, as premier and Chinese Communist Party general secretary, respectively. General Secretary Hu Yaobang visited in 1984 and 1985. Li Peng visited in 1985 and 1991, as deputy premier. In the 1990s, the only important Chinese visits were by General Secretary Jiang Zemin in 1990 and President Yang Shangkun in 1992. In 1999 Kim Yong-nam went to Beijing in the capacity of chairman (president) of the presidium of the SPA.[19]

Despite the appearance of political solidarity, North Korea had reason to be concerned about future relations with China. In 1979 China and the United States established diplomatic relations, presenting North Korea with the classic dilemma of witnessing its close friend become friends with its worst enemy. Of greater concern to Pyongyang was China's pragmatic approach to South Korea. In 1988 the Chinese, like the Russians, traveled to Seoul for the Olympics. In 1992 Beijing normalized relations with Seoul. Even though this was a great blow to the North Koreans, they could not afford to publicly criticize their only remaining big-power friend but did feel free to explore economic relations with Taiwan, in a sense adopting a two-China policy to mirror China's two-Korea policy.[20]

China had begun to trade with South Korea in 1980, and by 1985 China's trade with the South surpassed its trade with the North. In 1990 China-South Korea trade was almost ten times the volume of China-North Korea trade, even though after the collapse of the Soviet Union, China had become North Korea's largest trading partner. By 1997 (before the financial crisis struck South Korea) China-ROK trade was thirty-six times greater than China-DPRK trade ($24 billion versus $656 million).[21] In the early 1990s China announced that it would begin conducting trade with North Korea on a hard currency basis over a period of years, but this policy was never fully implemented. As the North Korean economy shrank during the 1990s, China became by default the North's largest trade partner.[22] Since the early 1980s the Chinese have been urging North Korea to follow their lead in adopting an economic open door policy, but the North Koreans have demurred. China and North Korea remain friends, although relations have cooled compared with the days of the cold war, and North Korea has become a growing economic burden for China. China has worked behind the scenes to try to resolve North Korea's nuclear disputes with the international community, realizing that nuclear proliferation on the Korean Peninsula would destabilize Northeast Asia. On the surface, relations throughout the 1990s appeared to remain solid, and the 1961 PRC-DPRK security pact remains in force, but in a meeting with U.S. congressional representatives in

1997, Premier Li Peng reportedly said, "North Korea is neither an ally of the PRC nor an enemy, but merely a neighboring country."[23]

Relations with Non-Aligned States

Wishing to avoid dependence on either of his powerful communist neighbors, Kim Il Sung applied the principle of Juche to foreign relations by trying to achieve independence from foreign influence and promote the democratization of the international order. The independence theme encompasses several of Kim's concerns. One, already mentioned in conjunction with Kim Il Sung's 1955 speech, was to eliminate competing domestic political factions originating in China and the Soviet Union. By the end of the 1950s these factions had been effectively eliminated. A second concern was to avoid domination by the Soviet Union's communist party, which considered itself the "mother party." Kim made it clear that the Korean Workers' Party (KWP) was independent of all other parties, though willing to cooperate with them in the spirit of proletarian internationalism—a concept that gradually lost its meaning as it became evident that the Chinese and Soviet communist parties were going their separate ways. A third concern was to promote Korean unification. North Korea consistently took the position that South Korea is an American colony, and that if U.S. forces were expelled from the peninsula the South Korean people would rally to Kim Il Sung and Juche. Since Chinese troops departed from the North in 1958, this theme of North Korean independence versus South Korean dependence has been central to Pyongyang's claim to sole political legitimacy on the Korean peninsula.

Finally, North Korea's concern for independence stems from Korea's historical experiences as a small state often at the mercy of larger states. The *tactical* problem Kim Il Sung faced was how to reconcile the need for aid from the Soviet Union and China with political independence. Until the end of the cold war, North Korea was relatively successful in keeping the aid pipeline from both countries open without leaning strongly toward either side. Because of its strategic location in East Asia, with borders on both China and the Soviet Union, and facing Japan and the American-allied South Korea, North Korea was a significant enough piece of political real estate to be wooed by both communist powers. The *strategic* problem that Kim Il Sung was never able to solve was how to apply Juche socialism principles to make his country economically and politically powerful enough to hold its own in the international arena. Pyongyang's political "declaration of independence," published in *Nodong Sinmun* on August 12, 1966, was a response to changes in Soviet policy since Khrushchev and to the instability of China during the Cultural Revolution.

Kim elaborated on his 1966 statement at the first session of the Fourth Supreme People's Assembly on December 16, 1967:

> We must not act on orders and instructions of others but, on the basis of the interests of our revolution and construction, settling all problems from the standpoint of Juche.... Needless to say, the international unity of the proletariat of all countries and the friendly alliance of the socialist countries in the revolutionary struggle against imperialist aggression ... are an important guarantee for safeguarding the revolutionary gains already obtained and winning new victories.... The decisive factor for victory in the struggle against imperialist reaction, however, is the internal forces of the country concerned.[24]

Pyongyang's foreign policy line was further developed by a speech Kim Il Sung gave to KWP's Sixth Party Congress in 1980, in which he introduced the three guiding principles of independence (*chaju*), friendly relations, and peace.[25] In his speech to the Supreme People's Assembly in 1990, the order of these principles was changed to independence, peace, and friendship, and this statement is found in article 17 of the 1992 and 1998 revisions of North Korea's constitution.

North Korea's declaration of independence from the Soviet Union and China was accompanied by a campaign to become a leader among that loose association of nonaligned states that had inaugurated a semiformal organization, the Non-Aligned Movement (NAM), in 1961.[26] North Korea was admitted to membership at the August 1975 NAM Foreign Ministers' meeting in Lima, Peru. South Korea, being aligned with the United States, was not considered eligible for membership in the group. Juche would seem well suited as a rallying cry for these nonaligned states, and North Korea put great effort into popularizing its political philosophy by establishing Juche study groups and sponsoring Juche seminars throughout the world. After the death in 1980 of Yugoslavia's Josip Tito, who had been the unofficial leader of NAM, Kim Il Sung aspired to take his place. But North Korea's close association with the communist states, the growing cult of personality surrounding Kim, and North Korea's sponsorship of international terrorism were repugnant to many NAM members. The high point of North Korea's participation in NAM was the multinational signing of the Pyongyang Declaration in 1987. During the 1990s, economic problems forced the Pyongyang government to close many of its embassies in third world capitals. In any case, the NAM never had the cohesive political, economic, or military power that could provide North Korea with a substitute for its reduced relations with the Soviet Union and China.

Relations with Japan

The North Koreans had no choice but to turn to the hated capitalists for diplomatic recognition and economic assistance. In his last New Year's address, Kim Il Sung replaced his usual foreign policy statement about developing friendly and cooperative relations with the peoples of socialist and non-aligned countries with "we will make positive efforts to unite with socialist countries and non-aligned countries and develop good neighborly relations also with capitalist countries which respect the sovereignty of our country."[27] Kim Jong Il's first major foreign policy address, delivered in 1997, took the same line: "We have no intention to regard the United States as our eternal sworn enemy; we hope to normalize the Korea-U.S. relationship.... Japan ... must sincerely reflect upon her past, give up her hostile policy toward our Republic.... Then we will take a friendly approach to Japan, our neighbor, and the abnormal relations between Korea and Japan will be improved."[28]

Japan has been viewed as an enemy by the North Koreans on two counts: as an unrepentant colonial aggressor and as the major Asian ally of North Korea's archenemy, the United States. For that matter, a reservoir of hostility has built up between the Japanese and Korean people over centuries. It is ironic that the cold war relationship between these two neighbors should continue, because Japan desires cordial relations with North Korea to stabilize the region, and North Korea needs Japanese capital and technology to rescue its economy.

An early period of rapprochement between the two governments in the mid-1950s (before Japan normalized relations with South Korea in 1965) came to nothing, although over the years the Japan Socialist Party (later renamed the Social Democratic Party of Japan) has been sympathetic toward North Korea. North Korea purchased several hundred million dollars' worth of capital equipment from Japan in the early 1970s but soon defaulted on payments, ruining any prospect that powerful Japanese business interests would lobby for an opening to North Korea. Japan imposed economic sanctions after North Korean agents staged the 1983 bombing in Rangoon that killed most of the visiting South Korean cabinet. Sanctions were lifted in 1985, only to be reinstated in 1987 after two North Korean agents blew up a Korean Air passenger plane.

South Korean President Roh Tae Woo's 1988 "northern policy," an attempt to defuse tensions in Northeast Asia, provided an opening for Japan and the United States to improve their relations with North Korea. In March 1989 Japan's Prime Minister Noboru Takeshita expressed Japan's "deep remorse" to all Koreans for past aggressions and suggested that Japan would welcome improved relations with North Korea. Needing a "southern policy" to respond to South Korea's "northern policy," the North Koreans invited the Japanese for a visit, and in September 1990 a political delegation headed by Shin Kanemaru of the Liberal Democratic Party (LDP) and Makoto Tanabe of the Japan Socialist Party visited Pyongyang as guests of the Korean Workers' Party. The representatives of the three parties issued a communiqué urging their respective governments to "resolve the abnormal situation existing between the two countries and establish diplomatic relations at an early date."[29] More controversially, the three parties acknowledge that Japan should "extend a thorough and official apology to, and provide compensation for, the Democratic People's Republic of Korea for the unhappiness and plight it caused the Korean people for thirty-six years in the past and for losses suffered by the Korean people in the forty-five years *following* the end of the war." North Korea's rationale for demanding compensation to cover the postwar period was that Japan's political and economic policies toward North Korea imposed economic hardship on the North Korean economy.[30]

South Korea had received $500 million in compensatory aid and trade credits when it normalized relations with Japan in 1965, and Japan was prepared to offer a similar compensation (adjusted for inflation) to North Korea. The North Koreans were hoping for something in the neighborhood of $5 billion to $10 billion, accompanied by an influx of private Japanese investment. An immediate benefit of the three-political-party talks was the release of two Japanese seamen who had been detained by North Korean authorities in 1983 on trumped-up charges of being responsible for the defection of a North Korean who had stowed away on their ship on a previous voyage to Japan.

For Japan, the communiqué paved the way for normalization talks, but for many reasons the Japanese delegation's efforts at détente did not bear fruit. First, many Japanese were critical of the communiqué since it was not a government-to-government agreement. Second, the idea of compensating North Korea for the period after the Japanese had left the peninsula was almost unanimously condemned in Japan. Third, by coincidence or intent, shortly after the delegation's visit, Washington provided Tokyo with satellite pictures of a North Korean nuclear reprocessing plant, suggesting that the North Koreans, in defiance of their obligations to the IAEA, were engaged in nuclear weapons research. Fourth, South Korea and the United States communicated their concern to Japan that an early normalization of Japanese-North Korean relations would deprive South Korea and the United States of leverage to force North Korea to engage in a political and economic opening. South Korea was insistent on this point, obtaining from Kanemaru (who traveled to Seoul to explain the agreement) a pledge to abide by "five principles" of diplomacy, essentially a promise to keep the ROK apprised of progress in Japan-DPRK relations.[31] The following year the Japanese government enunciated its own four principles of cooperative engagement:

(1) to conduct negotiations so as to promote peace and stability on the Korean peninsula; (2) to normalize relations with Pyongyang in such a way as not to undermine Japan's existing friendly relations with South Korea; (3) to make compensation for thirty-six years of colonial rule but not for any post-1945 "losses"; and (4) to seek Pyongyang's acceptance of international inspection of its nuclear facilities.[32]

A similar pledge made by the Japanese in November 1995 essentially gave South Korea veto power over Japan's foreign policy toward North Korea.

In January 1991 Japan and North Korea inaugurated a series of government-to-government discussions to explore issues related to the opening of diplomatic relations, but after eight meetings the talks broke off in November 1992. In the talks the two sides encountered a variety of obstacles, including disagreements over the scope and amount of Japan's compensation to North Korea, Japan's insistence that North Korea accept international inspections of its nuclear facilities, and North Korea's reluctance to disclose the fate of a Japanese woman who allegedly had been kidnapped to help train the terrorists who bombed the Korean Air plane. The relatively conservative LDP party in Japan lost its majority in the Diet in August 1993, and in 1994 Tomiichi Murayama, leader of the JSP, became prime minister at the head of a coalition government. Even though the socialists had traditionally been sympathetic to North Korea, the Murayama government was unable to make a breakthrough in diplomatic relations. In March 1995 a three-party Japanese delegation headed by the LDP's Michio Watanabe, a former foreign minister, visited Pyongyang to discuss the resumption of normalization talks. North Korea wanted normalization talks to progress on the basis of the 1990 three-political-party communiqué but finally agreed to resume talks with no preconditions. In May 1995 Pyongyang requested emergency food aid from Japan, which provided 500,000 tons and a half million dollars through the UN, but only after Pyongyang agreed to accept South Korean rice donations as well. In 1996 Japan contributed a further $6 million in food aid through the UN. But in deference to the feelings of the South Korean government, the Japanese were careful not to move too fast in engaging Pyongyang. The North Koreans, unmoved by Japan's food donations, continued to castigate the Japanese for failing to make an adequate apology for past transgressions, dragging their feet on normalization talks, and maintaining their security alliance with the United States.

Presently another issue came between the two governments. Between 1959 and 1984, 1,831 Japanese wives of Koreans living in Japan had returned with their husbands to North Korea. Over the years these women and their husbands were subjected to political, economic, and social discrimination in North Korea, and not a single Japanese wife had ever been permitted to return to Japan for a visit (although some of the wives corresponded with their Japanese relatives). The North Korean government's position was, "Any issue related to these women belongs to the sovereignty of the DPRK, which looks after their destinies in a responsible manner. No one else is supposed to poke his nose into this issue."[33] In October 1997 Japan donated $27 million in rice aid, and the following month the North Korean authorities finally permitted a select group of fifteen women to visit their families in Japan; another dozen followed in January 1998. All the women spoke glowingly of life in North Korea. But after the Japanese expressed dissatisfaction with the few visits permitted and with the North Korean selection process, Pyongyang ended the visitation program.

In 1997 yet another contentious issue emerged: the fate of ten Japanese who were allegedly kidnapped by North Korean commandos along the Japanese coast during the 1970s and 1980s. The North Koreans claimed to have no knowledge of the missing persons, but at Japan's insistence promised to conduct an investigation. Predictably, the North Korean investigation concluded that none of the individuals had ever been in North Korea. The Japanese government, not satisfied with this investigation, and viewing the kidnap issue and the visiting wives issue as humanitarian concerns, refused to grant North Korea's humanitarian request for further food aid, even though Japanese granaries were overflowing with surplus rice.

Whether these issues might have been resolved became irrelevant when North Korea, in August 1998, conducted the first test firing of its medium-range Taepodong 1 rocket, the first stage of which fell into the sea to the west of Japan, with the second stage and payload passing over the northern part of the main Japanese island of Honshu and falling into the sea well off the east coast. After a delay of several days, the North Koreans announced that the rocket had put a satellite into orbit, but this report was never verified by Japanese or U.S. space organizations. The Japanese were outraged at the rocket's trajectory and North Korea's failure to inform them before the launch. It is difficult to believe that the North Koreans viewed the rocket launch as a lever of negotiation with the Japanese; more likely, the firing was timed to coincide with Kim Jong Il's inauguration as the (re-elected) chairman of the National Defense Commission. If the launch was an international message, it was more likely directed at the United States, which was conducting missile nonproliferation discussions with the North Koreans. The Japanese were shocked. Tokyo announced that normalization talks with North Korea (which had been in the preparatory stage) would not convene in the near future, that no further food aid would be granted, and that Japan's signing of the KEDO agreement to contribute $1 billion toward the construction of two nuclear reactors in North Korea would be put on hold. The missile threat also prompted Japan to engage in talks with the South Koreans about the North Korean threat and sparked Japanese interest in participating with the United States in developing and deploying a theater missile defense system. In short, the rocket firing set back North Korea–Japan relations by several years.

Even though it seems likely that the governments (or at any rate the diplomats) of Japan and North Korea would like to improve relations, repeated military-like provocations from North Korea constantly keep the two nations on edge. In December 1998, four months after the Taepodong launch, three bodies clothed in North Korean military uniforms washed up on the shores of Japan, followed by another body in January 1999. In March, Japanese self-defense force boats and planes chased and fired upon two unidentified boats disguised as fishing vessels that fled Japanese waters into North Korean waters.[34] Evidence strongly indicates they were spy boats, although the North Koreans denied any involvement in the incident.[35]

In May 1999 the Diet passed enabling bills to support the U.S.-Japan Defense Guidelines. The guidelines, signed in September 1997, increased Japanese support for U.S. forces operating in the region to cope with "contingencies" (most likely, contingencies involving North Korea). The North Koreans strongly criticized the guidelines. Five days before the fifty-fourth anniversary of the liberation of Korea from Japan (August 15, 1999), the DPRK released a long official statement demanding that before the end of the millennium the Japanese apologize and atone for their past aggressions against the Korean people, and renounce their hostile stance toward North Korea, or "the DPRK will never miss the opportunity of meting out merciless retaliation but make Japan pay a high price for the blood shed by the nation and give vent to its century-old wrath."[36] In the face of such actions and words, it is not surprising that the Japanese people continue to harbor a hostile attitude toward the North Koreans, placing severe constraints on the foreign policy moves of the Japanese government. After an interval of more than seven years, Tokyo and Pyongyang resumed talks on normalizing relations in April 2000, after the Japanese had promised to send 100,000 tons of rice. The issues on the table had not changed, and neither side appeared to be optimistic about an early resolution to the problems that had for so long divided them.[37]

Relations with the United States

The beginnings of Korean-American relations were not auspicious. In the late nineteenth century the Choson dynasty pursued a policy of international isolation, quickly deporting sailors who were stranded on its shores. When the American merchant ship *General Sherman* attempted to sail into Korean waters in 1866, it was set afire and all hands perished. Attempts to ascertain the fate of the ship and its crew were rebuffed by the Koreans until a squadron of U.S. naval vessels defeated Korean troops in 1871. In 1882 a treaty was signed recognizing the Kingdom of Korea as an independent nation, much to the displeasure of the hegemonistic Chinese, who negotiated the treaty on behalf of Korea. In the 1905 Taft-Katsura memorandum, the United States renounced its interest in Korea by agreeing to respect Japan's preeminent interests on the Korean Peninsula.

The modern era of U.S.-Korean relations began in September 1945 when U.S. forces landed in Korea to accept the Japanese surrender south of the 38th Parallel. Unable to reach an agreement with the Soviet Union on how to unify Korea, the United States placed the Korean question before the United Nations, which subsequently oversaw elections in the southern half of the peninsula in May 1948. Elections held in the North in August 1948 were not recognized by the United Nations. Within a year of the inauguration of Syngman Rhee as South Korea's first president, virtually all American troops had been withdrawn from the peninsula. In a speech delivered in January 1950, Secretary of State Dean Acheson explicitly included Japan, Okinawa, and the Philippines in the U.S. defense perimeter but failed to mention South Korea. This speech and subsequent commentary by American political figures and press reporters may have helped convince Kim Il Sung that once again the United States had lost interest in Korea, and so he might successfully invade South Korea.

North Korean troops crossed the 38th Parallel on June 25, 1950. In an apparent reversal of foreign policy, the United States sent some 360,000 troops to Korea to fight the North Koreans and the Chinese: overnight South Korea had become an integral part of the U.S. alliance against communism. After the first year of fighting the war became a draw, with the two armies facing each other across the 38th Parallel. For two more years negotiation and fighting continued, until a truce agreement was signed by representatives of the Chinese, North Korean, and American-led UN forces. American troops remained in South Korea after the war, numbering some 60,000 in 1957, 40,000 by the mid-1970s, and 37,000 through the 1990s. Until the 1980s virtually the only official contact between North Korea and the United States was at the UN's Military

Armistice Commission meetings in Panmunjom inside the demilitarized zone, with an American general representing the UN side. At the beginning of the Korean War the United States imposed an economic embargo on North Korea, American passports became invalid for travel in North Korea, and American diplomats around the world were instructed to avoid contacts with their North Korean counterparts in third countries.

The low point in U.S.-North Korea relations came in the late 1960s. In January 1968 a thirty-one-man North Korean commando team staged an unsuccessful raid on the Korean presidential mansion in Seoul. Two days later, the North Koreans seized the U.S. reconnaissance vessel *Pueblo*, which they claimed was trespassing in their territorial waters, releasing the captain and crew eleven months later after the United States offered an apology. In April 1969, a U.S. Navy reconnaissance plane was shot down by the North Koreans, with the loss of forty-seven American lives.

Such actions served only to strengthen American resolve to protect South Korea and maintain a military presence in East Asia, while gaining a reputation for North Korea as one of the world's most violent state sponsors of international terrorism. Nixon's visit to China in 1972 was a hard pill for North Korea to swallow, but Pyongyang put the best possible face on the new U.S.-China détente: "Although he promptly called Nixon's July 1971 announcement that he would visit Beijing a sign of capitulation—'a trip of the defeated [that] fully reflects the declining fate of U.S. imperialism'— Kim appeared to look upon the development with a mixture of alarm and jealousy."[38] North Korea began rapprochement with the United States when it sent an open letter to the U.S. Congress in April 1973, pointing out that since the two Koreas were now conducting dialogue (as they did in 1971 and 1972), the United States should stop supplying weapons to South Korea and discontinue joint military exercises. In 1975 Kim Il Sung asked visiting members of Japan's Parliament to request the Americans to withdraw their troops from South Korea and consider signing a peace treaty with Pyongyang. The United States was in no mood to deal with the North Koreans.

In 1976 a group of North Korean soldiers attacked a contingent of American soldiers attempting to trim a tree in the demilitarized zone, hacking to death two U.S. Army officers. Yet hardly a year later, after President Carter had announced his intention to withdraw American ground troops from South Korea, the North Korean foreign minister sought to meet U.S. officials while attending a nonaligned meeting in New York. The North Koreans made another approach in 1979, but in both instances, the United States declined to meet the North Koreans.[39] When Ronald Reagan became president in 1981, the odds against U.S.-DPRK rapprochement lengthened considerably.

In October 1983 a North Korean commando team exploded a bomb which killed seventeen South Korean cabinet members and government officials visiting Rangoon. In response to a U.S.–South Korean proposal for tripartite talks made earlier in the year, a proposal initially rejected by North Korea, the DPRK's Central People's Committee sent an open letter to the U.S. Congress proposing talks to negotiate a peace settlement. The proposal was ignored. The first opening for U.S.–North Korean relations did not come until the late 1980s, and ironically that opening was made possible by South Korea.

On July 7, 1988, South Korea's President Roh Tae Woo unveiled a foreign policy initiative known as the "northern policy" or "Nordpolitik" (in imitation of West Germany's earlier Ostpolitik). This policy was aimed at achieving diplomatic cross recognition: South Korea would establish relations with communist states while encouraging noncommunist states, especially the United States and Japan, to improve relations with North Korea, so long as these relations did not impede progress toward unification. In October 1988 the Reagan administration slightly relaxed restrictions on trade and people-to-people exchanges with the DPRK, and permitted American diplomats to meet with their North Korean counterparts in third countries. From December 1988 to September 1993, North Korean and American officials at the political counselor level met in Beijing thirty-four times to discuss issues of mutual interest.

U.S.–North Korean relations improved only slightly as a result of the Beijing talks, and Pyongyang became more eager to move faster toward establishing relations with the United States and Japan to compensate for its flagging relations with China and the Soviet Union. South Korea's half of cross recognition had been stunningly successful: diplomatic relations had been established with the Soviet Union in 1990, with all the Eastern European states, and with China in 1992. Realizing the importance the United States places on nuclear nonproliferation, the North Koreans used their nuclear program to draw Washington into dialogue. Pyongyang's first move was to insist that it would discuss its nuclear program only with the United States, not with the International Atomic Energy Agency or with South Korea (with whom it had signed a Joint Declaration of a Nuclear Free Korean Peninsula in 1991). The United States, in hopes of moving North Korea toward honoring the Nuclear Non-Proliferation Treaty (NPT) and accepting the IAEA's nuclear inspections, agreed to hold talks at the undersecretary level in New York in January 1992. Eight days after the meeting North Korea signed the treaty, and the IAEA's nuclear inspections began.

When preliminary inspections suggested that North Korea was hiding some of its nuclear program, the United States threatened to seek UN economic sanctions to force North Korea to accept "special inspections" of the sort that had been imposed on Iraq. In response to this pressure (and also as a result of the resumption of U.S.-ROK Team Spirit military exercises in early 1993), North Korea in March 1993 announced its intention to withdraw from the NPT. To prevent the situation from deteriorating further, Washington agreed to hold a second round of high-level talks in June 1993, at which the North Koreans agreed to "temporarily suspend" their withdrawal from the NPT. Since no country had ever withdrawn from the NPT, not to mention "suspending" its withdrawal, no one could be sure what North Korea's status was in regard to the IAEA. In fact, from this time forward Pyongyang has insisted that it has a de facto special relation with the IAEA, subject to Pyongyang's own interpretation. American and North Korean negotiators held several subsequent meetings in 1993 and 1994, but North Korea still refused to open its nuclear program fully to IAEA inspections. Following a third round of talks in July 1994 (coincidentally on the day Kim Il Sung died), the United States and the DPRK reached a compromise in the form of an Agreed Framework, which was signed in Geneva the following October.

In the agreement the United States undertook to provide North Korea with two modern, proliferation-resistant reactors in exchange for a freeze on North Korea's current nuclear program. Furthermore, the United States agreed to supply half a million tons of heavy oil every year until the reactors went on line (intended to compensate North Korea for the forgone energy that its frozen reactors would have produced), gradually relax trade restrictions on the DPRK, enter into talks on establishing diplomatic relations, and provide a "formal assurance" that the United States would not use or threaten to use nuclear weapons against the DPRK. North Korea agreed to freeze operations of its nuclear reactors and related facilities. In support of the agreement, President Clinton sent a letter to "His Excellency Kim Jong Il" promising to "use the full powers of my office to facilitate arrangements . . . as long as the DPRK continues to implement the policies described in the Agreed Framework."[40]

The agreement was negotiated by the executive branch, and not being a formal treaty, did not receive the formal consent of Congress. For the moment at least the fear that North Korea would begin "turning out plutonium like sausages" was allayed (to quote the phrase of Defense Under Secretary Walter Slocombe).[41] But the agreement was widely criticized in the United States for providing too much to North Korea without a sufficient guarantee that the North Koreans, when the time came, would disclose the full extent of their nuclear program. In its defense the administration repeatedly stressed that the agreement was constructed in such a way that the North Koreans would have to hold up their end of the deal every step of the way or they would receive no more benefits.

President Clinton announced the removal of a few minor trade restrictions in January 1995 and a further relaxation on humanitarian trade in September 1995. Because of numerous obstacles put up by the North Koreans, the opening of liaison offices in Pyongyang and Washington was still only in the discussion stage six years later. The economic embargo remained largely in place. Yet after 1994 meetings between American and North Korean government officials became commonplace. Several issues were frequently discussed. The United States wanted North Korea's cooperation in locating the graves of soldiers missing in action from the Korean War. The United States also wanted North Korea to stop exporting missiles. North Korea wanted food aid, a peace treaty with the United States, the withdrawal of U.S. troops from South Korea, and a complete lifting of the economic embargo. Washington held to the negotiating principle that, except on the three issues of MIAs, missiles, and the nuclear freeze, U.S.-North Korean talks could only be conducted in parallel with South-North Korean talks. An ambitious attempt along this line was made when President Clinton proposed jointly with South Korea's President Kim Young Sam in April 1996 that North Korea join the two nations and China in four-party talks with an open agenda. The North Koreans were not enthusiastic about the proposition because they wanted to deal exclusively with the United States, but they did finally agree to the talks.

In summary, the U.S.-North Korean relationship opened up slightly in the 1990s, but the two sides realized that on the important issues such as the right of North Korea to pursue its own weapons development program, and the right of the United States to maintain a security alliance with South Korea, they were far apart, and their mutual hostility showed few signs of abating. The centerpiece of U.S.-North Korean relations was the Agreed Framework, characterized by its architect, Robert Gallucci, in the following manner: "It almost sounds hostile to say the agreement is not based on trust, and I don't mean to be hostile; what I mean to be is realistic. We do not have yet a relationship with the DPRK that could be based on trust."[42] Four years later the relationship was not much improved, to judge by the remark of State Department spokesman James Rubin, "We have no illusions about the difficulty of dealing with the North Korean government, and we do not trust North Korea, but we have a system in place now, a series of talks in which our concerns on the nuclear side and the missile side can be addressed if the North Koreans so choose."[43]

The North Koreans should have been able to understand that, in the eyes of the U.S. government and its people, the Agreed Framework was primarily an instrument to freeze North Korea's nuclear program, in no way implying an approval or acceptance of the Kim regime's policies, and that unless Pyongyang made significant changes in its domestic and foreign policies, the prospect of normalizing relations with Washington was dim.

Relations with South Korea

North Korea has good reason to keep its distance from South Korea in terms of government-to-government as well as people-to-people relations. Since the North Korean government refuses to recognize the legitimacy of the South Korean government, referring to it as a puppet government and to its president as the "person in authority" (less respectfully as "traitor" or "criminal"), government officials are loath to deal with their South Korean counterparts. As for dialogue between people, the Kim regime must control all aspects of inter-Korean contact to keep the North Korean people isolated and thus ignorant of the outside world.

Kim Il Sung's lifetime goal and his promise to the people was to reunite the two Koreas under communism. Having failed to achieve this goal in the Korean War, he turned increasingly to diplomacy to destabilize and delegitimize the Seoul government, while employing terrorist tactics as "a continuation of politics by other means." On only a few occasions have the two governments engaged in substantive dialogue (at least in public).

Following talks in 1971 between the Red Cross societies of the two Koreas on the subject of reunions of separated families, a series of secret and then public meetings was held between envoys of the two governments meeting in Panmunjom (along the demilitarized zone), Pyongyang, and Seoul. On July 4, 1972, delegates to the talks signed a joint communiqué in which they agreed to achieve unification through independent Korean efforts without being subject to external imposition or interference; by peaceful means; and to achieve "great national unity" by transcending differences in ideologies and political systems.[44] These would become known in North Korea as the three principles of independence, peaceful unification, and great national unity. A South-North Coordinating Committee was established to implement the agreement according to the supplementary recommendations, which included an agreement not to slander or defame each other, restore severed national ties and carry out social exchanges, but little was accomplished and North Korea cut off further dialogue in August 1973. Both sides continued to make occasional proposals for tension reduction and cooperation, but such proposals were never mutually acceptable.

During the latter half of the 1980s North Korea became more concerned about its own survival and less concerned about defeating South Korea. The two Koreas held a historic series of high-level talks, which led to the signing of two documents in the final days of 1991. The Agreement on Reconciliation, Nonaggression, and Exchanges and Cooperation was a more detailed version of the failed 1972 agreement. The Joint Declaration of a Nuclear-Free Korean Peninsula was designed to eliminate mutual threats of nuclear aggression—from the U.S. nuclear weapons that were presumed to be based in South Korea and from the nuclear weapons program that North Korea was suspected of developing. The negotiations leading up to these agreements opened a dialogue channel between the two governments, but North Korea was unwilling to implement the sweeping provisions of the reconciliation agreement or to open its nuclear program to the joint inspections provided for in the nuclear declaration; consequently, the two governments reverted to their traditional hostile relations, although nongovernmental trading relations continued to develop.

North Korea's long-standing goal of reunifying the two Koreas changed to a demand for the formation of a Korean confederacy consisting of "one nation, one state, two systems and two governments"—a strange political arrangement indeed but one that would presumably guarantee the survival of the North Korean government.[45] The challenge of truly unifying the country would be left to the efforts of "our posterity," as Kim Il Sung suggested in his 1991 New Year's address. The first-ever South-North summit was scheduled for the summer of 1994, but just two weeks before the historic meeting with ROK President Kim Young Sam, Kim Il Sung died of a heart attack. President Kim Young Sam refused to extend South Korea's condolences, insulting and angering the North Koreans, who refused to deal with President Kim for the remainder of his tenure.

North Korea's official policy toward South Korea has remained consistent since Kim's death. In his first major paper on unification and foreign policy, Kim Jong Il in 1997 pledged to continue his father's policies embodied in the Three Charters for the Reunification of the Fatherland, which are the three principles of independence, peaceful reunification, and great national unity, the Ten-Point Guideline for All-Korean Unity, and Kim Il Sung's proposal for the formation of a Democratic Confederal Republic of Koryo (DCRK).[46] The three principles were agreed to in the 1972 North-South joint communiqué, although the two Koreas interpret them differently. By the principle of independence (that is, Juche), North Korea means that American forces should be withdrawn from South Korea and the U.S.-ROK security alliance should be abrogated. The North Koreans consider this step the touchstone principle for

Korean unification. The principle of peaceful unification means that South Korea should stop its arms buildup and end joint military exercises with the United States. The principle of national unity means that the ROK government's National Security Law should be abolished and its National Intelligence Service disbanded, so that all peoples and parties in South Korea, not just government officials, could participate in discussions on Korean reunification with the North Korean government and its front organizations.

Kim Il Sung's ten-point guideline, first presented in 1980 and updated in 1993, is a more specific statement of the three principles, with an emphasis on confederal coexistence between the two Koreas.[47] If South Korea were to abide by the spirit of North Korea's confederation formula, it would be required to cut itself off from the international community and play out the game of domestic politics on an enclosed playing field. This state of affairs would be admirably suited to North Korea's brand of totalitarian communist politics, which was so successful in the late 1940s that the communists under Kim Il Sung were able to gain control of the northern half of the peninsula without significant bloodshed.[48]

The crisis of North Korean food shortages beginning in 1995 provided an opportunity for inter-Korean contact. Even before the devastating summer floods, ROK President Kim Young Sam had offered to supply grain and other goods to North Korea, sending the vice minister of finance and economy to Beijing in June to meet with a North Korean "nongovernment" official to discuss food aid. The first shipment of South Korean rice headed for North Korea on the South Korean cargo ship *Sea Apex*, which was forced to fly the North Korean flag upon arrival in port, thereby insulting the South Korean government. Following strong South Korean objections, an apology from the North Korean rice negotiator opened the way for a resumption of rice shipments. A crew member on another South Korean rice ship was detained by the North Koreans for taking pictures, further dampening South Korean ardor to assist North Korea.

After the summer floods North Korea's appeals for food grew more urgent. The United States limited its initial donation to a symbolic $25,000, South Korea donated $50,000, and Japan supplied $500,000 in flood relief. Since 1995, World Food Program appeals have boosted the scale of donations. From June 1995 to the end of 1998, the donations from all international sources had reached $1.08 billion, with South Korea donating $316 million.[49]

South Korea's Kim Dae Jung government, inaugurated in early 1998, adopted a "sunshine policy" toward the North, taking the position that individuals and organizations could legally provide aid to North Korea (something that until then was a violation of the National Security Law), but that tax dollars could only be spent on aid if the public was behind it. After being stung by North Korea's hostile reaction to early food donations, the public wanted reciprocity as a condition for continued humanitarian aid, asking that North Korea take steps toward opening its borders—especially to the members of separated families—and reform its economy in return for continued aid. The North Korean press belittled the quid pro quo concept as characteristic of the thinking of a money-hungry traveling salesman.[50]

Juche Foreign Relations

In the memorable words of Thucydides, "The strong do what they want and the weak bear what they must." Historically, Korea has suffered invasions from the North and from the South. In the modern era, international organizations—especially the United Nations—have softened the harshness of international relations with dialogue, coordination, and constraints. North Korea has demanded that the sovereign rights of nations be respected by the international community. Yet in modern times the reality of power politics still exists: some nations are more equal than others. When President George Bush spoke of a "new world order" in which the United States would be the only superpower, North Korea was incensed. The Juche principle calls for the democratization of the international order, consistent with the principle that all members of the international community have equal rights and privileges. In his 1994 New Year's address, Kim Il Sung pledged, "The government of our Republic will work hard to abolish the old international political and economic orders of domination and subordination, establish new ones on the basis of equality, justice and fairness, and develop South-South [that is, third world] Cooperation on the principle of collective self-reliance."[51]

Like many third world states, North Korea has demanded changes in the United Nations; specifically, expanding the Security Council to include more Asian nations (although the North Koreans bitterly oppose Japan's bid for a permanent seat on the council), eliminating the veto power of the permanent members, and shifting more power to the General Assembly.[52] In its relations with the international community, North Korea's most insistent demand has been noninterference in its domestic affairs and the removal of all troops and military bases from foreign countries—especially American troops in South Korea and Japan. But the Kim regime is not naive about its hopes for a democratic world order. The *Kangsong Taeguk* (militarily and economically strong nation) campaign seeks to guarantee North Korea's place in the world order by virtue of its strength, not relying on democratic principles. In support of the *Kangsong Taeguk* and "military-first" campaigns of Kim Jong Il in 1998 and 1999, the North Korean press has frequently stressed the importance of military power in the international arena, as in this passage from a *Nodong Sinmun* article:

> The U.S. doctrine of war is to commit military aggression on any coun-
> try weak in national power that goes against the grain with it and takes
> a stand against it. NATO military operations against Yugoslavia are moti-
> vated by the U.S. doctrine of war. A country weak in national power is
> conquered by the imperialists. . . . The dignity, sovereignty and peace of
> a nation are guaranteed by its own strong military power.[53]

While defending its own highly dubious record on human rights, North Korea criticizes the application of the Western conception of human rights values to other countries on three counts. First, from a traditional Marxist view-point, "The 'human rights' standard and mode of the West cannot be a 'common standard' of human rights of universal significance . . . because the 'human rights' advocated by Western countries is a camouflage to cover reactionary bourgeois politics with the veil of 'democracy' and only serves for a handful of privileged classes."[54] A second criticism—one voiced by other Asian nations—is that Western individualism threatens the "freedom from chaos" provided by strong social order. A third criticism is based on the sanctity of national sovereignty. "To arbitrarily assess the human rights in other countries and impose one's will on others is an infringement on their sovereignty and interference in their internal affairs."

According to Juche, "The priority in the settlement of the human rights problem should be set in conformity with the historical and cultural features of each region and country and the stages of their development."[55] The forty-ninth meeting of the UN Sub-Commission on Human Rights in 1997 passed a resolution calling on the DPRK to respect international human rights standards and submit a report on its implementation of these standards. North Korea's response, reminiscent of its 1993 response to the IAEA's call for nuclear inspections, was to announce its withdrawal from the human rights convention:

> [The resolution] is an unbearable violation of the DPRK's dignity and
> rights to independence. . . . In this regard the DPRK government decided
> to withdraw from the "international convention." . . . We have provided
> our people with genuine freedom and rights on a level far higher than
> the requirements of the "international convention."[56]

The international community was nonplussed, since no nation had ever withdrawn from the convention, just as no nation had ever withdrawn from the Nuclear Non-Proliferation Treaty (one of Pyongyang's favorite tactics is to flout diplomatic convention). Two years later the North Koreans announced that they were "ready to submit the second periodic report on the International Covenant on Civil and Political Rights that we prepared in 1997," presumably signaling a "return" to the convention.[57]

To what extent has North Korea's foreign policy over the years been a pragmatic response to changing conditions in the international environment, and to what extent has policy been dictated by ideology? B.C. Koh, a long-time observer of North Korea, offered an answer to this question (in 1986) by saying, "On balance . . . ideology seems to go a long way toward explaining North Korean behavior. If the past is any guide, even pragmatically induced change in Pyongyang's policy has a way of foundering on the rock of ideology. Sustained change, then, may require a mellowing of ideology and 'deradicalization.'"[58] North Korea's policies must somehow be reconciled with Juche ideology. As Sang-Woo Rhee, another veteran student of North Korea points out, "When North Korea is confronted with a serious situation that dictates policy changes, it first reformulates its official ideology so that the policy change does not jeopardize ideological integrity."[59] Partly because of the broadness of Juche and partly because the only person who can interpret it is the leader, the ideology can be stretched to fit diverse situations. Rhee says, "The *Chuch'e* scheme is . . . really a Gladstone bag for North Korea, flexible enough to accommodate all that North Korea pursues without tarnishing the integrity of the official ideology."[60]

How responsive North Korea is to the outside world, and how much its view is distorted is at the heart of the question of change and conservatism in North Korea. The argument here is that the Kim Il Sung-Kim Jong Il regime, in its domestic and foreign policies, is out of touch with reality. This theme is central also to Adrian Buzo's view of North Korean foreign policy. "On many occasions the DPRK displayed a crude, predatory outlook on foreign relations, embracing support for international terrorism, bribery, petty forms of coercion, smuggling, and widespread abuse of diplomatic privileges including arms, drugs and currency dealing . . . a foreign policy which renders a country isolated and widely reviled cannot be either well-conceived or well-executed."[61] The "major part" of Buzo's answer to why the DPRK has pursued such a seemingly ruinous foreign policy is that the policy reflects "the extent to which Kim Il Sung lost touch with reality."[62]

Since the United States began serious talks with North Korea in the early 1990s, North Korea's negotiation tactics have received considerable attention. Michael J. Mazarr's study of the background and negotiations relating to North Korea's challenge to the Non-Proliferation Treaty illustrates the complexities involved in negotiating over such high-stakes issues.[63] Leon Sigal presents the view that in the U.S.-North Korean nonproliferation negotiations, the Americans were "remarkably doctrinaire" in their attitude toward North Korea, whereas the North Koreans responded pragmatically to Washington's carrots and sticks.[64] The strengths of the "take-chargism" nature of North Korea's negotiating strategy, ultimately directed by one man—Kim Jong Il—are well illustrated in a study by Chuck Downs and James M. Lee of the DPRK's negotiating strategy.[65] Scott Snyder argues that not only is there a method to North Korea's seemingly bizarre diplomacy, but the DPRK is gradually adopting a less provocative negotiating style.[66] Several good studies of North Korean negotiating are also available in Korean.[67] Although opinions vary regarding how pragmatic Pyongyang's negotiating positions are and how much the North Koreans can be trusted, there seems to be a greater unanimity of views in regard to the actual experience of negotiating with them, an experience usually described as intense, protracted, and unpleasant.

"Low" Foreign Relations

Liberal democracies need little in the way of policy to guide people-to-people contact other than immigration and travel policies and trade and investment rules. Totalitarian regimes, however, must institute strict controls over international contact to maintain total control of society. North Korea has probably gone farther in this direction than any other contemporary state, imposing a policy of virtual isolation on its people. The *national* security goal of this policy is to keep all aspects of life in North Korea hidden from outsiders, who are suspected of seeking to use such information to undermine socialism. The *regime* security goal of this isolation policy is to prevent the North Korean people from obtaining information that would enable them to compare life under Juche socialism with life under capitalism or that would expose the lies on which the Kim family cult is built. The Kim regime might survive a revelation similar to that which Khrushchev made of Stalin's lies and deeds, but Kim Jong Il has no intention of making the test.

North Korea's people-to-people exchanges have been as selective and controlled as its government-to-government relations have been prickly. The Koreans are a relatively homogeneous people who have traditionally kept apart from their neighbors. In this sense they are more like the Japanese, who maintain a distinct cultural identity, than like the Chinese, who have interacted more extensively with other Asian cultures. The Korean people originally came from the region of the Altai Mountains in Central Asia and are thus distinct from the Han Chinese, although related to some degree (by how much is vigorously debated) to the Japanese.

For the most part, the historical contacts that Koreans have had with foreigners have not been pleasant, given that as a state Korea was often weaker than neighboring states. North Korea closed its borders after the Korean War; the demilitarized zone became a bamboo curtain more impenetrable than the iron curtain separating the two Germanys, both in keeping people inside the country and keeping them ignorant of the world outside. But the isolation was not complete. Some ordinary North Koreans had limited contact with people in the northeastern areas of China and the eastern regions of the Soviet Union, and with the North Korean community in Japan.

China

Approximately 2 million ethnic Koreans live in China, mostly in the three provinces bordering North Korea: 1.1 million in Jilin (1982 figure), which includes the Yanbian Korean autonomous prefecture with its 800,000 Koreans (1987 figure); 440,000 in Heilongjiang (1985 figure), and 200,000 in Liaoning (1986 figure).[68] Some Koreans have lived in China for centuries: a Korean kingdom called Parhae existed in what is now northeastern China from the early 700s to 926, although most of its citizens were later dispersed. It is probably safe to assume that in the modern era more Koreans in China came from the northern part of Korea than from the more distant southern parts. Those Koreans who did emigrate from the southern regions tended to go up the eastern coast, settling in Heilongjiang near the Russian border, whereas emigrants from the North settled in Jilin directly to the north or in Liaoning to the northeast. The first major wave of emigrants to China were fleeing from droughts in Korea in the 1860s, and the emigration pace increased with the building of railways later in the century. A second wave of emigrants left Korea after the Japanese annexed the country in 1910, and throughout the colonial period many political refugees and freedom fighters fled, as Japan tightened its hold on Korea. Koreans also emigrated for economic reasons; for example as Japanese colonial subjects sent to Japan's new state of Manchukuo (Manchuria) in northern China to settle the country and engage in agriculture.[69]

Among the 2 million Koreans living in China today, most have little sympathy for the Kim regime, which they consider to be a personality-cult regime rather than a communist government. Nor are the Koreans in China sympathetic to the South Korean government, which they consider too dependent on the United States, although as pragmatists (as are most Chinese) they favor South Korea's economic policies. The border between North Korea and China has become more closely controlled in the 1990s, but it is still porous. The volume of cross-border trade is difficult to estimate. In 1995 border trade by peddlers was estimated at some $300 million, over half of the total trade volume of $550 million.[70] More recent figures are unavailable, but the volume may well have declined as North Korea finds it more and more difficult to produce items to trade.

Russia

The ethnic Korean population in the former Soviet Union numbered an estimated 460,000 in 1995, with the largest populations living in the republics of Uzbekistan, Kazakhstan, and Russia, including Sakhalin Island.[71] Since these republics are relatively distant from Korea (except for Russia's short border with North Korea in the far Northeast), the Koreans in Russia have had only limited contact with North Korea. An estimated 15,000 to 25,000 North Korean citizens work under difficult conditions in sixteen Siberian logging camps under a contract between the two governments.[72] As many as 2,000 may have escaped from the camps over the years, but their status as refugees in Russia is unclear. An undetermined number of North Koreans also work on construction projects in eastern Russia. When relations between the two countries were good, hundreds of North Koreans were enrolled in Soviet universities and military training programs.

Japan

In 1994 the Japanese government estimated that 680,000 Koreans resided in Japan, most of them as resident aliens.[73] Approximately 369,000 were believed to be pro-South Korean, and 247,000 pro-North Korean. Most Koreans in Japan live within their own social communities.

Koreans began emigrating to Japan first by the thousands and then the tens of thousands after World War I to seek employment in mining and construction.[74] Almost 1 million Koreans were living in Japan in 1939, the year the Japanese government instituted a draft in its Korean colony to import men and women for its growing war effort. Most of these drafted laborers, who numbered another 800,000 throughout the war years, spent two years in Japan before returning to Korea, but working conditions were harsh and many died before returning. The Japanese also drafted Korean men into the Japanese army to fight overseas, and Korean women as "comfort women" to provide sexual services for overseas Japanese troops.[75]

In the first year after the end of the war some 640,000 Koreans returned to their homeland, but the mass exodus quickly slowed as news spread that living conditions in postwar Korea were harsh even compared with conditions in Japan. The Koreans who remained in Japan as resident aliens set up a social-political association under the name of *Chaeil Chosonin Ryonmaeng*, abbreviated *Choryon* (League of Korean Residents in Japan), which soon became linked to the Japan Communist Party (JCP), and was consequently disbanded by the Japanese government in 1949. Koreans who objected to the left-leaning politics of Choryon formed their own organization: *Chaeil Han'guk'in Koryumindan* or *Mindan* (Association for Korean Residents in Japan), which initially served as a social rather than political organization but which evolved into a pro-South Korean organization.

In the early 1950s the North Korean government provided more political and financial support to Koreans in Japan than did the South Korean government, and a pro-North Korean association of Korean residents was formed in 1955: *Chaeilbon Chosonin Ch'ongryonhaphoe* or *Choch'ongnyon* (General Association of Korean Residents in Japan), known in Japanese as *Chosen Soren* or *Chosoren*. This organization became more politically, economically, and socially active than Mindan, even though only a minority of the Korean residents had originally come from the northern half of Korea. In 1957 the North Korean government began sending money to Choch'ongnyon for educational support, making annual donations at the time of Kim Il Sung's birthday.

Choch'ongnyon actively appealed to North Korea to help Koreans repatriate. The North Korean government was initially lukewarm to this appeal, but as the North's economy grew stronger, Pyongyang changed its policy and asked Tokyo to sign an agreement on repatriation. The agreement was signed in 1959, and with the Japan Red Cross acting as intermediary, eventually 93,000 Koreans emigrated to North Korea.[76] When the Japanese-North Korean repatriation agreement expired in 1967, the exodus slowed to a trickle, virtually stopping by 1984. None of the repatriated Koreans or their Japanese wives were allowed to return to Japan.

In 1975 North Korea began requesting money from Choch'ongnyon, and requests became more urgent in the 1980s and 1990s as the North's economy contracted. The flow of money has come from several sources. Choch'ongnyon runs many businesses in Japan and has its own banks and credit unions. In 1992 the total value of such businesses (including 38 financial institutions and 176 other businesses) was estimated at 10 trillion yen (about $80 billion), not counting financial deposits in banks and Choch'ongnyon credit unions.[77] It is estimated that 30 percent of the highly profitable pachinko (pinball) industry is owned by Choch'ongnyon Koreans.[78] The amount of money sent to North Korea is extremely difficult to estimate; annual contributions of $600 million (or more) in the early 1990s have been suggested, although by the late 1990s the amount is likely to have fallen to $100 million or less.[79] Besides contributions by Choch'ongnyon and its businesses, Koreans in Japan who travel to Korea to visit relatives take along cash and gifts as an "admission price." Choch'ongnyon membership has declined as North Korea's political and economic situation has deteriorated and as older members of Choch'ongnyon die. There is believed to have been a fall-off in membership after the death of Kim Il Sung in 1994, and by 1998 the number who were active members in Choch'ongnyon was estimated to be only 56,000, as members leave Choch'ongnyon for Mindan, marry Japanese wives, or take Japanese citizenship.[80]

At Choch'ongnyon's Eighteenth Congress, convened in May 1998, the obligatory letter of congratulations to Kim Jong Il followed the standard North Korea line. "All of our achievements made since the 17th congress in September 1995, despite severe trials, are precious ones ascribable exclusively to your wise leadership and benevolent consideration. Your Excellency, Beloved General is really the symbol of victory, glory and the splendid future of Choch'ongnyon and all Korean residents in Japan."[81]

The congress got down to discussing how to cope with a shrinking membership. It is revealing that for want of a better candidate the Eighteenth Congress re-elected a ninety-one-year-old chairman who had headed Choch'ongnyon for forty-three years. The organization's headquarters staff was reduced, and its newsletter was published only twice a month rather than twice a week as formerly. Choch'ongnyon continues to exert some political influence in Japan, but the organization is a shadow of its former self. Choch'ongnyon business investments in North Korea have been small and mostly unprofitable. Yet politically and economically Choch'ongnyon remains an important ethnic link between North Korea and the outside world.

To halt the decline in Choch'ongnyon membership, Kim Jong Il reportedly instructed Choch'ongnyon in April 1999 to make itself less of a North Korean mouthpiece and more of an intermediary between Japan and North Korea.[82] Toward that end, Kim reportedly suggested that the pictures of himself and his late father need not be displayed in every classroom in Choch'ongnyon schools, that students not be required to wear the distinctive Korean dress to school, and that Choch'ongnyon not mimic North Korea's criticisms of the Japanese government. But given demographic, economic, and political trends, the future of Choch'ongnyon as a strong Japanese support base for North Korea appears bleak.

The United States

Approximately 1 million Korean-Americans reside in the United States.[83] The first significant influx of Korean immigrants came in the wake of the Korean War, but they numbered only 6,000 from 1956 to1960. Immigration accelerated between 1986 and 1990, totaling 173,000 (up to the 1990 census). Many Koreans live and work in their own communities, especially during their first generation of residence abroad, and many organizations, especially churches, provide a sense of community. In the United States there are no large Korean organizations affiliated with South or North Korea, and no statistics appear to be available on how many Korean Americans profess loyalty to or support for the North Korean government. There is, however, deep concern on the part of many Koreans for the economic plight of the North Korean people, and many organizations, especially churches, have sent charitable donations to North Korea since the mid-1990s. The number of Korean Americans traveling to North Korea annually is difficult to estimate, but probably does not exceed a few hundred, largely on humanitarian missions. The number of North Korean officials who visit the United States each year numbers even less than that, so the amount of people-to-people contact between the United States and North Korea is negligible.

Foreign Visitors, Travelers, and Tourists

The North Korean government goes to great lengths to keep its citizens from coming into contact with foreigners, thereby preventing them from learning about the outside world and preventing the foreigners from learning about conditions in North Korea. Except for an occasional visiting delegation housed under the watchful eyes of security personnel in one of Pyongyang's hotels and given a brief automobile tour of the city or nearby countryside, the only tourists who have access to North Korea are Choch'ongnyon members paying visits to family members. What they learn is usually kept secret for fear of harming their North Korean family. In 1998 the North Korean government entered into negotiations with South Korea's Hyundai company to permit South Korean tourists to travel to the scenic Mount Kumgang by boat, but they are restricted to this remote site and carefully supervised by North Korean security personnel. By April 2000, more than 200,000 people joined the tour.[84] Another 8,000 South Koreans traveled to North Korea to other destinations and for other purposes between February 1998 and November 1999.[85] Members of foreign aid organizations have been permitted to enter North Korea under escort to assess the food and health situation in some parts of the country and to distribute food, but the government prefers not to permit Korean-speaking personnel to enter the country.

The small expatriate business community living in North Korea—mostly in Pyongyang's Koryo Hotel—has no freedom to travel around the city or into the countryside. In 1991 the Najin-Sonbong foreign trade zone was established in the remote northeastern corner of the country for the purpose of hosting foreign businesses. The zone is surrounded by barbed wire, and only carefully screened, politically reliable North Korean citizens are permitted to live within the zone. Noted North Korean economic reformer Kim Dal Hyon, who disappeared from political view, is reported to have said, according to one North Korean defector, "Let's consider the Najin-Sonbong area as a pigsty. Build a fence around it, put in karaoke, and capitalists will invest. We need only to collect earnings from the pigs."[86] The foreign personnel who are managing the construction of the KEDO nuclear reactors live at another remote site on the southeastern coast. The only business people who are relatively free to come and go from North Korea are the Koreans who live in China. These traders regularly travel back and forth across the border, but their influence is largely restricted to the border area.

Principles and Pragmatism in Foreign Policy

Since China and Russia have redefined their relations with North Korea as simply "neighborly," North Korea has turned to the capitalist states for aid and recognition in the quixotic hope that they will accept the Kim regime on its own terms as a totalitarian socialist state.

Pyongyang's foreign relations are unique in at least two respects. First, the preeminent foreign policy goal is to keep the Kim regime in power, regardless of what happens to the economy. The preservation of the regime requires that Kim keep the people isolated from outside influences. Second, Pyongyang must conduct foreign relations in such a way as to maintain independence from its larger and more successful Korean neighbor in the South. This means that the North must remain loyal to Juche socialism—which distinguishes it from the political and economic system of South Korea—while trying to undermine South Korea by fomenting domestic discontent and weakening its ties with other countries, especially the United States.

Pyongyang's security environment has become increasingly hostile. Even its strongest supporter, China, would be happy to see the Kim regime replaced by a more pragmatic (communist) one. In the face of this surrounding threat and hostility, North Korea must not show any weakness; hence the belligerent nature of its foreign policy negotiations. North Korea's reputation in the international community as a pariah on issues such as terrorism, smuggling, and debt repayment curiously enables the government to negotiate with relatively few restrictions, having little fear that its reputation will be further besmirched. With its back to the wall, the Kim Jong Il regime can dispense with the niceties of international etiquette and single-mindedly pursue its goals.

North Korea's foreign policy is beset by a stark dilemma: to conduct a successful diplomatic policy in pursuit of such goals as international recognition, prestige, and foreign aid, the regime must open its doors to people-to-people relations. But since these interpersonal relations would expose the North Korean people to outside information that they could use to evaluate their condition and their government, such relations must be avoided, thus poisoning diplomatic relations. This is the straightjacket in which North Korea's foreign policy is confined.

A good example of this linkage is embodied in the Agreed Framework. An important article of the agreement, arguably the most important to South Korea (which is paying the lion's share of the KEDO bill), stipulates, "The DPRK will engage in North-South dialogue, as this Agreed Framework will help create an atmosphere that promotes such dialogue." Behind this ambiguous wording is the intention of the American negotiators that North-South dialogue is a key requirement for completing the KEDO project successfully. Yet the North Koreans quickly provided their own interpretation of this clause; namely, that inter-Korean dialogue was *contingent* on improvement in U.S.-DPRK relations. Once the agreement was signed, the North Koreans asserted, "Implementing the DPRK-US Agreed Framework and North-South dialogue are completely separate matters." "The United States is confusing the problem, stubbornly insisting on dragging in a perpetrator [that is, the ROK] who has been entirely excluded from discussions since the very beginning of the adoption of the agreement."[87]

Not surprisingly, political figures in Washington are wary of appearing too friendly toward the Kim regime. The North Koreans, in turn, have complained that their expectations of a better relationship based on the Agreed Framework have been disappointed.

The refusal by North Korea to link government-to-government relations with people-to-people relations means that North Korean agreements are severely limited in their consequences. For example, the North-South 1991 Basic Agreement on Reconciliation, Nonaggression, and Exchange and Cooperation provides for the free travel and communication of people from the two Koreas. It is difficult to imagine that the North Korean negotiators ever intended for this exchange to be realized. The agreement remains a useful propaganda tool for Pyongyang, which can point to it as evidence that it is pursuing inter-Korean relations, and therefore that other nations have no need to interfere in what is essentially a domestic issue.

Given the serious constraints under which the Kim regime operates—poverty, international stigma, commitment to socialism—it has done remarkably well in conducting foreign policy. By relying on military strength it has kept South Korea and other regional powers off balance. North Koreans are tough bargainers, sticking to their agenda and not concerning themselves with cultivating goodwill. Their Western counterparts in negotiations do not find the experience a pleasant one. North Korea's ideal of foreign relations is pure *Realpolitik*: build a militarily strong nation that is impervious to foreign threats; avoid foreign entanglements; keep the borders closed. In short, the kind of foreign policy that a medieval kingdom might pursue—until finally overwhelmed by a stronger power.

It is difficult to discern what *realistic* agenda Kim Jong Il is pursuing. *Realpolitik* is only realistic if conducted with a fine perception of the international environment and changing trends. In the short term, he may hope that foreign humanitarian aid and payoffs from governments worried about the proliferation of North Korea's weapons of mass destruction will be sufficient to keep him and his military in good health, while the masses fend for themselves. In the long term—if indeed Kim has any coherent long-range plans—he may hope that an end to the U.S.-led economic embargo will open the floodgates to foreign investors who will pay the regime for use of its slave labor. With the proceeds from foreign business payments going into government and party coffers (foreign businesses can not pay their North Korean workers directly), the Kim regime might hope to strengthen the economy sufficiently to deal with South Korea from a position of strength.

CHAPTER EIGHT

Dealing with
the DPRK

We do not want to regard the United States as the sworn enemy, and if the U.S. recognizes our sovereignty and the freedom of option, and approaches us with good faith, we are ready to develop relations with the U.S. on the principle of equality and mutual benefit. What we cannot overlook is the fact that the United States professes "improved relations" before us but behind the scenes it is persistently trying to wrest a unilateral concession from us, while pursuing a hostile policy to isolate and stifle us at any cost.[1]

It is difficult for Washington to focus on North Korea and its secretive, hostile regime. North Korea is half a world away in the part of the globe less familiar to Americans—Asia rather than Europe. And troublesome as North Korea may be, it is one of a number of foreign policy hot spots that Washington monitors. North Korea becomes visible only in the context of threats such as military provocations and weapons proliferation or humanitarian disasters such as the food crisis of the 1990s. But what brings North Korea to the world's attention are only symptoms of the basic problems on the Korean Peninsula. The proliferation of weapons of mass destruction is not a core problem, nor is militarism, or even a collapsed economy. The basic problem is that the principles that the Kim regime pursues, in its domestic and foreign policies are incompatible with the principles of the dominant Western states. Threatened by this incompatibility, the Kim regime resorts to harsh totalitarian measures to keep its people isolated and under control, while pursuing a policy of military strength and state-sponsored crime to carve out a place in a post–cold war environment that is becoming increasingly hostile to oppressive regimes. These policies threaten the democracies, and so the spiral of hostility continues.

The foregoing chapters have examined North Korea today. Before discussing U.S. policy toward North Korea, we review our conclusions.

Ideology

Juche, the idea underpinning North Korea's domestic and foreign policies, began as a simple idea of nationalism. Combined with socialism, building on Confucianism, and turned to the purpose of glorifying the Kim family, Juche has kept North Korea out of the mainstream of late twentieth century life and thought in the global community. To outsiders, Juche in its full-blown form is bizarre and irrational—especially in light of North Korea's ruined economy. Yet many aspects of Juche make sense to North Koreans. The principles of inviolable national sovereignty and international equality are appealing to citizens of many third world states. The communist goals of sharing and equality have been dreamed of by millions of people at many times and in many places. Dictatorship *over* the proletariat rather than *of* the proletariat can be rationalized by the North Korean leaders as letting the end justify the means.

Although Juche is not without its attractions to the masses, and not without its usefulness to the ruling elite, it will destroy those who try to live by it. For Juche, especially in its later forms, is riddled with falsehoods and lies— propositions that squarely contradict the state of the world as it is known to those who are free to inquire. At its core, it wrongly predicts that socialism as a stage in historical evolution must inevitably replace capitalism. It lies about economic and social conditions in South Korea and fabricates economic and social achievements for North Korea. And it lies about the biography and accomplishments of the ruling Kim family.

Do the elite believe in Juche? Probably they believe in the attainability of socialism, the virtues of nationalism, and the heroic qualities of the late Kim Il Sung. Yet even while believing, they realize something has gone badly wrong, perhaps because Kim Jong Il is not applying Juche correctly. Do the masses believe in Juche? Probably so, even to the extent that many believe Kim Jong Il, true to his revered father's wishes, is doing his best to make North Korea a socialist paradise on earth while he struggles against natural disasters, a venal bureaucracy, and the machinations of foreign capitalists who are said to be strangling the North Korean economy and preparing to launch an invasion.

Errors and lies impose consequences. Errors in principles and policies stifle growth. Lies multiply, one lie covering another, their aftereffects rippling through society and reverberating in time.[2] Lies destroy the fabric of society, for who knows what to do or in what direction to go if there is no way to separate truth from falsehood? The Kim regime is built on lies: leaders lie to their followers and followers lie to their leaders. If the truth is ever revealed, the Kim regime will collapse.

The Economy

The state of the North Korean economy provides an obvious measure of the consequences of refusing to face the truth and change with the times. North Korea's economic illness is reflected in macroeconomic statistics and in the declining health of the people. Kim Jong Il has tried to shift the blame for economic failure elsewhere, but regardless of how well he has succeeded in dodging responsibility, the failed economy provides neither political legitimacy for his leadership nor validation of his Juche theory.

North Korea's economic planners have never recovered from their early successes. Kim Il Sung's Stalinist heavy-industry mass-mobilization strategies successfully guided the economy as it recovered from the devastation of the Korean War. But these same principles failed to take North Korea to the next level of economic development in the late 1960s and into the 1970s. Kim, who had no training in economics, could not unlearn the early methods that had succeeded so well. In the wisdom of his final years he came to see the need for changes, but by then he lacked the energy to implement them. The instructions in his "behest"—to develop agriculture, light industry, and foreign trade—came thirty years too late. The North Korean economists who had advocated these economic strategies had long since been purged, and economic technocrats in the government today are unlikely to repeat their predecessors' mistakes of candor.

Kim and his economic planners may have searched for a "third way" between socialism and capitalism, but no attractive models are available. In China Deng Xiaoping's economic reforms, launched in 1978, are marginalizing the central government and the Chinese Communist Party. In any case, Deng did not have to worry about keeping the Chinese people isolated from the outside world to prevent them from discovering a "big lie." Russia's example is no more appealing: the adoption of political pluralism and a botched transformation toward unregulated capitalism has seriously damaged the Communist Party and the economy. Some of the Eastern European states have done better economically, but many of their former Communist Party officials have lost their positions; in East Germany some officials were tried and convicted of cold war crimes; in Romania Kim Il Sung's good friend President Nicolae Ceausescu was executed.

The tentative reforms adopted in North Korea since 1984 may be more of a hindrance than a help to Kim's economic planners, for while they provide the appearance of reforms, they are too slight to be of any real value. The lesson that Kim should have learned from other transforming socialist economies is that economic reform and opening are painful for the rulers and the ruled. Even if Kim Jong Il institutes reforms, he is likely to receive more blame than credit for his efforts. Recovering from a half century of misguided economic plans will be slow and painful. North Korea's best hope of improving its economy lies outside the socialist system in the people's markets and private farming plots, but Kim will not receive credit for successes in this sector because they are achieved by individual labor rather than state-supported collective action. More bad news for Kim is that these individual and local achievements loosen his control over people's lives.

The prediction that the North Korean government will refuse to make substantial changes in its economic system in a timely manner is a watershed assumption, dividing two schools of thought about North Korea's future. Those who believe North Korea is already reforming counsel patience and prescribe assistance in helping Pyongyang make a "soft landing."[3] Those who interpret the post-1984 modifications in economic policies as desperate muddling-through responses to preserve totalitarian communism have given up on the Kim regime.

Leadership

It appears that Kim Jong Il, indebted though he may be to the military for its support, has firmly taken control of political power. When foreigners deal with North Korea, they are dealing with Kim Jong Il, who makes all important decisions behind the scenes. As the North Korean press boasts, Kim is the "central brain" and the people are his body.

Kim is not without leadership qualifications: he is an intelligent man with well-developed political survival skills. But his leadership suffers from lack of enlightened support from the people, including his closest associates, who fear to give him accurate information and good advice. His view of the world is skewed away from reality. His orders are often capricious. The situation in Kim Jong Il's "court" can be compared with the situation in Germany during Hitler's later days, as described by Albert Speer, Hitler's minister for war production:

> In normal circumstances people who turn their backs on reality are soon
> set straight by the mockery and criticism of those around them, which

makes them aware they have lost credibility. In the Third Reich there were no such correctives, especially for those who belonged to the upper stratum. On the contrary, every self-deception was multiplied as in a hall of distorting mirrors, becoming a repeatedly confirmed picture of a fantastical dream world which no longer bore any relationship to the grim outside world.[4]

Kim controls the elite with rewards and punishments, and they are by turns grateful to him and fearful of him. It is unlikely that many top cadres like or respect him, but they support him to preserve their lifestyle and protect their families and friends. They also support him out of Confucian-based respect for Kim Il Sung and out of belief in the basic principles of the elder Kim's Juche philosophy. The masses are becoming more and more alienated from their leaders, now that Kim Il Sung is gone, and the economy has collapsed. They resist by inertia, struggling to survive in a hostile environment. For years their leaders have told them that if they worked hard and placed their faith in Juche, they could accomplish anything. Instead, all they have accomplished is to maintain their independence from the imperialists—no small accomplishment, in their eyes, but not the goal they were promised. They remain faithful to Juche in the abstract, longing for the return of their Great Leader, but they are neither supporters nor opponents of Kim Jong Il.

In spite of years of propaganda and extensive control over the people, Kim Jong Il's leadership position is precarious. He dare not relax his control over the people or they may turn against him out of frustration with the economy. Since he has made Juche theory into a religion centered on himself, his father, and his mother, he must be extremely cautious about revising it. Kim is quoted as saying, "Expect no change from me," and in truth there is little room to change without destroying himself. To gain the political legitimacy his economic and military accomplishments fail to provide, Kim rules by his father's behest. For this reason, Kim Jong Il can be no better than his father, whose great accomplishments in nation building date to the 1950s and 1960s when the world was very different. Kim Jong Il is living in the past, going even farther back in time to a dynastic era when North Korea could live in relative isolation.

The Military

Kim relies on military power to control the people and to deal with the outside world. Since his father's death, he has transformed North Korea into a militarized state, which he governs as chairman of the National Defense Commission. As in most authoritarian states, the military is an important player in domestic politics. Kim Jong Il is smart enough to realize he cannot trust the military to provide him with the same unquestioning support it gave his father; thus, over the years he has strengthened the role of the Korean Workers' Party in the military to keep the generals firmly in line.

Military personnel are rumored to have attempted coups against the two Kims and are likely to do so again. Outsiders know very little about the top military leaders or their opinions of Kim Jong Il, but one can safely assume they are not satisfied with his economic leadership. Yet a successful broad-based coup, even from a discontented military, is not likely for several reasons. First, under Kim the military elite is a privileged class; even lower-ranking troops are treated better than civilians. Second, since the military is guilty of human rights abuses, top officers would be in jeopardy of facing punishment if North Korea were absorbed by South Korea in the wake of a regime collapse. Third, military leaders are unlikely to have ideas of their own about economic reform; their idea of earning money is to sell weapons. Fourth, top officers are watched closely by Kim's security services.

Rumored coup attempts may have failed in the past, but only one needs to succeed. Sooner or later a military or security officer, acting alone or in a small group, may succeed in eliminating Kim Jong Il. In such a case, the military may try to govern in its own name, but one military group is likely to fight with another, leading to a series of governments each weaker than its predecessor, until a group is able to strike a deal with the ROK government that would pave the way for formal reunification in return for generous pensions and immunity from prosecution for the ruling junta.

Social Control

Even among the isolated and politically uneducated masses, belief in Juche is not strong enough to elicit complete obedience to Kim Jong Il, under whose rule they have experienced nothing but misery. Since the death of his charismatic father, Kim Jong Il has relied on coercive social control mechanisms to keep the public behind him. During the past fifty years these control mechanisms have been developed enough to enable one individual to do a surprisingly good job of controlling 20 million other individuals. The keys to this success lie in overlapping security organizations and reciprocal surveillance. Several police forces, each communicating directly to Kim Jong Il but not communicating well with one another, keep track of almost everyone, from Kim's closest advisers to the poorest rural peasants. The surveillance system is not perfect: some people are missed, and many flout the system by bribing security officials. But for the most part the system works well. People watch each other, and security officials watch one another. No one can be sure what will be reported. Everyone becomes a prisoner facing the classic dilemma of not knowing whether to incriminate others or risk being incriminated himself. Punishment is meted out not just on the offender but on his family, relatives, and friends.

Defectors from the North almost unanimously predict that an "implosion"—that is, an uprising of the people against the government—is a remote possibility given the masses' lack of power and political ideas.[5] But implosions are by their nature surprises, as events in Eastern Europe in the late 1980s illustrate. Outsiders may not see any large cracks in North Korea's political facade, but the design of the structure suggests it may be more brittle than it appears.

Foreign Relations

North Korea's foreign relations are distinguished by their lack of substance. Within the socialist camp North Korea was as independent as Yugoslavia, as closed as Albania, as harsh a dictatorship as Romania, and as loyal to socialism as Castro's Cuba. North Korea has kept its borders closed more tightly than any other country, communist or noncommunist, cutting off the exchange of information and ideas that is the building block of international relations. This isolation originated in Korea's Hermit Kingdom culture and has been reinforced by the West's containment policy and the Kim regime's need for strong social order.

North Korea's diplomatic relations are based on the principles of preventing foreign interference in its domestic affairs, avoiding dependence on other states, remaining true to socialism, and winning the zero-sum contest of political legitimacy against South Korea. This last consideration should never be underestimated. North Korea is not a truly separate state; it is the less successful half of a divided nation. The conduct of North Korean foreign policy often appears crude and even self-defeating, yet given the principles on which foreign policy is based, and the fact that North Koreans in their international isolation have relatively little experience in managing foreign relations, Pyongyang has achieved some foreign policy successes.

North Korea's foreign relations have been relatively consistent over the years, within the constraints of a changing international order. From the Soviet Union it sought a security guarantee, industrial goods, and weapons, while keeping its distance to avoid coming under Moscow's influence. With the impoverished successor state Russia, North Korea has had only minimal relations. China is cultivated as a neighboring military power who would help guarantee North Korea's national security but distrusted as an economic revisionist. On the strength of Juche ideology, North Korea hoped to become a leader in the Non-Aligned Movement but proved too aligned and too strange to succeed in that role. Throughout history much bad blood has built up between Japanese and Koreans; moreover in the postwar era Japan has become a firm ally of the United States and thus a threat to North Korea's security. Beyond managing close (but faltering) relations with Japan's Choch'ongyon community, North Korea has never seriously considered developing amicable relations with Japan, although diplomatic normalization and $10 billion in reparations payments would be welcomed. As the cold war's leader of the anticommunist bloc and its foe in the Korean War, the United States has always been North Korea's archenemy. Any relations between these two countries will be based on calculated interest, not on trust. Finally, South Korea is viewed as an American puppet state, not an independent political entity. Consequently, North Korea refuses to deal in good faith with the South Korean government.

North Korea's leaders are political realists within the confines of their rather naive view of the world. For all their talk of peace they firmly believe that a successful foreign policy must be based on military strength. Accommodation with capitalists spells the end of the Kim regime and must therefore be avoided. Above all, Kim Jong Il seeks a negative security guarantee by which other powers pledge not to attack North Korea or interfere in its domestic affairs.

North Korea: A Nation in Its Own Style

North Korea's leaders are not irrational. To borrow a term from the cognitive scientist Herbert A. Simon (extending its meaning), their rationality is bounded—not just by human constraints on information processing and decisionmaking but by a view of the world that diverges in at least two respects from the views of most other states in the late twentieth century.[6] First, North Korea's leaders believe that communism can work. Second, they believe a state's domestic affairs can be free of interference from and dependence on the international community.

The Juche view of the world is logically cohesive, highly principled, and empirically wrong. North Koreans say they seek to build a self-sufficient, classless national community encompassing the Korean people in both halves of the peninsula. To prevent economic inefficiencies and deviant behavior, and to provide social cohesion, the community would be structured as a large family overseen by a stern Confucian-style father. The nation would enjoy international rights equal to those of other nations, regardless of size or power, including the right to manufacture, test, deploy, and sell weapons of mass destruction. The nation would also be accorded equal voting rights in the United Nations.

The Kim regime's domestic goals are those that many people throughout the world dream in their daydreams. The foreign policy goals are those that the superpowers strive for. But for North Korea, at the end of the twentieth century, they are the wrong goals to pursue, for they are too far beyond its grasp.

Yet the Kim regime seems in no hurry to revise its basic strategies, and North Korea watchers should be cautious about inferring policy change from what Aidan Foster-Carter calls the "obscure immediacies of day-to-day events in North Korea." Foster-Carter recommends applying principles of social science and seeking analogies from Korean history to understand regime dynamics and predict the future course of events in North Korea.[7] Indeed, the lesson of the past thirty years is that change will be slow in coming, even in the highly unlikely event that the Kim government endorses some form of glasnost and perestroika. Opening the DPRK will be like opening a spring-hinged door: the wider it is opened, the greater the force building up to slam it shut. Internally, the more North Korea opens up, the more the pressure builds on the government to keep lies hidden and people under control. Change will bring crackdowns, exemplified by the closing of farmers' markets and the purging of foreign economic officials.

The opening of North Korea from outside will be impeded by the very agents of that opening. North Korean human rights violations are far more serious than China's, yet because of the closed nature of North Korean society, little foreign protest has been heard. If the country opens up, human rights violations will be widely recognized and protested against by the international community, straining newly developing relations with the democracies. For business reasons, foreign investors will become more cautious about investing in the DPRK as the miserable state of its infrastructure and the hostility of its bureaucracy to business are revealed. Nine years after it opened, the Najin-Sonbong trade zone has just about come to a standstill for exactly these reasons.

Policy toward North Korea

A medium-sized Asian state with 20 million impoverished people and a limited international trade is unlikely to attract the attention of Washington policymakers unless that state poses a threat to U.S. interests. In recent years North Korea has brought itself to Washington's attention by following this very principle.

It is obvious, but too frequently overlooked, that threats are defined by the values and expectations of the threatened party. Threats are *perceptions* created in the mind of those who feel threatened by perceived harmful capabilities, hostile intentions, and focus of attention. Thus threats come and go, rise and fall, not only as the world changes but as people's views of the world change.

North Korea has numerous capabilities and expressed intentions that could be considered threatening to the United States, regional neighbors, and many other countries in the world community. Some threats are general and enduring, like North Korea's potential to develop, deploy, and sell weapons of mass destruction. Other threats are specific and fleeting, like the (unfounded) concern that the large Kumchang-ni tunnel complex near Yongbyon might house nuclear facilities.

In the late 1990s, the hierarchy of North Korean threats looks something like this to many American security specialists: nuclear weapons, medium- and long-range missiles, forward-deployed conventional forces, and chemical and biological weapons. A longer list of threats would include North Korean terrorism, drug trafficking, and counterfeiting. Even broader threats can be perceived. The DPRK's totalitarian socialist government can be considered a threat to the U.S. goals "to bolster America's economic prosperity" and "to promote democracy abroad."[8] North Korea's human rights violations stand as an affront to Western individualistic human rights values. The aggressions of North Korea's leaders toward their people and foreigners (in the Korean War and after) are inconsistent with belief in a just world where aggressors and evildoers are deservedly punished.

Since the United States lacks sufficient capabilities and resolve to deal with North Korea's threats unilaterally, the cooperation of regional allies, as well as China and perhaps Russia, is necessary. These countries perceive their own threats, which are overlapping but not identical to U.S. concerns. South Koreans are less worried about global proliferation and more concerned about conventional military threats, including the possibility of another Korean war, infiltration, chemical and biological attacks in time of war, and continuing threats to the welfare of relatives living in the North. The potential for medium- and long-range missiles to reach their islands, especially if they carry nuclear, chemical, or biological warheads, troubles the Japanese. They are also wary of North Korean terrorism and the potential influx of refugees should North Korea abruptly collapse.

The North Korean people fear an American-South Korean invasion (which their leaders tell them is imminent) and the everyday threats posed by a collapsed economy (which many of them blame on the U.S. economic embargo). More relevant to the security equation is what threats Kim Jong Il and his followers perceive. They see threats that are less military and more political. Opening North Korea's borders to people and information would threaten the Kim Jong Il cult. The adoption of a market economy would reduce Kim Jong Il's control over the people.

Cold War Containment

Throughout the cold war era, containment was Washington's policy of choice for dealing with North Korea. The containment policy relied on defense, deterrence, sanctions, nonproliferation, and counterproliferation (or the threat thereof). The U.S. nuclear umbrella over the ROK, and the forward-deployed U.S. forces stationed in East Asia (especially the trip-wire forces stationed along the Korean demilitarized zone) defended against and presumably deterred North Korean aggression. Nonproliferation treaties sought to discourage the spread of weapons of mass destruction; proposed counterproliferation programs—such as the Strategic Defense Initiative and the later theater missile defense programs—were intended to provide a shield against hostile proliferating states and organizations.

The treaty on nonproliferation has helped discourage states from developing nuclear weapons, although some proliferation has occurred, but the DPRK considers itself free from some of the constraints of the treaty by virtue of its nuclear agreement with the United States (the Agreed Framework).[9] Nor is the DPRK a member of the Missile Technology Control Regime or the Chemical Weapons Convention. When nonproliferation fails, a counterproliferation policy may be adopted, such as the U.S. Theater Missile Defense proposal, but counterproliferation programs by their nature invite an escalation of the programs they are designed to counter.

Economic sanctions imposed by the United States (and restrictions on lending by financial institutions like the World Bank, over which the United States has strong influence) have limited North Korea's economic development, forcing the North Koreans to conduct most of their business with fellow socialist states, whose technology lags behind that of the West. The effectiveness of deterrents and sanctions as policy tools is widely debated.[10] Deterrents, even when they deter, often trigger a spiraling arms race. Sanctions are often unsuccessful. Among the conditions that restrict the usefulness of sanctions, according to a series of case studies edited for the Council on Foreign Relations by Richard

Haass, the ability of authoritarian regimes to withstand sanctions is especially relevant to North Korea, where the Kim regime has already permitted the economy to collapse and hundreds of thousands or millions of people to die. A second caution, that unilateral sanctions are rarely effective, might be turned on its head in North Korea's case: if a single important supporter, namely, China, refuses to sanction North Korea, the effectiveness of sanctions by other states will be limited.[11] In a reflection of another principle, that sanctions are easier to impose than to end, Washington policymakers have yet to find a politically acceptable way to relax the sanctions that have already been imposed on North Korea. Proving that without the use of deterrents or sanctions different outcomes would result is difficult.[12]

Freezing the DPRK's Nuclear Program

A continuation of the containment policy in the post–cold war period might have been appropriate if Pyongyang had not gained a reputation as a potential nuclear threat. To try to achieve the nonproliferation goals that containment policies seemed unable to achieve, Washington adopted a limited engagement policy to supplement, but not replace, containment.[13]

The history of the U.S.–North Korea nuclear issue has been well covered and need not be told again.[14] Simply put, North Korea began a nuclear research program in the late 1950s. It began operating a small 5-megawatt (MW) reactor at Yongbyon in 1986, and began building a 50-MW reactor in 1984 and a 200-MW reactor in 1991.[15] The spent fuel from these uranium-fueled, graphite-moderated reactors can be processed into weapons-grade plutonium.

In the late 1980s U.S. spy satellites detected a large building under construction at Yongbyon which looked like a reprocessing plant. Although a signatory to the International Atomic Energy Agency's Treaty on the Non-Proliferation of Nuclear Weapons (NPT) North Korea had never signed the accompanying nuclear safeguards accord that would provide for IAEA inspection of its facilities. When pressed to sign, in 1993 North Korea announced its intention to "withdraw unavoidably" from the treaty, only to "temporarily suspend" its withdrawal when the United States offered high-level talks to resolve the nuclear issue. The talks made only limited progress. In May 1994 North Korea raised the stakes by shutting down its 5-MW reactor to unload spent fuel rods (from which fuel could be extracted for reprocessing) without IAEA supervision. Washington was on the point of requesting that the United Nations impose an economic embargo on the DPRK for its failure to abide by the treaty when former president Jimmy Carter traveled to Pyongyang in June 1994, where he announced that the North Koreans had agreed to freeze their nuclear facilities in return for a comprehensive package of benefits from the United States. The agreement was worked out in a series of meetings, and the Agreed Framework was signed in Geneva on October 21, 1994.

In essence, the agreement provided that in return for North Korea's freeze of its nuclear facilities at Yongbyon, the United States would provide a half million tons of heavy fuel oil every year until an international consortium had completed construction of two 1,000-MW light water-moderated reactors whose spent fuel would be much more difficult to reprocess into weapons-grade plutonium. The United States also promised not to threaten North Korea with nuclear weapons and agreed to gradually eliminate the U.S. economic embargo against the DPRK and work toward establishing diplomatic relations. In return, North Korea would seal and eventually relinquish the spent fuel it had unloaded, submit its entire program to IAEA inspection before the first new reactor became operational, and dismantle old reactors before the second new reactor became operational. Although the United States has sometimes fallen behind schedule in delivering the promised heavy fuel oil (because of a shortage of funds in the appropriate administration budget), and the construction of the reactors is several years behind schedule, both sides have honored the essentials of the Agreed Framework.[16]

Monitoring the Freeze

In 1998 public concern in the United States was raised by reports attributed to U.S. intelligence sources that one of North Korea's estimated 8,200 underground installations—admittedly a large one hosting a construction crew of some 15,000 at a mountainside near Kumchang-ni—might be a part of a hidden nuclear industry.[17] North Korea, insisting that it was a nonnuclear installation, refused to permit American inspection as part of the Agreed Framework, citing national sovereignty. Negotiations proceeded toward another deal.

The North Koreans refused to accept "inspections," but they said that a one-time "visit" would be permitted, if the United States would pay them "compensation" of $300 million or 600,000 tons of food aid for slander if it happened that the installation were not nuclear related. The United States refused to pay any compensation for what it considered a right granted by the Agreed Framework. A deal was struck in March 1999 whereby North Korea would permit the United States to "visit" Kumchang-ni. The United States, in a purely humanitarian gesture, would donate 500,000 tons of food aid through the World Food Program, and as a gesture of goodwill, provide 1,000 tons of potato seeds and an additional 100,000 tons of food to feed potato farmers who were engaged in Kim Jong Il's potato-growing campaign. At the installation the visiting inspectors found an empty tunnel.

Policy Review

At the end of August 1998, U.S. attention was diverted from North Korea's nuclear program to its missile program, when Pyongyang launched a three-stage Taepodong 1 rocket. Although the rocket apparently failed to place a satellite in orbit, its range of 4,000 kilometers far exceeded the 1,500-kilometer range of the Nodong series. Throughout 1999 the North Koreans appeared to be preparing to launch an even larger rocket, the Taepodong 2, whose estimated range of 6,000 kilometers would enable it to strike Alaska.[18] The U.S. Congress, alarmed that U.S. nonproliferation policy was failing in North Korea, urged the president to appoint a North Korea policy coordinator to review U.S. policy. Former secretary of defense William Perry accepted the appointment. After the Kumchang-ni incident had been resolved, and eight months after beginning his investigation, Perry presented his findings and recommendations to the administration.[19] Just as the immediate pressure under which the Agreed Framework was negotiated in 1994 was the need to gain control over the spent fuel that North Korea was unloading from its 5-MW reactor, so the pressure in 1999 came from the fear that North Korea was about to launch its Taepodong 2 rocket. After meetings with the North Koreans, Special Envoy for the Korean Peace Process Charles Kartman and his team succeeded in getting the North Koreans to agree not to launch the rocket while negotiations over the Perry proposal were in progress. The newly proposed policy was along the same lines as the Agreed Framework—a "comprehensive, step-wise package," including economic and diplomatic incentives in return for a North Korean freeze and eventually abandonment of its missile program.

The Perry Report rejects several policy alternatives. "Status quo," defined as strong deterrence and limited engagement, is rejected on the grounds that although it has been effective (according to the report) in freezing North Korea's nuclear program, it is not sustainable because periodic North Korean provocations threaten to derail the Agreed Framework. And the status quo does not address the perceived threat posed by Pyongyang's expanding missile program. "Undermining the DPRK" by weakening the Kim Jong Il regime (in unspecified ways) is rejected because, "even assuming it could succeed," it would only be accomplished after the North had developed a formidable nuclear and missile potential. Furthermore, an undermining strategy would not win the support of U.S. allies (presumably the ROK), might harm the North Korean people, and at worst, risks war.

The report says the alternative policy of "reforming the DPRK" would be viewed by North Korea in the same light as a confrontational undermining policy and, like undermining, would take too long to achieve its nonproliferation goals. "Buying" the objectives of nuclear and missile nonproliferation (the label that critics have frequently applied to current U.S. North Korea policy) was rejected because it would "only encourage the DPRK to further blackmail, and would encourage proliferators worldwide to engage in similar blackmail." Moreover, Perry believes a reform policy would not be supported by Congress.

The Perry Report proposes a "comprehensive and integrated approach: a two-path strategy," which would "in a step-by-step and reciprocal fashion, move to reduce pressures on the DPRK that it perceives as threatening." The reduction in threat would be intended to "give the DPRK confidence that it could coexist peacefully with us and its neighbors and pursue its own economic and social development." In short, the Perry approach consists of an offer to coexist peacefully with the DPRK and not interfere in its domestic affairs. The policy's proposed inducements are not unlike those offered in the Agreed Framework: "The United States would normalize relations with the DPRK, relax sanctions . . . and take other positive steps that would provide opportunities for the DPRK." The report adds that the ROK and Japan would be prepared to take similar steps. In return for these inducements, the DPRK would have to "move to eliminate its nuclear and long-range missile threats." If the Kim government does not agree to this framework, Perry recommends a second path, whose details are not available in the unclassified version of the report, which simply warns that "on the second path, we would need to act to contain the threat."

The advantages that the Perry Report attributes to its recommended alternative are that it has the full support of U.S. allies; draws on U.S. (unspecified) negotiating strengths; maintains U.S. deterrence of North Korea; "builds on" the Agreed Framework; "aligns U.S. and allied near-term objectives with respect to the DPRK's nuclear and missile activities with our long-term objectives for lasting peace on the Korean peninsula" (the latter being highly valued objectives of the ROK and Japan); and "does not depend on specific North Korean behavior or intent" (although the report seems to contradict itself on this important point).

The ROK's Engagement Policy

ROK President Kim Dae Jung unveiled his own engagement policy in the first days of his administration in early 1998.[20] The policy is aimed at changing North Korea's policies over the long term by offering aid and cooperation *without requiring short-term policy changes in return.* In proposing the policy, President Kim was seeking an alternative to his predecessor's quid pro quo policy, which had failed to improve inter-Korean relations.

Initially called the sunshine policy after the Aesop fable in which the sun succeeds in getting a man to remove his coat after the wind has failed to blow it off, ROK engagement is based on three principles: "not to tolerate armed provocation by North Korea"; "not to attempt a takeover or absorption of North Korea"; and "to broaden reconciliation and cooperation." The guidelines for implementing the sunshine policy included separating politics from business approaches to the North, pursuing engagement at a pace consistent with South Korean national consensus (Kim had dubbed his the "people's administration"), and encouraging the international community—especially the United States and Japan—to pursue its own engagement policies toward the DPRK. South Korean businesses were permitted (perhaps even actively encouraged) to contact and invest in North Korea, and the one million dollar ceiling on investments was lifted. The adoption of the sunshine policy enabled the founder of Hyundai, Chung Ju-yung, to invest hundreds of millions of dollars in a joint project with North Korea to enable South Korean tourists to visit the scenic Mount Kumgang, just across the border in the remote southeastern corner of the DPRK.

On the face of it, the sunshine policy seems to be a win-win deal for North Korea. Offers of aid and investment accompanied by the promise not to absorb the North would seem to answer the needs of the North Korean people and their leaders. Yet this appearance masks the importance of the intense zero-sum contest for political legitimacy on the Korean Peninsula. To Pyongyang, anything the government in Seoul proposes must be opposed as treason and contrary to the true interests of the Korean people.

Indeed, initially the Kim Jong Il regime did not respond positively to the sunshine policy. In June 1998 a small North Korean submarine was captured on the South Korean coastline. Its nine-man crew committed suicide. In July the body of a North Korean frogman outfitted for a spy mission washed onto another beach. In November a high-speed North Korean boat escaped from pursuing South Korean coastal patrol boats. And in December a North Korean semisubmersible craft was sunk by the South Korean navy off the southern tip of the peninsula.[21] Except for the stranded submarine (the second in as many years, both of which North Korea claimed were training missions that drifted into South Korean waters after encountering engine trouble), North Korea denied any involvement in these incursions.

Besides the continuing attempts at infiltration and espionage, the Pyongyang press roundly condemned the sunshine policy as an attempt to subvert North Korea's Juche culture. One of numerous examples of this criticism reads:

> There is a fable of a crow that made the whole audience laugh by his cawing attempt to imitate a nightingale. The South Korean authorities' words and actions remind one of this fable. As if wasting time with politics improvised with an empty rampage is not enough, they are bragging about doing something while coming up with the so-called sunshine theory.... They are merely colonial puppets that do not have the slightest independence, philosophy or their own political opinion.[22]

The inducements of the sunshine policy are aimed more directly at the North Korean people than at their leaders, who view it as "poison carrots" proffered to destabilize their regime.[23] Yet the North Korean government's response has dampened enthusiasm for the sunshine policy among many South Koreans. President Kim Dae Jung has persevered in this initiative, which has the triple virtues of putting pressure on North Korea's closed borders, providing aid to the hungry North Korean people, and reducing the danger of war that accompanies a confrontational policy. Former ROK foreign minister Han Sung-ju has cautioned that no immediate changes in North Korea should be expected to result from the sunshine policy, and that if the policy is pursued, it must be implemented with the flexibility required by any long-term policy.[24]

Policy Considerations

The following principles and assumptions are offered as a guideline for policy construction.

Goals

The first goal of any responsible policy must be to avoid provoking conflict on the Korean Peninsula. Most of the people killed in a second Korean conflict would be Koreans in the North and the South, and for a third party to trigger such a conflict would be unconscionable. North Korea has two faces: the face of the ruling elite who seek to remain in power at all costs and the face of 20 million ordinary people who have no understanding of international politics and who are physically and mentally starved. Policymakers in Washington, far from North Korea, debate the pros and cons of using carrots and sticks to influence North Korea, often without having a good understanding of the concerns of Kim Jong Il and his colleagues, and without sensitivity to the hostage plight of the North Korean masses. Policymakers in Seoul, however, look across the border and see millions of fellow Koreans. At close quarters the situation on the Korean Peninsula becomes more complex and more human.

The second policy goal should be to provide the North Korean people with the opportunity to move toward democracy (a specific example of the avowed U.S. policy of promoting democracy abroad) by penetrating the illusions under which the North Korean elites and masses live. This simply means telling the truth to the North Korean people as much as possible. Since the Kim regime is built on lies and oppression, truth telling will go a long way toward defeating it.

A third goal is to prevent the DPRK from proliferating weapons of mass destruction. The direct path to this goal, by buy-off, while probably necessary in the short term, is in the end self-defeating. Payment for a weapons freeze is likely to be rent, not an irrevocable purchase. Triggering a war to prevent the spread of weapons is seriously flawed policy.

Choices

The policy options available to achieve these goals are limited, calling to mind John Kenneth Galbraith's comment in a letter to Kennedy in 1962, "Politics is not the art of the possible. It consists in choosing between the disastrous and the unpalatable." The likelihood of establishing a genuine cooperative relationship with the current DPRK government is remote: the gulf between the values and assumptions of the Kim Jong Il government and of democratic governments, compounded by a legacy of distrust built up since the Korean War, are insurmountable obstacles. Although the North Korean people, misled as they are, share with people everywhere the same human qualities, their leaders have placed them in a different world, on the other side of the looking glass, so to speak.

Confrontation with North Korea would be a disastrous policy choice for the United States. As broached in 1994, this policy would have begun with a stronger U.S.-sponsored economic embargo (presumably by Japan, since the United States had already imposed an almost total embargo). Such an embargo would almost certainly have been ineffective without the cooperation of China. Air strikes against North Korea's nuclear facilities were mentioned as a follow-up option.[25] The confrontational approach was rejected as unworkable and risky. At best, military confrontation would temporarily deter or destroy part of the North's nuclear program at the cost of ruining any chances of developing a long-term solution (as long as the Kim regime remained in power). At worst, military confrontation would have triggered a second Korean War in which South Koreans—and perhaps Japanese—would pay a far higher price than Americans.

Another alternative, disengagement (also variously referred to as laissez faire, benign neglect, and strategic disregard), seems to open the way for North Korea to begin "turning out plutonium like sausages" to quote the phrase of former undersecretary of defense Walter Slocombe.[26] The proposition that the United States tolerate North Korea's development of nuclear weapons and missiles (as it tolerates similar programs in India, Pakistan, and Israel), while taking pains not to give the North Koreans reason to use those weapons against the United States and its allies, is not a popular option. To pursue a policy of disengagement, one must exercise great patience and hold to the conviction that time is on your side.

Containment, useful before North Korea developed and acquired the technology to build nuclear bombs and missiles, also does not address these threats, although as long as the United States remains suspicious of North Korea's intentions, containment as a backstop policy is likely to be used. Inducing the Kim regime to comply with nonproliferation regimes will require some form of quid pro quo reward. Counterproliferation, in the form of either a strategic missile defense system (for example, the Strategic Defense Initiative, or "Star Wars") or a more limited Theater Missile Defense (TMD) system, is in its technological infancy. Even if such a system is developed to a working level, its deployment is likely to stimulate the North Korean weapons industry (not to mention the Chinese defense industry), with predictable destabilizing effects in the region.

The most promising choice for changing North Korea and reducing its threats is some form of engagement, such as already formulated in the Agreed Framework and the ROK's sunshine policy.[27] But current engagement policies and proposals are incomplete in at least two respects. First, because their inducements target both the government and the people of North Korea but not strongly enough to move either one. Second, the success of the policies relies too heavily on the willingness of the Kim Jong Il government to voluntarily change its policies.

The effective employment of positive incentives is not as simple as might first appear.[28] An important consideration is that what counts as reward (or with negative sanctions, as punishment) must be defined as such by the party to whom the reward or punishment is administered. To Kim Jong Il and the elite, what counts as a reward is whatever they can use to maintain and enhance their power; for example, foreign currency with which to strengthen their security forces, and international respect and a promise of noninterference in their country's domestic affairs. Humanitarian aid is targeted not at them but at the suffering North Korean people. Humanitarian aid is valuable from the Western viewpoint of human rights but should not be expected to change the policies of Kim Jong Il.

So the problem is this: the kind of rewards that might reduce the Kim regime's hostility will strengthen that regime and will therefore prove unpopular among democratic donor states. The rewards that benefit the people will not decisively move the Kim government, although they will lessen popular discontent against the regime. A policy that placates the Kim regime while empowering the North Korean people to govern themselves is needed.

Policymakers should be careful about pursuing "comprehensive agreements" or "package deals." The advantage for Pyongyang of such comprehensive agreements is that the Kim regime can pick and choose which of the provisions of the agreement it wishes to honor, declining to implement the less desirable provisions by claiming that the other party (the United States, the ROK) has not held up its side of the bargain. North Korea has always sought such deals. In 1993 Pyongyang promised, "If the United States accepts the DPRK-proposed formula of package solution, all problems related to the nuclear issue including the compliance with the [IAEA] safeguards agreement will be solved and it will not take much time."[29] A year later Pyongyang promised that its relations with Seoul would be improved too: "It is only too clear that if a definite guarantee is given to provide a light water reactor, the hostile relations between the DPRK and the US are removed and the issue of confidence building is resolved at the third round of DPRK-US talks, leading to a practical improvement of the bilateral relations, a decisively favorable phase will be opened in North-South relations."[30] As it turned out, the nuclear issue has never been satisfactorily solved, and as soon as the deal was signed North Korea turned its back on South Korea, Japan, and the IAEA.

In a genuinely comprehensive resolution to the legacy of the Korean War, Pyongyang is unlikely to settle for less than an end to the U.S.-ROK security alliance, which is obviously targeted at the DPRK. It will not settle for less, but it will sign an agreement for less—and then hold out for more. Thus American negotiators seek such an agreement with a healthy skepticism often not communicated to the general public.[31] William Perry, speaking at a 1999 meeting at the Woodrow Wilson Center, was cautious about prospects for his proposal: "I've told [the president] that I am confident that pursuing talks with North Korea seriously and creatively is a good idea, but that I can not be confident that this process will actually lead to a peaceful peninsula. Therefore the United States should keep its powder dry."[32]

For the Short Term—Buying Time

The comprehensive engagement policy as outlined in the Agreed Framework appears to have succeeded in its short-term goal of freezing North Korea's nuclear activities at Yongbyon, and as far as publicly available information indicates, throughout the rest of the DPRK. But as a road map for improving North Korea's relations with the United States and with its neighbors, it is likely to fall far short of its goals. The alarms over Kumchang-ni and the Taepodong rocket launch illustrate the distrust that will threaten the implementation of the agreement. The Pyongyang regime's hostility, coupled with its insistence that it has nothing to open and no need for reforms, has disappointed the optimists who hoped that after North Korea's founder Kim Il Sung died, the country would begin to change. The expectations of those who predicted a collapse of the new Kim Jong Il regime have also been disappointed, as Kim Jong Il has been able to extract aid from the West while keeping his people oppressed. Five years after the signing of the Agreed Framework, the DPRK remains a nuclear threat, although arguably not as great a threat as it would have been if the framework had not been signed.

The review of North Korea policy conducted by the Perry team was warranted. Their conclusion that the Agreed Framework is unsustainable was also warranted, not primarily because "aside from a failure to address U.S. concerns directly, it is easy to imagine circumstances that would bring the status quo rapidly to a crisis," but because the basic premise that the DPRK will agree to relinquish its military deterrents is unrealistic. The major flaw of the Agreed Framework and the Perry proposal as long-term "comprehensive" policy is that they seek an exchange of military deterrents for civilian infrastructure.

North Korea's capability to develop weapons of mass destruction—missiles and chemical, biological, and (the Agreed Framework notwithstanding) nuclear—is vital to its national security, just as American weapons programs are considered vital to U.S. security. Pyongyang is unlikely ever to bargain away all its deterrent capabilities. These capabilities persuaded the United States to change its containment policy to one of limited engagement. The Kim regime will never trust security guarantees from Washington—nor should it, given the American propensity to resort to military intervention to back up its foreign policy. The mistrust is so high—not just between Pyongyang and Washington, but between Pyongyang and most of the international community—that significant arms reduction on the Korean Peninsula is highly unlikely, even though it would be a great blessing to the economies of both Koreas. Moreover, tension reduction would deprive the Kim regime of one of its best social control weapons.

Short of risking another Korean war, it is difficult to find a way to stop the DPRK's strategic weapons programs other than following the model of the Agreed Framework, which means paying the DPRK for a freeze. This is the "buy-out" option that the Perry Report rejects on the grounds that it encourages North Korea to continuously come up with new threats to be bought out. This reservation is valid, but the alternative—expecting the DPRK to freeze its strategic weapons programs in return for improved relations with the United States and the reduction in threat that is implied by improved relations—is far too weak an incentive for the suspicious Kim regime.

The North Koreans have offered to sell Washington their missiles to the rumored tune of $1 billion a year. They have already made a multibillion dollar deal for their nuclear program at Yongbyon. They negotiated a lucrative deal for the inspection at Kumchang-ni. And every year they negotiate a deal to conduct joint searches for the remains of American soldiers killed in the Korean War. Nonproliferating states who join the Nonproliferation Treaty have always required a quid pro quo for agreeing to limit their nuclear programs; the DPRK simply demands a higher price than most other states. If the American public wants to freeze North Korea's weapons programs, it must be willing to pay, at least in the short term.

For the Long Term—Proactive Engagement

For the long term a more proactive engagement policy is needed, a policy that, unlike the Agreed Framework or the Perry proposal, does not depend on "the willingness of the DPRK [government] to traverse [the path] with us."[33] A proactive policy must reach out to the North Korean people, while dealing in good faith but at arm's length with the Kim Jong Il regime. Foreign governments should not expect to change the Kim regime or to continue indefinitely to feed North Korea's people.

As Juche teaches, the North Korean people must take their fate into their own hands. But they will not do so unless they have information about the alternatives provided by other political and economic systems. The people must be moved. The first step in effecting change is to provide them with information with which they can make informed decisions about their governance. Psychologists John Thibaut and Harold Kelley have noted that people's satisfaction is influenced by how their situation compares with other experienced situations. The North Korean people are suffering. But their government reminds them that earlier generations suffered as much as they do or even more—in conflicts with the Japanese and Americans. Those conflicts ended in "glorious victories," and better days (in the 1960s and 1970s) eventually came. Today's North Koreans are taught to be patient. Thibaut and Kelley also note that what moves people to change their situation (regardless of how satisfied they may be with it) is something else: the knowledge that better alternatives currently exist.[34] Or to quote de Tocqueville, "Evils which are patiently endured when they seem inevitable become intolerable when once the idea of escape from them is suggested."[35]

North Korea is different in an important respect from other dictatorial and communist states in that the North Korean people are relatively sealed off from information about the outside world. This difference explains why the Kim Jong Il regime is potentially weakest at its greatest strengths: ideology and social control. The ideology is filled with falsehoods, which if exposed are likely to turn the people decisively against their leaders. Once they are shorn of their faith in Kim and his father, they can only be controlled by coercive methods, which will be taxed beyond the government's limit.

Three means to reach the people are by devoting more resources to infiltrating information into North Korea, using foreign aid to change people's attitudes toward foreign governments and toward their own government, and opening multiple channels of engagement that will prevent the Kim regime from controlling all access to North Korea. These initiatives would add a needed dimension to current engagement policies.

Knowledge Is Power

Articles in the North Korean domestic press helpfully provide the United States with a framework for enlightening the North Korean people. Ever since the transformation of the Eastern European and Soviet republics, the Pyongyang propaganda machine has churned out warnings of the dangers of "imperialist pollution." *Nodong Sinmun,* mixing its metaphors, cautions that unless a "mosquito net" is erected to block foreign influences, "the yellow wind of capitalism [will] spread among the people like a narcotic and paralyze their sound-thinking."[36] The list of pernicious influences includes foreign broadcasts above all, followed by "newspapers, magazines, pictures, photographs, documentaries, movies and music." "Once the people take an interest in bourgeois publications and lifestyles, they become unwittingly brain-dead and they begin to aspire for capitalism."[37]

Although most North Korean radio dials are permanently set to receive only domestic broadcasts, an undetermined number of radios can receive foreign broadcasts when they are not jammed. A recent defector from North Korea has said, "If someone asked me to do something for reunification, giving me enough resources, I would ship more than 10 million small radios to the North in the first place."[38] Enhanced use of radio, television, informational materials infiltrated through the border with China and information accompanying foreign aid and Korean travelers have the potential to change the minds of the elite and the masses in closed North Korea.

Doing Well by Doing Good

In a major published address to the Korean people in 1997, Kim Jong Il warned, "Nothing is more foolish and dangerous than pinning hopes on imperialist 'aid,' ... The imperialist 'aid' is a noose of plunder and subjugation aimed at robbing ten and even a hundred things for one thing that is given."[39] Yet the DPRK government, unable to provide for its people, continues to solicit aid, courting its own destruction.

Hwang Jang Yop, a former secretary of the North Korean Workers' Party and the highest ranking North Korean defector to date, is convinced that the key to reuniting the two Koreas is to remove Kim Jong Il and his associates from power. Hwang believes that if the people begin to receive massive foreign aid (millions of tons of food), they will realize that the food cannot be coming from their own government, which has failed them. Hwang has suggested that food aid be channeled through South Korea, to be transported to North Korea through the truce village at Panmunjom, to make it clear to as many North Koreans as possible that the government in the South, which they are taught is corrupt and evil, is willing to do what their own government cannot do for them. If the North Korean authorities blocked the shipments (as they most likely would, at least initially), Hwang suggests letting the food pile up to shame the Kim government in the face of the world, and—to the extent the news reaches them—in the face of its people.[40]

Hwang's proposal raises the interesting question of how to respond when the Kim government refuses to accept aid because of the terms of the aid package. The DPRK initially refused to accept proffered aid from the ROK, until Japanese aid was made conditional on the acceptance of ROK aid. The World Food Program has often failed to reach its distribution goals because North Korean officials have blocked distribution. Other aid groups have also curtailed their efforts or even withdrawn them completely. Future rejections are inevitable, especially if more strings are tied to aid. But the ROK's early experience with aid donorship offers a clue about how to respond to North Korea's aid refusals: if donors coordinate their demands for aid-related concessions,

North Korea will be unable to play one off against the other and will be more likely to give in to demands for concessions in its policies.

If foreign aid is to be used to inform the people about the benign intent of the "imperialists," its national and organizational origins must be clearly identified and aid distribution must be closely monitored to ensure that its provenance remains identified and that it reaches its intended target—the people rather than their leaders. The WFP and other aid organizations try to achieve transparency, but in seeking to keep aid channels open, they must necessarily be cautious about offending the North Korean government. But foreign aid *should* offend the Kim regime, which is responsible for North Korea's economic problems. An effective foreign aid program is one that not only feeds the North Korean people but enlightens them and shames their government.

The politicization of foreign aid is justified when the problem that created the need for the aid is political. Providing aid with no strings attached simply supports the perpetrators of the disaster. Attaching political goals to aid and pursuing these goals help overcome the lack of short-term rewards for aid donors, demonstrating that aggressive action is being taken to solve underlying problems.

Multichannel Engagement

A major source of frustration in negotiations with the DPRK is that all important decisions appear to be made by Kim Jong Il, who operates behind the scenes. Although reputed to be a bold thinker, Kim may be particularly cautious about making foreign policy decisions, considering not only the international ramifications but also how they will affect his political position in Pyongyang and whether the military would approve. As long as a single comprehensive package is presented to Kim from a single source, he can carefully study it. If diverse offers arrive in Pyongyang from multiple sources, negotiations will be backlogged. If the United States, Japan, Australia and other democratic countries establish embassies in Pyongyang, and North Korea establishes embassies in those countries, the Kim Jong Il surveillance system (of foreigners and its own diplomats) will be stretched thin. Extensive exchanges with South Korea would tax the Kim regime even more.

If the U.S. economic embargo were to be lifted, Kim would have to deal with a host of curious business delegations (who would likely drive hard bargains before investing). To the extent that aid offers and business propositions include benefits for various segments of North Korean society, it is likely that the cadres in Pyongyang, if not the common people, would recognize that they are missing out on attractive offers because Kim cannot handle the traffic. Moreover, ending the American economic embargo would communicate an important truth, for the North Koreans would discover that their perverted economic system rather than an embargo has destroyed their economy.

Proactive Engagement and Multinational Cooperation

To achieve U.S. goals on the Korean Peninsula, it is necessary to coordinate policy closely with the ROK, to a lesser extent with Japan, and to some degree with China, Russia, and the Western industrial powers. South Korea and Japan are already paying for most of the reactor construction that serves as the centerpiece of the Agreed Framework. The Perry Report also envisions the necessity of South Korean and Japanese involvement in any new comprehensive agreement. But the goals of South Korea and Japan are not identical with U.S. goals, and thus preferred policies may differ. All three countries share the goal of avoiding conflict, but this goal is paramount for the South Koreans, and it places strong constraints on any U.S. policy that claims to be an internationally cooperative endeavor. Moreover, many South Koreans still cherish the goal of reunification, not a goal in Washington (or Tokyo), where a divided Korea, as long as it is peaceful, may even be preferred.

Kim Dae Jung's sunshine policy seeks to reach the North Korean people in spite of the hostility of North Korea's government toward the government in Seoul. This is the correct approach. But the sunshine policy is overly cautious, separating humanitarian and business issues from political issues. The time frame for changing the North Korean government and achieving reunification is very long, certainly too long to achieve U.S. nonproliferation goals. For U.S. nonproliferation policy to succeed, U.S. policy may have to be more forceful than current ROK policy, without being belligerent.

The Japanese appear to have few illusions about the difficulty of overcoming the decades of animosity that have built up between them and the North Korean government. The Japanese are vulnerable to North Korean provocations and desirous of peace on the Korean Peninsula, but their policies are motivated more by the desire to avoid provoking North Korea than by the desire to change it. The Koreans (in North and South) and the Japanese would agree that Japan's role in Korea's political affairs should be limited.

Washington should have few illusions about obtaining cooperation from China, which is desirous of freezing the DPRK's weapons programs but is equally concerned about a collapse of the DPRK regime into the hands of the ROK, resulting in a strong Korean state on its borders. Russia shares similar concerns. Other states and international organizations, such as the European Union, share Washington's nonproliferation concerns but have always considered problems on the Korean Peninsula primarily a matter for the Americans to handle.

Consequences

A multiplicity of separate offers and different kinds of engagement might succeed all too well in overwhelming and discrediting the Kim Jong Il regime, leading to domestic anarchy in North Korea. The Perry Report rejects the policy of undermining the Kim regime, partly because of the fear that an attempt to do so would "risk destructive war" and "might harm the people of the DPRK more than its government." Presumably the forms of undermining that Perry was considering were more offensive than blowing the "yellow wind of capitalism" into North Korea.

There still remains the danger of anarchy and social collapse, whose costs to South Korea will be financially and socially significant.[41] In answer to this reservation, Nicholas Eberstadt, among others, has argued that supporting the current regime and hoping it will gradually change is highly uncertain in its effect and provides no guarantee that unification costs will not increase if reunification is delayed.[42] Moreover, the human rights abuses that the Pyongyang regime visits on its people, many of whom have been reduced to living like animals, must weigh on the conscience of those who have the means to end these abuses but choose not to.

Make no mistake, even a collapse of the Kim Jong Il government and reunification under the South Korean government does not achieve a long-term resolution of the proliferation issue. A unified Korea, like many other states, may decide to acquire certain weapons of mass destruction to provide for its national security. But at this stage U.S. nonproliferation concerns shift to the more global problem of sustaining a two-tiered proliferation regime.

If North Korea does collapse, the United States must come to the aid of the ROK in reuniting the country, for the United States was undeniably partially responsible for the division of Korea. To the extent that U.S. policy intentionally destabilizes the Kim regime, the United States will bear even greater responsibility. But compared with the cost of supporting the DPRK indefinitely and erecting an expensive counterproliferation shield, these reunification costs—a Marshall Plan for Korea—will be well spent.

No one can predict what will become of the North Korean regime. Judging by present trends, it will continue to oppress its people and resist change and opening, all the while presenting its neighbors with the maddening question of how to deal with a government that rejects the present world order.

Weakening the Kim Jong Il regime is only a first step to bring North Korea into the international community. Years of indoctrination have bred suspicion of foreigners—especially Americans and Japanese—in the minds of the North Korean people. Years of malnutrition have degraded their physical health. Socialist propaganda has warped their views about how economic systems work. Post-unification Korea will face almost insurmountable hardships. The sooner the re-education of North Korea begins, the better.

A proactive engagement policy hews to the truth as we know it. Truth telling may not be a priority in the formulation of foreign policy, but truth has a way of making itself known in the fullness of time, both to international and domestic audiences. A proactive engagement policy designed to bring the truth to the North Korean people refuses to cater to the ideologues in Pyongyang who claim that one-party socialism is a viable policy and that totalitarian socialist countries can live amicably with liberal democracies. Ironically, when the Pyongyang press declares that North Korea under Kim Jong Il "cannot live under the same sky" as Americans, it is finally telling the truth.[43]

Notes

Preface

1. Lewis Carroll, "Through the Looking Glass," in Martin Gardner, ed., *The Annotated Alice* (Bramhall House, 1960), pp. 184–85.

2. Kongdan Oh, "Security Strategies of South and North Korea: Through the Looking Glass," in Tae-Hwan Kwak, ed., *The Search for Peace and Security in Northeast Asia toward the Twenty-First Century*, a collection of papers presented at the eleventh conference on Korea-U.S. Security Studies, October 1996 (Seoul: Kyungnam University, 1997), pp. 45–59; and Edward Carr, "Survey: The Koreas: Through the Looking Glass," *Economist*, July 10, 1999, pp. 11–14.

Chapter One

1. "Be a Human Fortress to Defend Pyongyang," *Nodong Sinmun*, January 29, 1999, p.1.

2. Among a number of fine histories of Korea available in English, the following three, combined, provide a solid background in facts and interpretation. Carter J. Eckert and others, *Korea Old and New: A History* (Seoul: Ilchokak Publishers for the Korea Institute, Harvard University,1990); Han Woo-Keun, *The History of Korea*, translated by Lee Kyung-shik (Honolulu: East-West Center Press, 1970); and James B. Palais, *Politics and Policy in Traditional Korea* (Harvard University Press, 1975).

3. An empirical analysis of North Korean history education is provided by Chung Doo-

hee, "The Heritage of the Chosun Dynasty Appearing in the North Korean Description of History," *East Asian Review*, vol. 10 (Spring 1998), pp. 25–40.

4. Palais, *Politics and Policy*.

5. An anonymous reviewer of this book manuscript has suggested that a number of interesting parallels could be drawn between the Kim Il Sung cult and the Japanese imperial cult; and that, moreover, Kim Il Sung, who grew up in Japanese colonial Korea, may well have borrowed ideas from Japanese emperor worship.

6. A good analysis of the role of the Japanese in bringing capitalism to Korea is Carter J. Eckert, *Offspring of Empire: The Koch'ang Kims and the Colonial Origins of Korean Capitalism, 1876–1945* (University of Washington Press, 1991). Legal, social control, educational and media control policies adopted by the colonial administration to manage Korea are discussed in separate chapters by Edward I-te Chen, Ching-chih Chen, E. Patricia Tsurumi, and Michael E. Robinson, respectively, in Ramon H. Myers and Mark R. Peattie, eds., *The Japanese Colonial Empire, 1895–1945* (Princeton University Press, 1984).

7. See Chong-Sik Lee's discussion of imposed religion in *Japan and Korea: The Political Dimension* (Stanford: Hoover Institution Press, 1985), pp. 10–13.

8. See Michael Edson Robinson, *Cultural Nationalism in Colonial Korea, 1920–1925* (University of Washington Press, 1988).

9. The expatriate wartime activities of Kim Il Sung and his early days after returning to Korea are recounted in Dae-Sook Suh's authoritative biography, *Kim Il Sung, The North Korean Leader* (Columbia University Press, 1988). Additional information about this period in Kim's life can be found in an insightful monograph by Sydney A. Seiler, which draws on interviews of former North Korean officials published by the South Korean daily *Chungang Ilbo* in 1991. *Kim Il-song, 1941–1948: The Creation of a Legend, The Building of a Regime* (University Press of America, 1994).

10. See Bruce Cumings, *The Origins of the Korean War, Volume II: The Roaring of the Cataract, 1947–1950* (Princeton University Press, 1990), chap. 3.

11. The period leading up to the Korean War is covered by two carefully researched volumes by Bruce Cumings: *The Origins of the Korean War*, vols. 1, 2 (Princeton University Press, 1981, 1990).

12. In the context of Kim Jong Il's 1998 military-first policy, the North Koreans reiterated their view of war: "The Juche-based point of view on war is based on a scientific understanding of war. War is an extension of politics by means of a special form of violence. A counterrevolutionary war of the exploiting class that tramples underfoot the independence of the working masses and impedes social development is an unjust war whereas the revolutionary war of the working class that protects the independence of the people and promotes social development is a just war. To answer the imperialists' war of aggression with a revolutionary war and deal fire with fire is the nucleus of the revolutionary point of view on war. . . . In the event a war breaks out in our country, we will be waging a just war to safeguard the sovereignty of the country and reunify the fatherland. . . . A just war will surely end in victory. For truth and justice to triumph is the law of history. It is important to be full of fight and determined to fight some day against the U.S. impe-

rialists head-on to settle old scores once and for all." See Kim Myong-hui, "The Revolutionary Point of View on War," *Nodong Sinmun*, December 7, 1998, p. 3.

13. Korean War casualty figures from the ROK government-affiliated Yonhap News Agency's *Korea Annual, 1999* (Seoul: Yonhap News Agency, 1998), p. 299.

14. In the mid-1990s, before the precipitous slide in North Korea's economy, GNP was estimated at around $20 billion, with defense expenditures of approximately $6 billion. With a GNP twenty times greater, South Korea's defense budget was a proportionately modest $14 billion and rising. See, for example, *Defense White Paper, 1999* (Seoul: Ministry of National Defense, 1999), pp. 222, 225, 302.

15. Dae-Sook Suh, *Kim Il Sung, The North Korean Leader*, pp. 130–36.

16. Secretary Hwang has offered this description of North Korea in several published interviews. See, for example, "Table Talk: Hwang Jang Yop and Shin Sang-ok Talk about the Two Homelands They Have Experienced," *Wolgan Choson*, March 1999, pp. 609–41. Since leaving North Korea, Hwang has also published two books (neither is currently available in English): his autobiography, entitled *Nanun Yoksaui Chillirul Poatta* (I Saw the Truth of History) (Seoul: Hanul, 1999); and his thoughts on North Korea, presented in *Pukhanui Chinsilkwa Howi* (The Truth and Falsity of North Korea) (Seoul: Unification Policy Research Center, 1998).

17. Interview with twenty-nine-year-old truck driver trading with China, who defected in January 1996.

18. The observation that North Koreans, specifically the North Korean military, live in a "reality sealed off from the outside" is made by Kim Chong-min in an article for *Pukhan* entitled "Conscription System and Soldiers' Lives in North Korea," August 1999, pp. 134–45.

Chapter Two

1. Chong-pyo Chung, "Our Fatherland Is an Ideological Power," *Nodong Sinmun*, September 10, 1996, p. 3.

2. Carl J. Friedrich and Zbigniew K. Brzezinski, *Totalitarian Dictatorship and Autocracy* (Frederick A Praeger, 1966), p. 107.

3. Franz Schurmann, *Ideology and Organization in Communist China*, 2d ed. (University of California Press, 1968), p. 18.

4. Chung, "Our Fatherland," p. 3.

5. Robert A. Scalapino and Chong-Sik Lee, *Communism in Korea, Part II: The Society* (University of California Press, 1972), p. 869.

6. Alain (Emile-Auguste Chartier), *Propos sur la religion*, 1938, no. 74.

7. "DPRK's Socialist Constitution (Full Text)," Unofficial translation published by *The People's Korea*, no. 1825 (September 19, 1998), p. 4.

8. Reo M. Christenson and others, *Ideologies and Modern Politics* (Dodd, Mead & Company, 1971), p. 5.

9. Friedrich and Brzezinski, *Totalitarian Dictatorship*, pp. 88–89.

10. Ibid., p. 91.

11. In 1994 North Korean archaeologists claimed to have unearthed the tomb of Tangun, said to be the founder of the Korean people. According to legend, Hwanung, one of the gods, descended to earth and married a bear-woman, who bore Tangun, who founded the Korean nation in 2333 BC. Some versions of the legend say Tangun was buried on Mount Taebak near Pyongyang, while other versions say he was transformed into the god of Asadal mountain. Obviously there is no certainty that such a person ever existed, and foreign experts question the methodology used by the North Koreans to identify the bones and artifacts alleged to be Tangun's. The DPRK rebuilt Tangun's tomb to provide substance for the claim that Korea was founded near present-day Pyongyang. See Choi Mong-lyong, "Questions on Excavation of 'Tangun Tomb,'" *Korea Focus*, vol. 2 (November-December 1994), pp. 39–43.

12. Bruce Cumings, "The Corporate State in North Korea," in Hagen Koo, ed., *State and Society in Contemporary Korea* (Cornell University Press, 1993), pp. 197–230, quotation on p. 213.

13. Ibid., p. 214.

14. Han Shik Park, "*Chuch'e*: The North Korean Ideology," in C. I. Eugene Kim and B. C. Koh, eds., *Journey to North Korea: Personal Perceptions*, Research Papers and Policies Studies, no. 8 (Berkeley: Institute of East Asian Studies, 1983), pp. 84–98, quotation on p. 85.

15. "On the Juche Idea," KCNA (Internet Version), December 10, 1997.

16. Cumings, "The Corporate State in North Korea," p. 214.

17. Dae-Sook Suh, *Kim Il Sung, The North Korean Leader* (Columbia University Press, 1988). Suh's discussion of Kim's 1955 speech is found on pp. 306–07. At several points in chapter 17 Suh gives examples of how the North Koreans have fabricated or rewritten historical documents. He says Kim's 1955 speech was not published in English until 1964. Another source reports that the first publication was not until 1968. See Song-u So, "Kim Chong-il as New Leader," *Pukhan*, February 1994, pp. 60–67, translated by Foreign Broadcast Information Service, *Daily Report: East Asia*, 94-095, May 17, 1994, pp. 34–41; see p. 41. (Hereafter FBIS, *East Asia*).

18. Kim Il Sung, "On Eliminating Dogmatism and Formalism and Establishing Juche in Ideological Work," Speech to Party Propaganda and Agitation Workers, December 28, 1955, in *Kim Il Sung Works*, vol. 9, *July 1954-December 1955* (Pyongyang: Foreign Languages Publishing House, 1982), pp. 395–417, quotation on pp. 395–96. The talk, which is devoted ostensibly to the topic of ideological work, makes a strong appeal for studying and valuing Korean literature and art.

19. Kim Il Sung, "On Eliminating Dogmatism," pp. 404–05.

20. For an interesting discussion of the nationalism-internationalism issue related to Juche theory, see Jae-Jean Suh, "Theoretical Revision of Juche Thought and Nationalism in North Korea," *Korean Journal of National Unification*, vol. 2 (1993), pp. 7–30.

21. Kim Il Sung, "On Eliminating Dogmatism," p. 416.

22. Ibid., p. 403. Deng Xiaoping's injunction was, "It does not matter whether the cat is black or white, so long as it catches mice."

23. Kim Jong Il, "On Some Problems of Education in Juche Idea," *Nodong Sinmun*, July 15, 1987; translated by *The People's Korea*, July 25, 1987, pp. 2–3, quotation on p. 3.

24. Kim Il Sung, "On Some Problems of Our Party's Juche Idea and the Government of the Republic's Internal and External Policies (Excerpts), Answers to the Questions Raised by Journalists of the Japanese Newspaper *Mainichi Shimbun,* September 17, 1972," in the author's *On Juche in Our Revolution,* vol. 2 (Pyongyang: Foreign Languages Publishing House, 1975), pp. 425–36, quotation on p. 436.

25. As one of the reviewers of this manuscript noted, the concepts of *Kokutai* in imperial Japan and anticommunism in South Korea have been used by their governments in the same way, as a tool for maintaining power.

26. Kim Il Sung, "On Some Problems of Our Party's Juche Idea and the Government of the Republic's Internal and External Policies (Excerpts)," pp. 425–26.

27. Ibid., p. 430.

28. See, for example, Carol Barner-Barry and Cynthia Hody, "Soviet Marxism-Leninism as Mythology," *Political Psychology,* vol. 15 (December 1994), pp. 609–30.

29. Kim Il Sung, "On Some Problems of Our Party's Juche Idea," p. 434.

30. Ibid., p. 430.

31. In September 1973 Kim was elected to the KWP secretariat. Perhaps even earlier decisions were made that he would be the next leader. He may have been formally selected (within the party) as the next leader in a closed KWP meeting held sometime in 1974. None of this was made public. Kim was not introduced to the public as his father's successor until the Sixth Party Congress in October 1980. See Kong Dan Oh, *Leadership Change in North Korean Politics: The Succession to Kim Il Sung* (Santa Monica, Calif.: Rand, 1988), pp. 7–16; and Dae-Sook Suh, "Kim Jong Il and New Leadership in North Korea," in Dae-Sook Suh and Chae-Jin Lee, eds., *North Korea after Kim Il Sung* (Lynne Rienner, 1998), pp. 13–31, see esp. pp. 21–24.

32. For a discussion of "pure" ideology, see Seung-ji Kwak, "The Evolution of North Korea's Ideology," *Vantage Point,* vol. 21 (March 1998), pp. 30–39. Kwak borrows the term from Franz Schurmann.

33. Kim Jong Il, "Socialism Is a Science," *Nodong Sinmun,* November 1, 1994; in the translated version broadcast by KCNA, November 7, 1994; transcribed by FBIS, *East Asia,* 94-215, November 7, 1994, pp. 38–49, quotation on p. 40.

34. Kim Jong Il, "Socialism Is a Science," p. 42.

35. Ibid., p. 43.

36. Kim Jong Il, "On Some Problems of Education in Juche Idea," p. 2.

37. Ibid., p. 3.

38. Ibid., p. 4.

39. Kim Jong Il, "Socialism Is a Science," p. 48.

40. Kim Jong Il, "On Some Problems of Education in Juche Idea," p. 5.

41. Kim Jong Il, "Socialism Is a Science," p. 47.

42. Ibid., pp. 45, 47.

43. "The Nature and Originality of a Revolutionary View of the Leader," a dialogue broadcast by Pyongyang's Korean Central Broadcasting Network (KCBN), November 23, 1994; translated by FBIS, *East Asia,* 94-227, November 25, 1994, and entitled "Dialogue on 'Revolutionary View' of Leader, pp. 37–38; quotation on p. 37.

44. "The Nature and Originality of a Revolutionary View of the Leader," p. 38.

45. In the leadership literature, see, for example, Bernard M. Bass, *Leadership and Performance beyond Expectations* (Free Press, 1985) for a discussion of transformational and transactional leadership.

46. According to chapter 2 of the KWP charter, "All leading party bodies, from the lowest to the highest shall be democratically elected." Chapter 3 stipulates that the party congress meet every three years (its last meeting as of this writing was in 1980), and that between sessions the Central Committee of the party be convened every six months. Chapter 3, article 24, provides that this committee elect the general secretary. For the official announcement, see "Secretary Kim Jong Il Elected WPK General Secretary," KCNA, October 8, 1997.

47. See, for example, an article by the ROK's *Naewoe Tongsin*, no. 910 (July 21, 1994), pp. A1-A4; translated by FBIS, *East Asia*, 95-004, January 6, 1995, and entitled "Kim Chong-il's Ruling Style Analyzed," pp. 30–31.

48. "The Dear Leader Comrade Kim Chong-il Is the People's Great Leader," Unattributed talk on KCBN, September 28, 1994; translated by FBIS, *East Asia*, 94-189, September 29, 1994, and entitled "Kim Chong-il's Love, Trust in People Lauded," pp. 37–38.

49. "Wealth Serves People in Korea," KCNA, February 15, 1994; transcribed by FBIS, *East Asia*, 94-031-A, February 15, 1994, p. 40.

50. Slogan examples from an article broadcast by KCNA, February 6, 1998.

51. Kim Jong Il, "Our Socialism for the People Will Not Perish," a talk given to senior officials of the Central Committee on May 5, 1991, published in *Nodong Sinmun*, May 27, 1991, and republished in *The People's Korea*, no. 1517 (June 8, 1991), pp. 2–7; quotations on pp. 4, 5.

52. Kim Jong Il, "Historical Lesson in Building Socialism and the General Line of Our Party," a talk given to senior officials of the Central Committee on January 3, 1992, published in *Nodong Sinmun*, February 4, 1992, and broadcast on the same day by KCNA, transcribed by FBIS, *East Asia*, 92-024, February 5, 1992, pp.11–24, quotations from various pages.

53. Chon, "Reactionary Nature and Harmfulness of Bourgeois Life Style."

54. See, for example, Chu-kyong Kim, "Liberalization Wind, if Tolerated in the Ideological Realm, Destroys Socialism Completely," *Nodong Sinmun*, October 20, 1995, p. 6; translated by FBIS, *East Asia*, 96-016, January 24, 1996, pp. 43–45. Specifically, "An ideological struggle is a prelude to a political struggle, which inevitably leads to a power struggle" (p. 45).

55. Kim Jong Il, "Historical Lesson in Building Socialism," p. 23.

56. The evils of capitalism are described in Chong-ho Chon, "Reactionary Nature and Harmfulness of Bourgeois Life Style," *Minju Choson*, August 31, 1997, p. 2. On the same theme, a *Nodong Sinmun* article of November 7, 1998, p. 6, outlines what the newspaper considers to be the legacy of bourgeois ideas in former socialist countries: three million alcoholics in Russia; drug addicts and drug smugglers in Poland; teenage Czech, Slovak, and Polish prostitutes plying their trade in Germany; 2,000 murders in Albania, and so on.

57. See William J. McGuire, "Inducing Resistance to Persuasion: Some Contemporary Approaches," in Leonard Berkowitz, ed., *Advances in Experimental Social Psychology*, vol. 1 (Academic Press, 1964), pp. 191–229.

58. Richard Walker, *Hankuk eui chuok*, translated from English into Korean by Chong-soo Lee and YuSuk Hwang (Seoul: Hankuk Moonwon, 1998), pp. 241–42. The authors are grateful to an anonymous reviewer for providing the reference for this incident.

59. "Deceptive Nature of 'Freedom' of Ideology Chanted by Imperialists," KCNA report on a *Nodong Sinmun* article of June 29, 1995; transcribed by FBIS, *East Asia*, 95-125, June 29, 1995, p. 33.

60. Chong Chong-hwa, "The Mental Narcotic That Depraves and Corrupts Society and Mankind," *Minju Choson*, September 22, 1999, p. 6.

61. Song-kuk Ch'oe, "Imperialists' Wily Strategy of Disintegration," *Nodong Sinmun*, May 3, 1998, p. 6.

62. Kim Jong Il, "Historical Lesson," p. 19.

63. "Socialism Is Our People's Faith and Life," *Nodong Sinmun*, March 15, 1993, as broadcast on KCBN, March 15, 1993; translated by FBIS, *East Asia*, 93-052, March 19, 1993, pp. 16–19, quotation on p. 18.

64. Kim Jong Il, "On Preserving the Juche Character and National Character of the Revolution and Construction."

65. Mun-kyu Paek, "Revolution and Construction Will Be Ruined if 'Western Style' Is Introduced," *Nodong Sinmun*, September 14, 1997, p. 6.

66. Ibid.

67. Interview with middle-aged foreign currency official who defected in the mid-1990s.

68. Gilbert Ryle, *The Concept of Mind* (Barnes and Noble, 1949), p. 8.

69. "Vigilance Should Be Heightened against Tricks of Imperialists," *Nodong Sinmun*, December 7, 1996.

70. Kim Jong Il, "On Preserving the Chuche Character and National Character of the Revolution and Construction."

71. Nam-hyok Kim, "Adoption of the Market Economy Leads to Catastrophe," *Nodong Sinmun*, March 1, 1998, p. 6.

72. Paek-hyon Yun, "The Imperialists' Cunning Maneuver of Ideological and Cultural Infiltration," *Nodong Sinmun*, May 24, 1997, p. 6.

73. Chon Kyong-no, "An Important Question in Tapping Inner Reserves," *Minju Choson*, June 17, 1997, p. 3.

74. For a brief overview of the Red Banner philosophy, see "Red Banner Philosophy as Kim Jong-il's Ruling Tool," *Vantage Point*, vol. 20 (March 1997), pp. 16–18.

75. Chang-man Hwang, "The Source of Our People's Revolutionary Optimism," *Nodong Sinmun*, June 1, 1997.

76. "Let Us Further Intensify the Ideological Work of the Party to Suit the Demands of the Final Assault of the Arduous March," *Nondong Sinmun*, August 6, 1997, p. 1.

77. Ibid.

78. Hwang, "The Source of Our People's Revolutionary Optimism."

79. Kim Myong-hui, "The Revolutionary Spirit for Suicidal Explosion," *Nodong Sinmun*, December 29, 1998, p. 3.

80. See, for example, Gail Warshofsky Lapidus, "Society under Strain," in Erik P. Hoffmann and Robbin F. Laird, eds., *The Soviet Polity in the Modern Era* (Aldine Publishing Company, 1984), pp. 691–715.

81. Reinhart Schönsee and Gerda Lederer, "The Gentle Revolution," *Political Psychology*, vol. 12 (June 1991), pp. 309–30.

82. Interview a former North Korean government official who defected in the mid-1990s.

83. See Warshofsky Lapidus, "Society under Strain."

84. Interview with a former high-ranking North Korean government official who defected in the early 1990s.

85. Eric Scheye, "Psychological Notes on Central Europe: 1989 and Beyond," *Political Psychology*, vol. 12 (June 1991), pp. 331–44, quotation on p. 338.

86. Interview with a former North Korean university student in his thirties who defected while studying abroad in the early 1990s. The Korean words this student used to describe the belief system of his North Korean compatriots are particularly descriptive: *Chilli kyumyonge taehan popyonjokin yokkuga issodamyon yoksaui waegoki iroke kyesok toelliga obsotta.*

87. Ibid.

88. Christenson and others, *Ideologies and Modern Politics*, p. 16.

89. Blair A. Ruble, "Muddling Through," in Erik P. Hoffmann and Robbin F. Laird, *Soviet Polity in the Modern Era*, pp. 903–14, quotation on p. 912.

90. Georgi Shalchnazarov, an aide to Gorbachev, quoted by David Remnick in *Lenin's Tomb, The Last Days of the Soviet Empire* (Random House, 1993), p. 168.

91. Schönsee and Lederer, "The Gentle Revolution."

Chapter Three

1. "Let Us Adhere to the Line on Building a Self-Reliant National Economy to the End," special joint article carried in *Kulloja* [the KWP's theoretical journal] and *Nodong Sinmun* [the party's newspaper], September 17, 1998.

2. Chollima is a legendary Korean horse which could cover 1,000 ri (400 kilometers) in a day. The Soviet Union's Stakhanovite movement, dating to the 1930s, is named after Aleksei Stakhanov, a Russian miner credited with heroic production feats.

3. KCNA report under the heading "Korea Is Creating a 'New Chollima Speed, the Speed of Forced March,'" June 2, 1998.

4. Yong-song Kim, "An Account of My Personal Experience as a Battalion Commander of a Building Workers' Shock Regiment for the Construction of Kwangbok Boulevard, Pyongyang," *Wolgan Choson*, November 1994, pp. 37–44, translated by Foreign Broadcast Information Service, *Daily Report: East Asia*, 95-009, January 13, 1995, and entitled "Defector Describes North Construction Industry." (Hereafter FBIS, *East Asia*.)

5. For a well-structured review of North Korea's economic history, see Doowon Lee,

"North Korean Economic Reform: Past Efforts and Future Prospects," in John McMillan and Barry Naughton, eds., *Reforming Asian Socialism: The Growth of Market Institutions* (University of Michigan Press, 1996), pp. 317–36.

6. The organization and information in figure 3-1, as well as the following discussion, are largely based on Lee, "North Korean Economic Reform."

7. Joseph S. Chung, "The Economy," in Andrea Matles Savada, ed., *North Korea: A Country Study* (Washington: Federal Research Division, Library of Congress, 1994), pp. 103–64, see pp. 139–40.

8. Lee, "North Korean Economic Reform," p. 8.

9. Sang-In Jun, "A Maker of vs. a Victim of History: A Comparative-Historical Study of Economic Reforms and Developments in Vietnam and North Korea," *Korean Journal of National Unification*, special ed., 1993, pp. 59–96, see p. 73.

10. Yonhap News Agency, April 26, 1999.

11. Chon Kyong-no, "An Important Question in Tapping Inner Reserves," *Minju Choson*, June 17, 1997, p. 3.

12. Cost estimates for the festival, attended by 20,000 visitors, are from "Analysis: Summing Up—1989," *Vantage Point*, vol. 12, (December 1989), p. 12.

13. Lee, "North Korean Economic Reform," p. 8.

14. "Communiqué of Plenary Meeting of C.C., WPK on Fulfillment of Third Seven-Year Plan," KCNA broadcast of December 9, 1993; transcribed by FBIS, *East Asia*, 93-235, December 9, 1993, and entitled "KCNA Summarizes Communiqué," pp. 19–22, quotation on p.19.

15. "Communiqué of Plenary Meeting of C.C.," p. 21.

16. "Let Us Adhere to the Line on Building a Self-Reliant National Economy to the End."

17. "SPA Approves New State Budget, Focuses on National Defense, Economic Construction," *The People's Korea*, no. 1840 (April 14, 1999), pp. 1, 3.

18. For the text of the law, see *The People's Korea*, no. 1840 (April 21, 1999), pp. 2–3. Some excerpts follow. Article 3: "It is the consistent policy of the DPRK to manage and operate the people's economy under centralized and unified guidance." Article 25: "Organizations, enterprises and groups register people's economic plans if need be with the organs in charge. An unregistered people's economic plan does not receive required labor, facilities, materials or funds." Article 27: "It is mandatory for organizations, enterprises and groups to precisely implement people's economic plans." Article 36: "No items that are not included in people's economic plans can be produced." Article 48: "Those in charge of organizations, enterprises and groups, their staff and individuals who violate this Law and bring severe damage to the people's economic plans, assume administrative and penal responsibilities."

19. Information according to D-16, a North Korean journalist who defected in 1996.

20. Information on everyday life in North Korea is not easy to come by. Visitors to the country are rarely permitted to see life in its "unstaged" form. The single best source is testimony from. The information on standard of living is primarily from the following sources, most of them compiled by the ROK government: Hwang, Eui-Gak, *Pukhan Kyongjeron:*

Nam-Pukhan Kyongjeui Hyonhwang'gwa Pigyo (The North Korean Economy: The Current Situation and a Comparison of South-North Korean Economies) (Seoul: Nanam, 1992); *Pukhan Kaeyo '95* (An Introduction to North Korea, '95) (Seoul: Ministry of National Unification, 1995) pp. 285–301; *Topyoro-bon Pukhanui Onul* (Today's North Korea Seen through Charts) (Seoul: Ministry of Information, 1993). A thorough English language source devoted to North Korean life, based on information gleaned from defectors by the CIA in the 1970s, is Helen-Louise Hunter, *Kim Il-song's North Korea* (Westport, Conn.: Praeger, 1999).

21. Hunter, *Kim Il-song's North Korea*, p. 160.

22. According to D-18, a medical professional who defected from North Korea in the mid-1990s, this is just one of many similar phrases used by the government to justify withholding food from the people, even as they starve.

23. Many articles are available on the food crisis in North Korea and its impact on the physical and mental condition of the people. See, for example, Chang Namsoo (a professor of food and nutrition at Ewha Women's University in Seoul), "Status of Food Shortage and Malnutrition in North Korea," *Korea Focus*, vol. 7 (January-February 1999), pp. 47–55; Philo Kim, "The Sociopolitical Impact of Food Crisis in North Korea," *Korea and World Affairs*, vol. 23 (Summer 1999), pp. 207–24. From July to September 1998, 440 North Korean immigrants in Northern China at fifteen randomly selected sites were interviewed in a program sponsored by a Johns Hopkins team. Survey results of food intake and mortality estimates are reported in W. Courtland Robinson and others, "Mortality in North Korean Migrant Households: A Retrospective Study," *Lancet*, vol. 354 (July 24, 1999), pp. 291–95.

24. Besides the previously cited sources, see Andrew Natsios, "The Politics of Famine in North Korea," special report (Washington: U.S. Institute of Peace, August 2, 1999). Natsios served as assistant administrator of the Agency for International Development's Bureau of Food and Humanitarian Assistance and as vice president for World Vision, an international relief agency.

25. *Pukhan Kaeyo '95* (An Introduction to North Korea, '95), pp. 285–301. See also *White Paper on Human Rights in North Korea, 1996* (Seoul: Research Institute for National Unification, 1996), p. 63.

26. For example, Kim Il Sung, "New Year Address," *The People's Korea*, no. 1544 (January 18, 1992), p. 2.

27. "News conference by DPRK Air Force Pilot Yi Chol-su," KBS-1 Television Network [Seoul], May 28, 1996; translated by FBIS, *East Asia*, 96-104 (May 29, 1996) and entitled "DPRK Defector's 28 May News Conference," pp. 18–24, especially p. 20.

28. News conference by Yong-hwan Ko, KBS-1 Television Network, September 13, 1991; translated by FBIS, *East Asia*, 91-179, September 16, 1991, and entitled "North Defector Gives News Conference," pp. 18–23, quotation on p. 20.

29. For example, see Janos Kornai, *The Socialist System: The Political Economy of Communism* (Princeton University Press, 1992).

30. "Episodes That Bloomed on That Day," *Nodong Sinmun*, November 26, 1998, p. 3.

31. Chong Kwang-pok, "Improving the Quality of Products," *Nodong Sinmun*, July 31, 1999.

32. An observation from a North Korean journalist who defected in 1996.

33. See Kim Jong Il's November 4, 1994, treatise entitled "Socialism Is a Science," broadcast by KCNA on November 7, 1994, transcribed by FBIS, *East Asia*, 94-215, November 7, 1994, and entitled "'Full' Text of Kim's 'Socialism Is a Science,'" pp. 38–49, quotation on p. 46.

34. Ho-ik Chang, "The Rational Utilization of Economic Levers for Promoting the Development of Science and Technology," *Kyongje Yongu*, August 20, 1998, pp. 21–23.

35. WheeGook Kim, *The Impact of Regional and Global Developments on the Korean Peninsula*, paper presented to the Joint Conference on Change and Challenge on the Korean Peninsula, Washington, Center for Strategic and International Studies and the Korea Institute for National Unification (Washington: East-West Institute, 1995).

36. A good analysis of North Korea's agricultural policies and the agricultural management system may be found in Hong Sun-chik, "North Korea's Agricultural Management," *Tongil Kyongje*, May 15, 1998, pp. 99–107.

37. Kwon T'ae-chin, "Agricultural Policy," *Tongil Kyongje*, September 1999, pp. 10–15.

38. Rather than allow their families to starve, farm workers "preharvested" grain when the government grain rations were reduced, especially after 1995. The World Food Program estimates that half of the 1996 corn harvest went missing. Defectors report cases of farm house roofs collapsing under the weight of grain hidden in the rafters. See Natsios, "Politics of Famine."

39. Larry Niksch, "North Korean Food Shortages: U.S. and Allied Responses," *CRS Report to Congress* (Washington: Congressional Research Service, 1997); and Kim Woon-keun, "Recent Changes in North Korean Agricultural Policies and Projected Impacts on the Food Shortage," *East Asian Review*, vol. 11 (Fall 1999), pp. 93–110.

40. Natsios, "Politics of Famine."

41. Kwon, "Agricultural Policy."

42. In the (exaggerated) expression of a young man who defected from North Korea in 1996.

43. Kap-che Cho, "Recorded Tape of Kim Chong-il's Live Voice—60 Minutes of Astonishing Confessions Similar to That of a Reactionary," *Wolgan Choson*, October 1995, pp. 104–28; translated by FBIS, *East Asia*, 95-213, November 3, 1995, and entitled "Transcript of Kim Chong-il 'Secret' Tape Viewed," pp. 40–52, quotation on p. 45.

44. A review of forty studies on North Korea's prospects may be found in Kongdan Oh and Ralph Hassig, "North Korea between Collapse and Reform," *Asian Survey*, vol. 39 (March-April 1999), pp. 287–309.

45. Nicholas Eberstadt, "North Korea: Reform, Muddling Through, or Collapse?" *NBR Analysis* (National Bureau of Asian Research), vol. 4 (September 1993). A few additional shortcomings of the North Koreans' approach to economic affairs are listed in Eberstadt's "South Korea's Economic Crisis and the Prospects for North-South Relations," *Korea and World Affairs*, vol. 22 (Winter 1998), pp. 539–49.

46. Hong Soon-jick, "North Korea's Industrial Management System," *East Asian Review*, vol. 10 (Summer 1998), pp. 94–105; see also Hy-Sang Lee, *North Korea: A Strange Socialist Fortress* (forthcoming).

47. Yim Ul-ch'ul, "End of Experiment for Opening Najin-Sonbong?" *Hangyore 21* (Chollian database version), February 4, 1999.

48. Andrew Pollack, "Rajin Journal; The Real North Korea: The Bustle of a Mausoleum," *New York Times*, September 23, 1996 (electronic version).

49. Hong, "North Korea's Agricultural Management."

50. Vasily Mikheev, "Reforms of the North Korean Economy: Requirements, Plans and Hopes," *Korean Journal of Defense Analysis*, vol. 5 (Summer 1993); reprinted in the ROK National Unification Board's *Information Service*, 1993, no. 3 (June 30, 1993), pp. 52–66.

51. Mikheev, "Reforms of the North Korean Economy," p. 56.

52. Ch'oe Son-yong, "Truth about the Accounting Department of the DPRK Kumsusan Assembly Hall: Caretaker of the Kim Jong Il Family Assets," Yonhap News Agency, December 2, 1999, pp. E1-E2.

53. David E. Kaplan, "The Wiseguy Regime," *U.S. News & World Report*, February 15, 1999, pp. 36–39.

54. Kwon Kyong-pok, "Reorganization of DPRK Trade Offices and Its Implication," *Tongil Kyongje*, July 1999, pp. 79–87.

55. Yim Ul-ch'ul, "End of Experiment for Opening Najin-Sonbong?" See also Im Kangt'aek, "Foreign Trade Policy," *Tongil Kyongje*, September 9, 1999, pp. 16–23.

56. *DPRK Report No. 8*, a product of a joint project between the Center for Nonproliferation Studies (Monterey Institute of International Studies) and the Institute for Contemporary International Problems at the Diplomatic Academy, Moscow. Reported in NAPSNet e-mail.

57. "KCNA on Japan's False Propaganda," KCNA, September 8, 1999.

58. A wealth of information exists on North Korea's secondary economies, much of it gleaned from defectors. An excellent brief overview is provided by Chun Hong-taek, "The Characteristics and Function of the Second Economy in North Korea," *Vantage Point*, vol. 20 (April 1997), pp. 28–37; and Chun, "The Second Economy in North Korea," *Seoul Journal of Economics*, vol. 12 (1999), pp. 173–94. The article also appeared in *Tongil Kyongje*, February 1997, pp. 48–67. A broader view of North Korea's economy, including consideration of the second economy, may be found in Kwon O-hong, "A Study of North Korean Commercial Practices: Practical Approaches and Mistakes," *Tongil Kyongje*, October 1, 1997, pp. 42–62. For a book-length examination, see the analysis (in Korean) by fourteen South Korean economists in Choi Su-young, ed., *Pukhanui Che 2-Kyongje* (The Second Economy of North Korea) (Seoul: Korean Institute for National Unification, 1997).

59. Deng's economic reforms were endorsed by the third plenary meeting of the 11th Chinese Communist Party (CCP) Congress, which met in December 1978. Excellent sources on Chinese reforms are Minxin Pei, *From Reform to Revolution: The Demise of Communism in China and the Soviet Union* (Harvard University Press, 1994) on which the following account is based; Harry Harding, *China's Second Revolution, Reform after Mao* (Brookings, 1987); and Jean C. Oi, *Rural China Takes Off: Institutional Foundations of Economic Reform* (University of California Press, 1999).

60. Pei, *From Reform to Revolution*, p. 119.

61. Ibid., p. 127.

62. David Remnick, *Lenin's Tomb: The Last Days of the Soviet Empire* (Random House, 1993), pp. 409, 410.

63. Remnick, *Lenin's Tomb*, p. 212.

64. Ibid., p. 313.

65. Hwang Kyong-o, "Principal Economic Laws That Function in the Market Economy," *Kyongje Yongu*, February 10, 1997, pp. 20–23.

66. Ch'oe Yong-ok, "The Trade Policy Presented by Our Party Today and Its Correctness," *Kyongje Yongu*, April 10, 1997, pp. 13–18. Emphasis added.

67. Ch'oe, "Trade Policy."

68. To take two examples: Kim Nam-sun, "The Way to Do a Good Job of International Settlements Resulting from External Trade," *Kyongje Yongu*, November 15, 1997, pp. 22–25, and Song-hui Yi, "Intrinsic Features of Joint-Venture Companies and Their Role," *Kyongje Yongu*, April 10, 1997, pp. 39–41.

69. Ki-song Yi, "The Direction of Economic Management for the Present Period and Correct Use of the Potential of the Self-Dependent National Economy as Elucidated by the Great Leader Comrade Kim Chong-il," *Kyongje Yongu*, November 15, 1997, pp. 2–6.

70. See, for example, Lee Young-hwa, *Pyongyang Pimil Chiphueui* (Pyongyang Night with Secret Gatherings) (Seoul: Dong-A Publication, 1994), p. 220.

71. Kil-Nam Oh, a South Korean economist who had Marxist inclinations, emigrated to North Korea from Germany, where he received a rude awakening. He managed to escape a year later, and has written an insider's view of the "daydreaming" economic plans of the Pyongyang elite. "Pukhan Chonggwonui Kyungje Chongch'ack: Punsokkwa Chonmang" (Economic Policy of the DPRK Regime: Analysis and Prospects), in An Chong-Su and others, eds., *Pukhan Chonggwonui Haengdong: Punsokkwa Chonmang* (Behavior of the DPRK Regime: Analysis and Prospects) (Seoul: Munwusa, 1993), pp. 157–206.

72. Lewis Carroll, *Through the Looking Glass*, in Martin Gardner, ed., *The Annotated Alice* (Bramhall House, 1960).

73. "New Year's Address by Comrade Kim Il Sung," Pyongyang Domestic Service, January 1, 1990; translated by FBIS, *East Asia*, 90-001, January 2, 1990, and entitled "Kim Il-song Delivers 1990 New Year's Address," pp. 11–16, quotation on p. 12.

74. "New Year Address of President Kim Il Sung," *The People's Korea*, No. 1544 (January 18, 1992), pp. 2–4, quotation on p. 2.

75. "New Year Address by President Kim Il Sung," *The People's Korea*, No. 1633 (January 15, 1994), pp. 2–3.

76. "Let Us Advance Vigorously in the New Year, Flying the Red Flag," Joint Editorial of *Nodong Sinmun, Choson Inmingun*, and *Nodong Chongnyun*, *The People's Korea*, no. 1726 (January 13, 1996), pp. 5–7.

77. "Let Us Build Our Country, Our Fatherland, to Be Richer and Stronger under the Great Party's Leadership," Joint Editorial of *Nodong Sinmun, Choson Inmingun*, and *Nodong Chongnyun*, January 1, 1997.

78. "Let Us Push Ahead with the General March of the New Year, Following the Great

Party's Leadership," Joint Editorial of *Nodong Sinmun* and *Choson Inmingun*, December 31, 1997.

79. "Let's Make This Year Mark a Turning Point in Building a Powerful Nation," Joint Editorial of *Nodong Sinmun, Choson Inmingun*, and *Chongnyun Chonwi, The People's Korea*, no. 1833 (January 16, 1999), pp. 2–3.

80. Kim Chin-o, "We Can Do Our Farming without Chemical Fertilizer, Vinyl Sheet," *Nodong Sinmun*, February 21, 1999.

81. KCBN television broadcast, July 20, 1997, translated by FBIS, *East Asia*, March 4, 1999.

82. An excellent analysis of the North Korean economy, which supports the conclusion that no fundamental reforms will be adopted, is Chun Hongtack and Kim Sang-gi, *Pukhan Kyongjeui Hyunhwanggwa Silsang* (The Current Situation and Reality of the North Korean Economy) (Seoul: Korea Development Institute, 1997).

83. *Nodong Sinmun*, January 27, 1999. The article says that "Rabbit raising is something that is worth a try for anyone, and is a work to be carried out by the entire masses. Each person has had experience in raising rabbits. Therefore, rabbit raising can be carried out in schools, homes, work sites or any other places. People often think that rabbit raising is a work for children. However, this is not true. It is an important policy-level issue for implementing the party's policy." A few months later the vice minister of agriculture weighed in with his advice on rabbit raising. He noted that the government was in the process of taking "overall control and command of the rabbit-raising movement" and had also organized a Rabbit Society. From an article by Kye Song-nam entitled "Another Drive with the Force of a Gale: Remarks of a Vice Minister of Agriculture," *Nodong Sinmun*, July 30, 1999, p. 3. Rabbits (and other grazing animals) are not the only home-grown sources of meat. For some years visitors to Pyongyang have been told that apartment dwellers have taken to raising livestock in their apartments as a means of supplementing their food rations.

84. Douglas Farah and Thomas W. Lippman, "The North Korean Connection," *Washington Post*, March 22, 1999, pp. A21, A22.

85. "Let Us Adhere to the Line on Building a Self-Reliant National Economy to the End."

86. Oh, "Pukhan Chonggwonui Kyungje Chongch'ack."

Chapter Four

1. "Kim Jong Il Emerges as the Lodestar for Sailing the 21st Century," *New York Times* [headline from a full-page advertisement], December 16, 1997, p. A21.

2. The most authoritative English-language source on Kim Il Sung is Dae-sook Suh's *Kim Il Sung, The North Korean Leader* (Columbia University Press, 1988). More recently, Adrian Buzo's *The Guerilla Dynasty: Politics and Leadership in North Korea* (Westview Press, 1999) depicts Kim as a leader in the Stalinist mold rather than a modern-day Confucian-style leader.

3. Buzo, *The Guerilla Dynasty*, p. 241.

4. The mythology of Kim Jong Il's early years is peeled away in the following sources:

Osamu Megumiya, "Secret of Kim Chong-il's Birth and Life of His Mother, Kim Jong-suk," *Seikai Orai*, August 1992, pp. 34–39; and in an ROK government publication, *The True Story of Kim Jong-il* (Seoul: Institute of South-North Korea Studies, 1993). Kim's later life is covered in a series of articles by So Song-u, Chon Hyon-chun, Kim Chong-min, and an uncredited resume of Kim, published in the February 1994 issue of *Pukhan*; translated by Foreign Broadcast Information Service, *Daily Report: East Asia*, 94-095, May 17, 1994, pp. 34–41. (Hereafter FBIS, *East Asia*.) The official North Korean version of Kim's life, a hagiography of highly dubious veracity, is entitled *Kim Jong Il, The Lodestar of the 21st Century*. It is being published serially on the KCNA-affiliated website maintained by a pro-North Korean Japanese organization: www.kcna.co.jp/works/work.htm (accessed February 2000).

5. Megumiya, "Secret of Kim Chong-il's Birth," pp. 34–39.

6. Kong Dan Oh, *Leadership Change in North Korean Politics: The Succession to Kim Il Sung*, R-3697-RC (Santa Monica: Rand, 1988), p. 7.

7. Oh, *Leadership Change*, p. 8.

8. Morgan E. Clippinger, "Kim Chong-il in the North Korean Mass Media: A Study of Semi-Esoteric Communication," *Asian Survey*, vol. 21 (March 1981), pp. 289–309.

9. *A Handbook on North Korea*, first rev. (Seoul: Naewoe Press, November 1998), pp. 16–17.

10. Lee Yang-gu, *Kim Jong Il kwa kuui ch'ammodul* (Kim Jong Il and His Brain Trust) (Seoul: Shintaeyangsa, 1995), pp. 283–90, 374. See also Kang Myong-do, *Pyongyang un mangmyongul kkumkkunda* (Pyongyang Dreams of Defection) (Seoul: *Joong-Ang Daily News*, 1995), pp. 66–69.

11. Interview with a former North Korean diplomat who defected in the early 1990s.

12. Shiozuka Mamoru, "Watch on North Korea—Secretary Kim Jong Il's Financial Resources and Connections: We Hear from Ko Yong-hwan, Ex-DPRK Diplomat" (in Japanese), *Sankei Shimbun*, November 21, 1992, morning edition, p. 4.

13. Oh, *Leadership Change*, p. 14.

14. See, for example, "Kim Jong-il Era Dawns, with Military's Status Enhanced," *Vantage Point*, vol. 21 (September 1988), p. 1.

15. Teresa Watanabe, "N. Korean Heir Apparent Is a Bizarre Enigma," *Los Angeles Times*, July 10, 1994, p. 1.

16. "Sacred Traces Which Replaced the New Year's Speech," talk on KCBN, January 28, 1998.

17. The 1997 meeting with Baeri is described in Tetsuo Sakamoto, *Sankei Shimbun*, October 17, 1992, morning ed., p. 4. The 1994 meeting with Valori is described in *The People's Korea*, no. 1660 (August 6, 1994), p. 1.

18. "Hwang Chang-yop Answers Reporters' Questions," KBS Television, Seoul, July 10, 1997, translated by the BBC Summary of World Broadcasts, July 15, 1997.

19. Megumiya, "Secret of Kim Chong-il's Birth," pp. 34–39.

20. Ian Buruma, "Following the Great Leader," *New Yorker*, September 19, 1994, pp. 66–74, quotation on p. 71.

21. See "Table Talk: Hwang Jang Yop and Shin Sang-ok Talk about the Two Homelands They Have Experienced," *Wolgan Choson*, March 1999, pp. 609–41.

22. Yi Ki-pong, "Kim Jong Il's Pathological Womanizing," *Chugan Choson*, April 12, 1992, pp. 74–77, translated by FBIS, *East Asia*, 92-097, May 19, 1992, pp. 25–27.

23. Interview with Yi Nam-ok, niece and adopted daughter of Kim Jong Il, in *Bungei Shunju*, February 1998, pp. 274–92.

24. Kap-che Cho, "Recorded Tape of Kim Chong-il's Live Voice—60 Minutes of Astonishing Confessions Similar to That of a Reactionary," *Wolgan Choson*, October 1995, pp. 104–28, translated by FBIS, *East Asia*, 95-213, November 3, 1995, pp. 40–52. While residing in the United States, the film director Sang-ok Shin and his actress wife Eun-hi Choi authored a two-volume work (available only in an out-of-print Korean edition) about their experiences in North Korea: *Choguk-un chohanul chomolli* (Diary: The Motherland Is Beyond the Sky and Far Away) (Pacific Palisades, Calif.: Pacific Artist Corporation, 1988). See also "Table Talk: Hwang Jang Yop and Shin Sang-ok Talk about the Two Homelands They Have Experienced."

25. A North Korean, who worked as an intelligence agent and defected in the early 1990s, says he heard that Kim Jong Il became angry with the arrogant behavior of one of his closest associates, Chang Song-taek (Kim's brother-in-law), and shot Chang's assistant to teach Chang a lesson.

26. Interview with a former North Korean diplomat who defected in the early 1990s.

27. Mike Chinoy, *China Live: Two Decades in the Heart of the Dragon* (Atlanta: Turner Publishing, 1997), p. 318.

28. The most serious coup attempt, by the military, is described by Kwang-chu Son, "Kim Chong-il and the Military," *Sindong-a*, October 1997, pp. 210–37. This incident is reviewed in chapter 5.

29. Interview with a former North Korean security officer who defected in the early 1990s.

30. Interview with Yi Nam-ok by *Bungei Shunju*.

31. Report on an interview with Carlo Baeri by Tetsuo Sakamoto in *Sankei Shimbun*, October 17, 1992.

32. Hyun-sik Kim and Kwang-ju Son, *Documentary Kim Jong Il* (in Korean with these title words written in Hangul) (Seoul: Chongji Media, 1997), p. 202.

33. "Table Talk: Hwang Jang Yop and Shin Sang-ok Talk about the Two Homelands They Have Experienced."

34. "Three Commanders' Exploits Glorified," KCNA, March 3, 1999.

35. KCNA, March 13, 1998.

36. Kim and Son, *Documentary Kim Jong Il.*

37. "Story about Kim Jong Il's Lunch with Workers," KCNA, July 31, 1998.

38. "General Kim Jong Il's Simplicity," KCNA, March 5, 1998.

39. Ch'il-nam Cho'oe and Ch'ol Pak, "Sacred Three Years," *Nodong Sinmun*, July 2, 1997, pp. 3–4.

40. "Traffic Control Women's Appearance Renewed," KCNA, January 31, 1997.

41. *Kim Jong Il, The Lodestar of the 21st Century* .

42. "Table Talk: Hwang Jang Yop and Shin Sang-ok Talk about the Two Homelands They Have Experienced."

43. For accounts of Kim's first days back in Korea under the Russians, see Sydney A. Seiler, *Kim Il-song, 1941-1948: The Creation of a Legend, The Building of a Regime* (University Press of America, 1994). An interesting eyewitness account of this period by the Russians is provided in an article by Leonid Vasin, "Steps Toward the Throne, Kim Il-song: Who Is He?" *Nezavisimaya Gazeta*, September 29, 1993, p. 5; translated by FBIS, *East Asia*, 94-021, February 1, 1994, pp. 28–34.

44. Kim Il Sung, "On Eliminating Dogmatism and Formalism and Establishing Juche in Ideological Work," Speech to Party Propaganda and Agitation Workers, December 28, 1955, in *Kim Il Sung Works*, vol. 9 (Pyongyang: Foreign Languages Publishing House, 1982), pp. 395–417, quotation on p. 396.

45. Ibid. p. 400.

46. A young North Korean medical professional who fled to China in the middle 1990s says, "I was going through a magazine [while visiting the ROK embassy in Beijing]. One journal was familiar to me: *Red Army* [a Russian military journal]. The journal carried an article about President [Boris] Yeltsin's recent visit to South Korea, and his delivering some archival material on the Korean War. I read the article and found out that the war was triggered by Kim Il Sung. I did not believe it, and asked a man at the embassy. He laughed and told me what he knew. If the journal had not been from Russia, I still would have believed the article was fabricated by South Korea. . . . I had not believed in Juche, but I did believe in Kim Il Sung. . . . So I decided to go to South Korea to learn more."

47. Early in his political career (by the end of the 1960s), Kim Jong Il was referred to as "Dear Leader Comrade" (*Chinaehanun Jidoja Tongji*). Two days before his father's death, he was referred to for the first time in *Nodong Sinmun* as *Yongdoja* (Leader). Beginning in January 1995 he began to be referred to as *Widaehan Yongdoja* (Great Leader). He is routinely equated with his father, the *Suryong*, but so far as we are aware, has never been addressed by that most exalted title in the North Korean press. See Young Whan Jo, *Maeu Tukpyolhan Inmul Kim Jong Il* (Very Special Person, Kim Jong Il) (Seoul: *Jisik Kongjakso*, 1996), pp. 220–27.

48. In an update on the "revolutionary view of the leader," *Minju Choson* in 1999 insists that "The great Comrade Kim Jong Il is exactly the same as the respected and beloved leader [Kim Il Sung] in ideology, leadership, and moral influence—he is today's Comrade Kim Il Sung." Hwang ch'ol-su, "The Revolutionary View of the Leader," *Minju Choson*, August 22, 1999, p. 2.

49. "Let Us Accomplish Revolutionary Cause of Chuche under Leadership of the Great Comrade Kim Chong-il," *Nodong Sinmun*, June 19, 1996, cited by KCNA on June 19, 1996, and translated by FBIS, *East Asia*, 96-120, June 20, 1996, entitled "*Nodong Sinmun* Commemorates Kim Chong-il's WPK Career," p. 21.

50. David C. McClelland, *Human Motivation* (Scott Foresman, 1985).

51. Headline from a full-page advertisement in the *New York Times* taken out by a Japanese entity called "The Committee for Translating and Publishing Kim Jong Il's Works," December 16, 1997, p. A21.

Chapter Five

1. Pak Nam-chin, "Immortal Course during Which the Military Assurance for the Consummation of the Chuch'e Cause Has Been Provided," *Nodong Sinmun,* June 26, 1997, p. 3.

2. Although the 1998 constitution does not make the chairmanship of the NDC the highest state position, this ranking was explicitly made by SPA Presidium Chairman Kim Young Nam, the formal head of state, when he introduced Kim Jong Il to the Assembly. See "Kim Jong Il's Election as NMC [that is, NDC] Chairman Proposed," KCNA, September 5, 1998.

3. See, for example, an article by Hwang Ch'ang-man, "The Great Leader Who Leads the Socialist Cause by His Military-First Revolutionary Leadership," *Nodong Sinmun,* February 28 1999, p. 2.

4. See, for example, the paper by Jinwook Choi, *Changing Relations between Party, Military, and Government in North Korea and Their Impact on Policy Direction* (Palo Alto, Calif.: The Asia/Pacific Research Center, Institute for International Studies, Stanford University, July 1999).

5. Kong Yong-un, "Resumption of Strategic and Diplomatic Relations between the DPRK and Russia after the Lapse of Ten Years," *Munwha Ilbo* (Internet version), February 10, 2000.

6 . Cho Kap-che, "Recorded Tape of Kim Chong-il's Live Voice—60 Minutes of Astonishing Confessions Similar to That of a Reactionary," *Wolgan Choson,* October 1995, pp. 104–28, translated by Foreign Broadcast Information Service, *Daily Report: East Asia,* EAS-95-213, November 3, 1995, and entitled "Transcript of Kim Chong-il 'Secret' Tape Viewed," pp. 40–52, quotation on p. 47. (Hereafter, FBIS, *East Asia.*)

7. Estimates of underground installations made by the ROK's Ministry of National Defense have been published in *Chungang Ilbo* (Internet version), December 8, 1998.

8. "KPA Will Answer U.S. Aggression Forces' Challenge with Annihilating Blow—Statement of KPA General Staff Spokesman," KCNA, December 2, 1998, reprinted in *The People's Korea,* no. 1831 (December 12, 1998), p. 2.

9. *Pukhan Ch'ongram* (A Comprehensive Summary of North Korea) (Seoul: Pukhan Yong'uso (Institute of North Korean Studies, 1983), p. 1460.

10. See, for example, "Paper on Gen. Secy. Kim Chong-il's Military Feats," KCNA, November 4, 1997.

11. For a discussion of irrationality and deterrents, see Robert Mandel, "The Desirability of Irrationality in Foreign Policy Making: A Preliminary Theoretical Analysis," *Political Psychology,* vol. 5 (December 1984), pp. 643–60.

12. "Sooner or Later the U.S. Will Be Aware of What the Korean War Method Is Like," KCNA, December 19, 1998.

13. *Pukhan Ch'ongram,* p. 1460.

14. A survey of North Korea's military capabilities may be found in the ROK's annual *Defense White Paper* (Seoul: Ministry of National Defense, Republic of Korea); see also Joseph S. Bermudez Jr., *The Armed Forces of North Korea* (Sydney, Australia: Allen & Unwin, 1999); a good Korean-language source is Yu Suk-Ryul, *Pukhanui Wigi Chejewa Hanbando Tongil*

(The Crisis Regime of North Korea and the Unification of the Korean Peninsula) (Seoul: Pakyongsa, 1997).

15. According to a KWP cadre who defected to South Korea, North Korea's regular army is backed up by a million reservists ("provincial forces"), 650,000 Young Red Guards (the KWP's young adult organization), and 5 million Worker-Peasant Red Guards. If this esti-mate is correct, one out of three North Koreans is enlisted in some form of military organization. See Kim Chong-min, "Conscription System and Solders' Lives in North Korea," *Pukhan*, August 1999, pp. 134–45.

16. Nicholas Eberstadt and Judith Banister, *The Population of North Korea* (Berkeley, Calif.: University of California Institute of East Asian Studies, 1992).

17. See, for example, Yim Ul-ch'ul, "Evaluation and Prospects of DPRK's Missile Indus-try and Technology," *Tongil Kyongje*, August 1999, pp. 96–104. In the United States, Joseph S. Bermudez Jr. has been a diligent observer of North Korea's missile program. His articles appear frequently in *Jane's Intelligence Review*.

18. See, for example, Joseph S. Bermudez Jr., "North Korea's Chemical and Biological Warfare Arsenal," *Jane's Intelligence Review*, vol. 5 (Asia-May 1993), pp. 225–28. See also John M. Collins, Zachary S. Davis, and Steven R. Bowman, *Nuclear, Biological, and Chem-ical Weapon Proliferation: Potential Military Countermeasures*, CRS Report for Congress, 94-528S (Washington: Congressional Research Service, June 28, 1994). The DPRK has not signed the Chemical Weapons Convention, but it has ratified the Biological and Toxin Weapons Convention. For Defense Department estimates of DPRK NBC capabilities, see Office of the Secretary of Defense, *Proliferation: Threat and Response* (Government Print-ing Office, November 1997), pp. 4–8.

19. "Army Mainstay of Revolution," KCNA, March 9, 1998.

20. Kim Myong-hui, "The Revolutionary Spirit for Suicidal Explosion," *Nodong Sinmun*, December 29, 1998, p. 3.

21. Ch'ung-il Ch'oe, "Core of the Chuch'e-Type Revolutionaries' Ideological and Men-tal Features," article in *Nodong Sinmun*, May 17, 1998, p. 2.

22. Formerly known as the Ministry of Public Security, the MPS received its new name at the Third Session of the Tenth SPA, April 2000.

23. See for example Ul-ch'ul Yim, "Trend and Outlook of North Korea's Recent Shift to Market Economy System," *Tongil Kyongje*, March 1999, pp. 82–89.

24. The "pillar" theme began receiving prominence in early 1997, to be followed in 1998 by the "economically and militarily strong nation" theme. The role of the military and the pillar concept are elaborated in Nam-chin Pak, "Immortal Course."

25. Chong-p'yo Sung, "The Programmatic Masterpiece That Has Made It Possible to Augment Dramatically the Political, Economic and Military Strength of Our Revolution," *Nodong Sinmun*, July 3, 1997, p. 3.

26. Son Kwang-chu, "Kim Jong Il and the Military," *Sindong-a*, October 1997, pp. 210–37.

27. "NHK News 7" documentary on Kim Jong Il, NHK Television (Tokyo), February 29, 1996, translated by FBIS, *East Asia*, February 29, 1996, 96-041, and entitled "NHK Obtains 'Documentary Program' on Kim Chong-il," p. 11.

28. "Comrade Kim Chong-il's Experience of War," KCNA, October 1, 1997.

29. Pak, "Immortal Course."

30. Kim Hong-Kun, "The Respected and Beloved Supreme Commander," *Nodong Sinmun*, April 23, 1998, p. 2.

31. Sung, "The Programmatic Masterpiece."

32. Adrian Buzo, *The Guerilla Dynasty* (Westview Press, 1999).

33. " 'Moving Story' Associated with Ch'ol Ridge," KCNA, October 6, 1999.

34. Kim made thirty-two visits to military sites, eleven visits to nonmilitary sites including economic installations, twenty visits to art and cultural sites, and eight visits to historical spots according to "General Secretary Kim Jong Il's On-the-Spot Guidance Given on Total of 71 Occasions in 1998," *The People's Korea*, no. 1834 (January 30, 1999), p. 2.

35. *Kim Jong Il, The Lodestar of the Twenty-First Century.* This biography is a continuing serial publication found on the KCNA-affiliated website maintained by a pro-North Korean Japanese organization, www.kcna.co.jp.

36. Ibid.

37. Pak, "Immortal Course."

38. *Kim Jong Il, The Lodestar of the 21st Century.*

39. Ibid.

40. To take an example from his biography: "The Supreme Commander Kim Jong Il's responses to the Team Spirit 93 U.S.-South Korean maneuvers, which began early in January 1993, and pressures for nuclear inspections, were his second psychological war against the United States [the first was the capture of the *Pueblo* in 1968, now said to have been directed by Kim].... In this tense situation, the General was full of confidence and free and easy, and telephoned a cadre of the Ministry of People's Armed Forces, when hundreds of thousands of enemy troops were attacking the country from the sky, land and sea and asked him about progress on the construction of a memorial monument.... On March 8, as the situation reached a peak, Leader Kim Jong Il issued Supreme Commander Directive No. 0034, ordering that the entire army, people and country be placed on a semi-wartime footing. The United States was flustered, taken aback by this unexpected order.... In the face of Korea's resolute response, the United States was compelled to terminate Team Spirit early. ... This is recorded in history as the 15-day battle without gunfire." Ibid.

41. Kim, "The Respected and Beloved Supreme Commander."

42. Ibid.

43. Ibid.

44. "Evasion of Military Service by Children of Ranking Cadres Widespread," *Naewoe T'ongsin*, February 5, 1998, pp. F1–F4.

45. Conditions in the KPA are described in the following articles: Pak T'ae-yong, a former Air Force senior lieutenant, in *Wolgan Choson*, August 1999, pp. 62–96; and Kim, "Conscription System."

46. Hwang, "The Great Leader."

Chapter Six

1. Chong-hon Choe, "Thoroughly Establishing the Revolutionary Law-Abiding Spirit Is a Demand to Consolidate the Socialist Foundation like Bed-Rock," *Minju Choson*, January 30, 1997, p. 2.

2. Mike Chinoy, *China Live: Two Decades in the Heart of the Dragon* (Atlanta: Turner Publishing, 1997), p. 5.

3. Ian Buruma, "Following the Great Leader," *New Yorker*, September 19, 1994, pp. 66–74, quotation on p. 68.

4. Don Oberdorfer, *The Two Koreas: A Contemporary History* (Reading, Mass.: Addison-Wesley, 1997), p. 234.

5. Interview with Koh Young-hwan, first secretary of the DPRK embassy in the Congo, before he defected in 1991.

6. Michael Shapiro, "Kim's Ransom," *New Yorker*, January 31, 1997, pp. 32–41, especially p. 37.

7. In 1994 a South Korean real estate company won the bid to rent out office space at the hotel, according to a Yonhap News Agency report of December 28 1994, transcribed by Foreign Broadcast Information Service, *Daily Report: East Asia*, 94-249, December 28, 1994, and entitled "Firm to Rent Office in DPRK's Ryukyong Hotel," p. 43.

8. The three churches are the Bongsu and Chilgol (Bansok) Protestant churches erected in 1986 and 1989, respectively, and the Changchun Catholic Church, built in 1989. For information about religion and worship in North Korea, see the excellent article by Kang In Duk, "North Korea's Policy on Religion," *East Asian Review*, vol. 7 (Autumn 1995), pp. 89–101.

9. Korean Central Television Network, a translated compilation of reports by FBIS, *East Asia*, 95-149, August 3, 1995, on short programs broadcast between July 26 and August 2, 1995, pp. 47–48.

10. Interview with a senior medical professional who defected in the mid-1990s.

11. Shapiro, "Kim's Ransom."

12. Kim Yong-song, "An Account of My Personal Experience as a Battalion Commander of a Building Workers' Shock Regiment for the Construction of Kwangbok Boulevard, Pyongyang," *Wolgan Choson*, November 1994, pp. 37–44, translated by FBIS, *East Asia*, January 13, 1995, and entitled "Defector Describes North Construction Industry," pp. 37–44.

13. *Pukhan Ch'ongram* (A Comprehensive Summary of North Korea) (Seoul: Pukhan Yon'guso [Institute of North Korean Studies], 1983). *Pukhan Kaeyo '92* (An Introduction to North Korea, '92) (Seoul: Ministry of National Unification, 1992), pp. 266–69. *White Paper on Human Rights in North Korea, 1996* (Seoul: Research Institute for National Unification, 1996), pp. 77–82.

14. *White Paper on Human Rights in North Korea, 1999* (Seoul: Korea Institute for National Unification, 1999), pp. 16–17.

15. Ibid., pp. 3–4. In the report, the 1997 U.S. State Department estimate of 150,000-200,000 is mentioned.

16. The inhumane conditions in concentration camps are described by former prison-

ers and guards. An excellent survey is provided by Yoon Hyun, "'The Gulag Archipelago': North Korea, Past and Present," *East Asian Review*, vol. 10 (Autumn 1998), pp. 38–55. Testimony of An Myong-chol, a former prison camp guard who defected in 1994, is presented in *Political Prisoners' Camps in North Korea* (Seoul: Center for the Advancement of North Korean Human Rights, 1995). Another firsthand account of prison conditions is provided by Im Kyong-su, a former security officer who fled to China, in his memoir, "The Inside of DPRK Ministry of Public Security: A Prison Empire of Corruption, Conspiracy, and Torture," *Wolgan Choson*, June 1999, pp. 340–70.

17. "'There Is No Human Rights Problem in Our Country': DPRK," *The People's Korea*, no. 1661 (August 13, 1994), p. 8.

18. Interview with a KPA officer who defected in the mid-1990s.

19. A good description of the MPS is provided by Im, "The Inside of DPRK Ministry of Public Security: A Prison Empire of Corruption, Conspiracy, and Torture."

20. Koh Young-hwan, *Wonderland* (Seoul: Institute of North Korean Affairs, 1994).

21. Im, "The Inside of DPRK Ministry of Public Security: A Prison Empire of Corruption, Conspiracy, and Torture."

22. For information on security in the military, see "Organization and Role of Military Political Organs," *Naewoe T'ongsin* (Seoul), January 15, 1998, pp. B1–B6.

23. "Purges, Rising Status of Military Examined," *Chungang Ilbo* (Internet version), October 1999.

24. For information on the Security Command, see Yi Chong-hun, "We Uncover the Veils of the Security Command of the North Korean Army," *Sisa Journal*, November 6, 1997, pp. 72–73.

25. Yong-chong Yi, "'Security Command Engineers Purges in DPRK,' - Hwang Jang-yop," *Chungang Ilbo* (Internet version), February 11, 1999.

26. Ul-ch'ul Yim, "Trend and Outlook of North Korea's Recent Shift to Market Economy System," *Tongil Kyongje*, March 1999, pp. 82–89.

27. According to Hwang Jang Yop, the KWP's agriculture secretary, So Kwan-hui, was publicly executed in 1997 ostensibly for corruption in office but in reality as a scapegoat for the inability of the agricultural sector to recover from the natural disasters that struck the country beginning in 1995. See "Table Talk: Hwang Jang Yop and Shin Sang-ok Talk about the Two Homelands They Have Experienced," *Wolgan Choson*, March 1999, pp. 609–41.

28. "One More North Korean 'Surprise,'" *Korea Herald* (Internet version), October 7, 1997.

29. According to a report of *Korea Times* (Internet version), June 29, 1999; and Kim Ji-ho, "Nightmare Haunts Housewife Detained during Kumgang Tour—Under Close Scrutiny for Mental Duress, Min Young-mi Says North Korea Used Her to Save Face," *Korea Herald* (Internet version), July 27, 1999.

30. "S. Korean Rulers Urged to Discontinue Anti-North False Propaganda," KCNA, July 3, 1999.

31. According to South Korea's *Chungang Ilbo* (Internet version), March 8, 1999, North

Korean residents in border areas are shown a film entitled "The Actual State of Those Who Betrayed the Fatherland," which includes fake footage of South Korean soldiers shooting North Korean defectors to death. Also interview with a medical professional who defected in the mid-1990s.

32. Two defectors whom we have interviewed claim they engineered their release from prison by such means. One was a medical professional and the other was a truck driver and foreign currency earner who defected in the mid-1990s.

33. Interview with Koh Young-hwan, 1997.

34. Nicholas Eberstadt and Judith Banister, *The Population of North Korea* (Berkeley, Calif.: University of California, Institute of East Asian Studies, Center for Korean Studies, 1992), pp. 75–79.

35. Helen-Louise Hunter, *Kim Il-song's North Korea* (Praeger, 1999), p. 7.

36. Choi Eun-soo, "North Korea's Educational Policy," *Vantage Point*, vol. 19 (December 1996), pp. 25–31.

37. Choi Young-gyun and Kim Hung-ju, *Pukhan-gwa Chungguk-ui Kyoyuk Chedo Pigyo Yon'gu* (Comparative Studies of the Education Systems of North Korea and China) (Seoul: Korea Institute of Education Development Research, 1988), p. 174, cited in Kim Hyung-chan, "Chodung Kyoyuk" (Primary Education), pp. 227–55, in Kim, ed., *Pukhan-ui Kyoyuk* (Education in North Korea) (Seoul: Eulyu Munhwasa, 1990), p. 248.

38. Dongho Jo, *The Quality of North Korean Labor and Implications for Inter-Korean Economic Cooperation*, Working Paper (Korea Development Institute, November 1996), p. 8.

39. Kim Hyung-Chan, "Chodung Kyoyuk," pp. 219–51.

40. Hunter, *Kim Il-song's North Korea*, p. 214.

41. Ibid.

42. "Haksaengddul-e taehan sahoe kyoyuk-ul kanghwahalde taehan tang-ui pangchim-gwa silhyun" (The Party's Principle and Implementation to Strengthen Social Education of Students), *Nodong Sinmun*, October 4, 1973. Cited in Choi Un-sil, "Pukhan-ui sahoe kyoyuk: sahoe kyoyuk-ui cheje-wa silche" (Social Education in North Korea: System and Reality), in Kim, "Chodung Kyoyuk," p. 319; and Hunter, *Kim Il-song's North Korea*, p. 216.

43. Ibid., "Pukhan," pp. 318–35.

44. Interview with a North Korean graduate student who defected while studying in China in the mid-1990s.

45. Interview with Koh Young-hwan, 1997.

46. Interview with a DPRK public official who defected in the mid-1990s.

47. Interview with an employee of a North Korean foreign-currency-earning firm who defected in the mid-1990s.

48. Interview with a North Korean college student who defected in the early 1990s.

49. Interview with Koh Young-hwan, 1997.

50. Chung Suk-hong, *Nam-Pukhan Bigyron* (Comparative Studies of North and South Korea) (Seoul: Saram-gwa saram Publishing, 1997), p. 49.

51. Victor N. Shaw, *Social Control in China: A Study of Chinese Work Units* (Praeger, 1996).

52. These children, like the swallow that darts from flower to flower, move from one place to another. The Korean phrase originally referred to young prostitutes. *White Paper on Human Rights in North Korea, 1999*, p. 5.

53. For a good review of the history and function of farmers' markets, see Song-kuk Hong, "Realities of North Korean Farmers Market and Its Implications," *Tongil Kyongje*, February 1999, pp. 82–90.

54. Yonhap news report on KBS-1 Radio, January 24, 1999.

55. Interview with a noncommissioned officer in the Korean People's Army who defected in the early 1990s.

56. Interview with an employee of a North Korean foreign-currency-earning firm who defected in the mid-1990s.

Chapter Seven

1. "Let's Make This Year Mark a Turning Point in Building a Powerful Nation," Joint Editorial of *Nodong Sinmun, Choson Inmingun*, and *Chongnyun Chonwi*, in *The People's Korea*, no. 1833 (January 16, 1999), pp. 2–3. This formula is similar to foreign policy statements in previous years.

2. John K. Fairbank, Edwin O. Reischauer, and Albert M. Craig, *East Asia, Tradition and Transformation* (Houghton Mifflin Company, 1978), p. 610.

3. The sources for this brief history are the same as those in the first chapter; especially, Carter J. Eckert and others, *Korea Old and New: A History* (Seoul: Ilchokak Publishers for the Korea Institute, Harvard University, 1990).

4. This is somewhat similar to the distinction between high and low politics in international relations, with high politics referring to military-security issues and low politics referring to social and economic issues. Military-security issues are more likely to be dealt with at the government level, and economic and social issues are often shaped by encounters between business organizations and people.

5. Sydney A. Seiler taps recently released documents to chart Kim Il Sung's activities during World War II and immediately thereafter: *Kim Il-song 1941-1948: The Creation of a Legend, The Building of a Regime* (University Press of America, 1994).

6. Vladimir Yakubovsky, "Key Pages of the History of Russian-Korean Relations: An Attempt at a New Reading," *Korean Journal of Defense Analysis*, vol. 8 (Winter 1996), pp. 315–62.

7. Bruce Cumings, *The Origins of the Korean War: Liberation and the Emergence of Separate Regimes, 1945-1947* (Princeton University Press, 1981). In his study of events leading up to the Korean War, John Merrill points out that by the time of the June 25 invasion, more than 100,000 Koreans from the North and the South had already been killed in border clashes. See John Merrill, *Korea: The Peninsular Origins of the War* (University of Delaware Press, 1989).

8. Yakubovsky, "Key Pages," pp. 315–64.

9. Ibid., quotation on pp. 331–32.

10. Doug Joon Kim, ed., *Foreign Relations of North Korea during Kim Il Sung's Last Days* (Seoul: Sejong Institute, 1994), p. 492.

11. Yakubovsky, "Key Pages," p. 342. Emphasis added.

12. Ibid., p. 361.

13. Ibid., p. 345.

14. *Nodong Sinmun* commentary, October 5, 1990, cited in "Pyongyang Raps Moscow on Diplomatic Ties with Seoul," *The People's Korea*, no. 1491 (October 13, 1990), pp. 1, 8, quotation on p. 8.

15. Yong Chool Ha, "Russo-North Korean Relations in Transition," in Kim, *Foreign Relations of North Korea*, pp. 331–56, especially p. 344.

16. "Mind Your Own Business," KCNA headline reporting on a *Nodong Sinmun* article of April 24, 1993, transcribed by Foreign Broadcast Information Service, *Daily Report: East Asia*, 93-078, April 26, 1993, pp. 28–29. (Hereafter FBIS, *East Asia*).

17. See table 3-3 in chapter 3 for trade volume between 1985 and 1998.

18. "China-N. Korea Treaty Does Not Mean Dispatch of Troops," *Yonhap*, November 14, 1995, transcribed by FBIS, *East Asia*, 95-219, November 14, 1995, entitled "Friendship Pact Does Not Mean Troop Dispatch," p. 54.

19. Taeho Kim provides a 1989–97 visit chronology in English in "Strategic Relations between Beijing and Pyongyang," in James R. Lilley and David Shambaugh, eds., *China's Military Faces the Future* (Washington: American Enterprise Institute Press, 1999), pp. 307–08. Buk-han Gaerjo, *Outline of North Korea* [in Korean] (Seoul: Tong-il Won Chungbo Bunsuksil, 1995).

20. The dynamics of China-Taiwan-North Korea relations are discussed by O Chin-yong, "Sino-North Korean Relations Standing at the Crossroads," *Pukhan*, March 1999, pp. 80–89.

21. Statistics and analyses of Chinese and South Korean trade and their economies are well covered in Doowon Lee and Jason Z. Yin, eds., *Comparison of Korean and Chinese Economic Development: Forecasting Korean-Chinese Bilateral Economic Relations* (Seoul: Yonsei University Press, 1999). Recent trade statistics may be found in Young Rok Cheong, "Prospects for Sino-Korean Economic Cooperation: An Institutional Appraisal," pp. 15–42.

22. See table 3-3, chapter 3, for North Korea-China trade volume between 1985 and 1998.

23. Report by Pak Tu-sik, *Choson Ilbo*, April 17, 1997, p. 2.

24. Kim Il Sung, *The Non-Alignment Movement Is a Mighty Anti-Imperialist Revolutionary Force of Our Times* (Pyongyang: Foreign Languages Publishing House, 1976), especially pp. 10, 11, 15, 16.

25. Nam Sik Kim, "Policy-Making Process and Concepts in Formulating North Korea's Foreign Policy," in Kim, *Foreign Relations of North Korea*, pp. 69-112, see p. 76.

26. Dae-Ho Byun, *North Korea's Foreign Policy: The* Juche *Ideology and the Challenge of Gorbachev's New Thinking* (Seoul: Research Center for Peace and Unification in Korea, 1991), especially pp. 49ff.

27. See "New Year Address of President Kim Il Sung," *The People's Korea*, no. 1633 (January 15, 1994), p. 3.

28. "Let Us Carry Out the Great Leader Comrade Kim Il-song's Instructions for National Reunification," a work published by Kim Jong Il, August 4, 1997, from a KCNA broadcast of August 20, 1997.

29. Kim, *Foreign Relations of North Korea*, p. 509.

30. Hong Nack Kim, "North Korea's Policy toward Japan in the Post-Cold War Era," in Doug Joong Kim, *Foreign Relations of North Korea*, pp. 159–92, especially p. 168. Emphasis added.

31. Kang In-duk, "Efforts to Form a New International Order among the Powers Surrounding the Korean Peninsula," *East Asian Review*, vol. 9 (Winter 1997), pp. 3–19, especially p. 13.

32. Hong Nack Kim, "Japan's Policy toward the Two Koreas in the Post-Cold War Era," *International Journal of Korean Studies*, vol. 1 (Spring 1997), pp. 131–58; see p. 140.

33. "Statement Made by KAPPC (Korean Asia-Pacific Peace Committee) on Issue of 'Japanese Wives,'" *The People's Korea*, no. 1796 (August 2, 1997), p. 6.

34. A comprehensive account of the Japanese encounter with the two boats is Shunji Taoka, "The Grand Sea Chase, Why the Spy Boats Could Not Be Captured," *Sekai no Kansen*, June 1999, pp. 110–13.

35. A DPRK Foreign Ministry spokesman said, "We have no idea of the 'mysterious ships.' At the present juncture, the loud-mouthed 'mysterious ships pursuit case' cannot be construed otherwise than one more anti-DPRK fiction invented by the Japanese reactionaries on purpose. . . . History and facts go to clearly prove that as the general situation turned unfavorable to them this time, they orchestrated their clumsy drama of 'mysterious ships pursuit case' in a bid to justify their militarization moves and break the DPRK-U.S.–DRPK-Japan relations." See "'Mysterious Ship Pursuit Case,' Anti-DPRK Fiction, Statement of Spokesman for DPRK Foreign Ministry," KCNA headline, March 27, 1999.

36. "Japan Cannot See in the 21st Century as Long as Relations with the DPRK Remain Unsettled, Statement of the DPRK Government," *The People's Korea*, no. 1848 (August 28, 1999), p. 6.

37. Report on the rice aid from Japan's Kyodo news agency, March 17, 2000. The pessimism of the head of the Japanese delegation is reported in a Kyodo report of March 28, 2000. North Korean commentary on the talks is summarized in a KCNA report of April 5, 2000, "Head of DPRK Government Delegation Calls Press Conference." The joint communiqué released by the two sides is reported by KCNA on April 7, 2000.

38. See Byung Chul Koh, *The Foreign Policy Systems of North and South Korea* (University of California Press, 1984), p. 87.

39. Manwoo Lee, "Pyongyang and Washington: Dynamics of Changing Relations," *Asian Perspective*, vol. 19 (Fall-Winter 1995), pp. 131–51, especially pp. 134-35.

40. The full text of the agreement and President Clinton's letter, with a brief analysis, can be found in *Success or Sellout? The U.S.–North Korean Nuclear Accord*, the report of an independent task force cosponsored by the Council on Foreign Relations and the Seoul Forum for International Affairs (Council on Foreign Relations, 1995).

41. Barry Schweid, "Diversion of Fuel by North Koreans Angers Donor U.S.," *Washington Times*, February 18, 1995, p. 6.

42. Comments by Ambassador-at-Large Robert Gallucci at a press conference at the Foreign Press Center, Washington, October 27, 1994, in *Nautilus Daily Report*, October 28, 1994.

43. Thomas W. Lippman, "U.S. Sets Accords with N. Korea, Aiming to Defuse Tension," *Washington Post*, September 11, 1998, p. A25.

44. An extensive discussion of the 1972 communiqué and reunification events before and since is provided by Bong-youn Choy, *A History of the Korean Reunification Movement: Its Issues and Prospects* (Peoria, Ill.: Research Committee on Korean Unification, Institute of International Studies, Bradley University, 1984), especially chap. 6.

45. The confederacy proposal was first presented by Kim Il Sung in 1960; the formal proposal for a Confederate Republic of Koryo was presented in October 1980, at the Sixth Party Congress.

46. "Let Us Carry Out the Great Leader Comrade Kim Il-song's Instructions for National Reunification."

47. See, for example, the discussion in "Pyongyang Announces '10-Point Program for Unity,' 4 Preconditions for Unification Dialogues Included," *Vantage Point*, vol. 16 (April 1993), pp. 11–13. See also Young Whan Kihl, "Unification Policies and Strategies of North and South Korea," *International Journal of Korean Studies*, vol. 1 (Spring 1997), pp. 231–44. The principles are listed and explained in *A Handbook on North Korea, 1st Revision* (Seoul: Naewoe Press, 1998), pp. 123–26.

48. The many potential problems involved in making a confederation work are discussed by Tae Hwan Ok in his case study of confederations. Tae Hwan Ok, "A Case Study of Confederations," *Korean Journal of National Unification*, vol. 3 (1994), pp. 275–92.

49. *Yonhap* report, June 27, 1999.

50. "Stray Notes: 'Peddler,'" Radio Pyongyang, June 21, 1998, translated by FBIS, *East Asia*, June 26, 1998.

51. "New Year Address of President Kim Il Sung."

52. "Establishment of Fair International Relations Is Demand of Present Era," *Minju Choson* article cited by KCNA, November 16, 1996.

53. *Nodong Sinmun* signed article reported on the same date (May 25, 1999) by KCNA.

54. "Western 'Standard of Human Rights' Cannot Work," KCNA headline of August 5, 1993, citing a *Nodong Sinmun* article of the same date, transcribed by FBIS, *East Asia*, 93-150 (August 6, 1993), pp. 15–16, quotation on p. 16.

55. "A Human Rights Problem Must Not Be Used for Political Purpose: Leader of DPRK Delegation," KCNA, June 24, 1993, transcribed by FBIS, *East Asia*, 93-120, June 24, 1993, pp. 12–13.

56. "DPRK's Withdrawal from 'International Convention' Is a Legitimate Step," KCNA, August 28, 1997.

57. Reported in *Korea Times* (Internet version), August 5, 1999.

58. B. C. Koh, "Ideology and North Korean Foreign Policy," in Robert A. Scalapino and

Hongkoo Lee, *North Korea in a Regional and Global Context* (Berkeley, Calif.: Institute for East Asian Studies, 1986), pp. 20–36, quotation on p. 36.

59. Sang-Woo Rhee, "*Chuch'e* Ideology as North Korea's Foreign Policy Guide," in Scalapino and Lee, *North Korea*, pp. 37–54, especially p. 37.

60. Rhee, "*Chuch'e* Ideology," p. 45.

61. Adrian Buzo, *The Guerilla Dynasty* (Westview Press, 1999), p. 244.

62. Ibid., p. 245.

63. Michael J. Mazarr, *North Korea and the Bomb: A Case Study in Nonproliferation* (St. Martin's Press, 1995).

64. Leon V. Sigal, *Disarming Strangers: Nuclear Diplomacy with North Korea* (Princeton University Press, 1998), quotation on p. 252.

65. Chuck Downs, *Over the Line: North Korea's Negotiating Strategy* (Washington: American Enterprise Institute Press, 1999).

66. Scott Snyder, *Negotiating on the Edge: North Korean Negotiating Behavior* (Washington: U.S. Institute of Peace, 1999).

67. On North Korean negotiating, see Kwak Tae-Hwan and others, *Pukhanui Hyopsang Chollayakkwa Nam-Pukhan Kwangye* (North Korea's Negotiation Strategy and North-South Relations) (Seoul: Institute for Far Eastern Studies, Kyungnam University, 1997; and Kim Do-tae and Cha Jae-hoon, *Pukhanui Hyopsang Chonsul Tuksong Yon'gu: Nam-Puk Taehwa Saryerul Chungsimuro* (A Study of the Characteristics of North Korea's Negotiating Tactics: Case Studies of North-South Dialogues) (Seoul: Korea Institute for National Unification, 1995).

68. Bernard Vincent Olivier, *The Implementation of China's Nationality Policy in the Northeastern Provinces* (San Francisco: Mellen Research University Press, 1993), especially pp. 266–69, 276.

69. Carter J. Eckert, *Offspring of Empire: The Koch'ang Kims and the Colonial Origins of Korean Capitalism 1876-1945* (University of Washington Press, 1991), pp. 162–64.

70. Report by Song Ui-tal in *Choson Ilbo*, August 19, 1996, p. 9.

71. Kwon Hui-young, *Segyeui Hanminjok: Tonkrip Kukka Yonhap* (Koreans around the Globe: Federation of Independent States) (Seoul: Ministry of National Unification, 1996), p. 157.

72. See Pak Song-yong article in *Korea Times*, April 3, 1994, p. 2; transcribed by FBIS, *East Asia*, (April 5, 1994), and entitled "Number of 'Escapees' on Increase," p. 44. Difficult as the conditions may be, the Russian logging job is highly sought after for its pay: only one out of 20 or 30 candidates is accepted. Successful applicants are judged to be politically reliable and have an above-average education. Interview with former North Korean lumberjack who defected from a Russian logging camp in the mid-1990s.

73. U Chong-chang, "Making a Living Is More Important Than Ideology—Members of General Association of Korean Residents in Japan, Chongnyon, Are Wavering," *Chugan Choson*, May 12, 1994, pp. 18-21; translated by FBIS, *East Asia*, 94-093 (May 13, 1994) and entitled "Article on 'Wavering' of Choch'ongnyon Members," pp. 38–42.

74. Background on Koreans in Japan may found in Changsoo Lee and George De Vos,

Koreans in Japan: Ethnic Conflict and Accommodation (University of California Press, 1981). Immigration figures from p. 37.

75. A thorough and objective account of the comfort women practice is provided by George Hicks, *The Comfort Women: Sex Slaves of the Japanese Imperial Forces* (Singapore: Heinemann Asia, 1995).

76. Lee and De Vos, *Koreans in Japan*, pp. 106–97.

77. "Forced Support of North Korea Hastening Chongnyon's Organizational Collapse," *Naewoe Tongsin*, no. 980 (November 23, 1995), pp. B1–B4; translated by FBIS, *East Asia*, 96-017 (January 25, 1996) and entitled "Increased Conflicts within Choch'ongnyon Reported," pp. 35–37.

78. Mary Jordan and Kevin Sullivan, "Pinball Wizards Fuel North Korea," *Washington Post*, June 7, 1996, p. A25.

79. Ibid.

80. Che Myong-sok, "Will Choch'ongnyon, 'the Chuch'e Tower' of Japan, Collapse?" *Sisa Journal*, June 20, 1998, pp. 50-51.

81. "Pyongyang Is Desperate to Save the Collapsing Chongryon," *Vantage Point*, vol. 21 (June 1998), p. 1.

82. Toshimitsu Shigemura, report in *Mainichi Shimbun*, August 6, 1999, Morning Edition, p. 5.

83. Eui-Young Yu, "The Korean American Community," in Donald N. Clark, ed., *Korea Briefing, 1993* (Westview Press, 1993), pp. 139–62.

84. Tourist figures from the *Korea Herald* (Internet version), March 22, 2000.

85. Figures for South Korean visits to North Korea were made public in a Ministry of Unification White Paper issued in early 1999, with highlights published in the *Korea Times* (Internet version), February 16, 2000.

86. Interview with North Korean reporter who defected in the mid-1990s.

87. The first quotation is from KCBN, February 8, 1995, in a commentary by Kim Ho-sam entitled "Implementing the DPRK-U.S. Agreed Framework and North-South Dialogue Are Separate Matters"; translated by FBIS on February 8, 1995, and entitled "Agreed Framework, N-S Talks 'Separate Matters'"; FBIS, *East Asia*, 95-026, pp. 17–18. The second quotation is from KCBN, March 29, 1995, in a commentary by Kim Ho-sam entitled "It Is Not an Issue for Intrusion by a Third Party"; translated by FBIS on the same date and entitled "ROK Inclusion in Framework Agreement Denounced"; FBIS, *East Asia*, 95-060, pp. 29–31.

Chapter Eight

1. "U.S. Urged to Show Faith," KCNA headline, July 26, 1999, reporting on a statement by a spokesman of the DPRK Foreign Ministry.

2. A highly readable refutation of the view that lies are harmless and necessary in public and private life is provided by Sissela Bok, *Lying, Moral Choice in Public and Private Life* (Vintage Books, 1989). George Orwell's description, in *1984*, of bureaucrats slaving away

in the Ministry of Truth, constantly revising history to accommodate the party's latest line, is a not-so-fictional example of the complications of lies.

3. See, for example, Selig Harrison, "Promoting a Soft Landing in North Korea," *Foreign Policy*, no. 106 (Spring 1997), pp. 57–75.

4. Albert Speer, *Inside the Third Reich: Memoirs*, translated by Richard Winston and Clara Winston (Avon Books, 1971), p. 379.

5. This conclusion may have to be re-examined in the future. Defectors in 1998 and 1999 are reporting that people are beginning to dissent more openly, although there are still no credible reports of organized resistance to the Kim regime.

6. Simon's concept of "bounded rationality" describes the model of problem solving in which a person, limited by memory and computational capacity, resorts to cognitive short-cuts to achieve an approximation to rational decisionmaking. See, for example, Herbert A. Simon, "Human Nature in Politics," *American Political Science Review*, vol. 79 (1985), pp. 293–304.

7. Aidan Foster-Carter, "Regime Dynamics in North Korea: A European Perspective," in Chung-in Moon, ed., *Understanding Regime Dynamics in North Korea* (Yonsei University Press, 1998), pp. 113–39, quotation on p. 134.

8. To name the second two national goals (following the enhancement of our security) listed in *A National Security Strategy for a New Century* (Washington: White House, May 1997), p. i. A more specific strategy for East Asia and the Pacific, based on the 1997 national security strategy, may be found in Office of International Security Affairs, *The United States Security Strategy for the East Asia-Pacific Region, 1998* (Department of Defense, November 1998).

9. Pyongyang has never permanently rescinded its 1993 withdrawal from the Non-Proliferation Treaty, taking the position that by signing the framework its nuclear program has become a bilateral issue with the United States. In 1998 North Korean Ambassador Kim Chang-guk told the UN General Assembly that the DPRK "does not have unilateral obligations to allow the IAEA to conduct monitoring activities when the US is not fulfilling its obligation," referring to the fact that U.S. heavy oil shipments were tardy, the construction project was behind schedule, and Washington had failed to lift economic sanctions against North Korea. Quoted in *Korea Times* (Internet version), November 5, 1998. Repeated IAEA complaints of Pyongyang's failure to permit necessary inspections have been ignored.

10. On deterrents, see, for example, Robert Jervis, "Introduction: Approach and Assumptions," in Robert Jervis, Richard Ned Lebow, and Janice Gross Stein, eds. *Psychology and Deterrence* (Johns Hopkins University Press, 1985), pp. 1–12; and Jervis' "Perceiving and Coping with Threat," pp. 13–34, in the same volume. See also Philip E. Tetlock, Charles B. McGuire, and Gregory Mitchell, "Psychological Perspectives on Nuclear Deterrence," *Annual Review of Psychology*, vol. 42 (1991), pp. 239–76.

11. Richard N. Haass, ed., *Economic Sanctions and American Diplomacy* (Washington: Council on Foreign Relations, 1998).

12. On the analysis of "what might have been," see, for example, Philip Tetlock and Aaron Belkin's edited volume, *Counterfactual Thought Experiments in World Politics: Logical, Methodological and Psychological Perspectives* (Princeton University Press, 1996).

13. Among the many treatments of American policy toward North Korea, a concise and perceptive view that touches on a number of ideas expressed in this chapter is Park Jongchul's "U.S. Policy towards North Korea: Strategy, Perception, and Inter-Korean Relations," *Journal of East Asian Affairs*, vol. 12 (Summer-Fall 1998), pp. 529–52.

14. Michael J. Mazarr provides extensive coverage of the North's nuclear program in *North Korea and the Bomb* (St. Martin's Press, 1996). We have discussed the nuclear issue (in much less detail) in several articles, including Kongdan Oh and Ralph C. Hassig, "The North Korean Bomb and Nuclear Proliferation in Northeast Asia," *Asian Perspective*, vol. 19 (Fall 1995), pp. 153–74; and Kongdan Oh and Ralph Hassig, "North Korea's Nuclear Program," in Young Whan Kihl, ed., *Korea and the World: Beyond the Cold War* (Westview Press, 1994), pp. 233–50. As the major issue of contention between the United States and the DPRK, the nuclear issue is also dealt with in some detail by the negotiation studies cited in chapter 7 in this volume, by Chuck Downs, Leon Sigal, Scott Snyder, Kwak Tae-Hwan and others, and Kim Do-tae and Cha Jae-hoon.

15. The output of nuclear reactors can be measured in thermal units (how much heat is produced) or electrical units (how much electricity can be produced). The more practical (and conservative) measure is megawatts electrical (MWe), which is used here. A valuable discussion of North Korea's nuclear sites may be found in Joseph S. Bermudez Jr., "North Korea's Nuclear Infrastructure," *Jane's Intelligence Review*, vol. 6 (February 1994), pp. 74–79.

16. Ralph A. Cossa has provided valuable updates on the status of the Agreed Framework. See for example *The U.S.-DPRK Agreed Framework: Is It Still Viable? Is It Enough?* Occasional Paper (Honolulu: Pacific Forum, Center for International and Strategic Studies, April 1999).

17. The figure for underground sites is reported by *Chungang Ilbo* (Internet version) on December 8, 1998.

18. The Two-Stage Taepodong 1 with a 700–1,000 kilogram warhead has an estimated range of 1,500–2,200 kilometers. The three-stage launch version of the rocket probably carried a payload of only 100 kilograms and thus achieved a range of 4,000 kilometers, although it apparently failed to place its payload in orbit. The 4,000 to 6,000 estimated range of the Taepodong 2 is with a 700–1,000- kilogram payload. Estimates provided to the authors in a copyrighted chart by Joseph S. Bermudez Jr., "DPRK Ballistic Missile Characteristics," December 19, 1998.

19. *Review of United States Policy toward North Korea: Findings and Recommendations.* Unclassified Report by Dr. William J. Perry, U.S. North Korea Policy Coordinator and Special Advisor to the President and the Secretary of State, Washington, October 12, 1999. (www.state.gov/www/regions/eap/991012_north korea_rpt.html [accessed April 2000]).

20. In many respects, the sunshine policy is an example of the psychologist Charles Osgood's tension-reduction model called Graduated Reciprocation in Tension-reduction (GRIT), designed (originally in the context of U.S.–Soviet Union cold war competition) to overcome the suspicions of a hostile government. Charles E. Osgood, *An Alternative to War or Surrender* (University of Illinois Press, 1962).

21. A good chronology of North Korean provocations is Rinn S. Shinn, *North Korea:*

Chronology of Provocations, 1950-1998 (Congressional Research Service, January 4, 1999), pp. 11, 12, 13.

22. Commentary entitled "The So-Called Sunshine Policy Is a Revised Version of the Anti-North Confrontation Theory," *Nodong Sinmun*, August 7, 1998.

23. In an insightful article, Paul Bracken, using the "poison carrots" analogy, suggests that the Kim regime is constructing a virtual "doomsday machine" that would consume the region in chaos and destruction if the regime were threatened to the point of collapse. Bracken, "Risks and Promises in the Two Koreas," *Orbis*, vol. 39 (Winter 1995), pp. 55–64.

24. Han Sung-chu, "Fiction and Reality of Sunshine Policy," commentary by former foreign minister, *Chungang Ilbo* (Internet version), July 5, 1998.

25. In 1995, Defense Secretary Perry said "serious consideration" had been given to military strikes against North Korea in 1994. See Thomas W. Lippman, "U.S. Considered Attacks on N. Korea, Perry Tells Panel," *Washington Post*, January 25, 1995, p. A4.

26. Undersecretary Slocombe's quotation may be found in Barry Schweid, "Diversion of Fuel by North Koreans Angers Donor U.S.," *Washington Times*, February 18, 1995, p. 6.

27. The parameters of engagement as a policy alternative to confrontation and containment seem not to have been closely analyzed. See Victor Cha, "Dealing with Rogue Regimes: North Korea and the Argument for Enhanced Engagement," *Asian Survey*, forthcoming.

28. Discussions of the use of rewards in foreign policy can be found in David A. Baldwin, "The Power of Positive Sanctions," *World Politics*, vol. 24 (October 1971), pp. 19–38; and Thomas W. Milburn and Daniel J. Christie, "Rewarding in International Politics," *Political Psychology*, vol. 10 (December 1989), pp. 625–45. A discussion of inducements in the context of U.S.-DPRK relations may be found in Ralph C. Hassig, "Rewarding North Korea: Three Views," in Kongdan Oh and Craig S. Coleman, eds., *Restarting the Peace Process on the Korean Peninsula* (Los Angeles: Korea Society/Los Angeles, 1995), pp. 59–79.

29. "We Have No Idea of Having Dialogue under Pressure, DPRK FM Spokesman," KCNA headline, November 29, 1993, transcribed by FBIS, *East Asia*, 93-228, November 30, 1993, and entitled "Spokesman Warns U.S. against Applying Pressure," p. 13.

30. "Solution of Nuclear Issue May Be Impeded, If Improvement of North-South Relations Is Set as Precondition: Foreign Ministry Spokesman," KCNA headline, July 25, 1994, transcribed by FBIS, *East Asia*, 94-142, July 25, 1994, and entitled "Spokesman on 'Precondition' for U.S. Ties," pp. 58–59.

31. Expressions of distrust by Robert Gallucci, who negotiated the Agreed Framework, and by a U.S. State Department spokesman four years later, have already been cited in the chapter on foreign relations.

32. *Report on the North Korea Policy Review*, The Honorable William Perry, presentation at the Woodrow Wilson Center, November 29, 1999.

33. In an analysis of U.S. policy toward North Korea, Hyung-kook Kim makes a similar point, that "the U.S. must manage the changes in North Korea rather than follow them." Several of the six policy suggestions offered by Professor Kim are similar to our own (offer more economic deals, continue to pursue normalization talks). He advocates putting more

pressure on North Korea (short of military action) to move the U.S.-DPRK relationship from "seemingly endless engagement" to "constructive engagement." His idea of "a bigger stick but the same carrot" sounds somewhat similar to Alexander George's generic foreign policy of "coercive diplomacy": "to back one's demand on an adversary with a threat of punishment for noncompliance that he will consider credible and potent enough to persuade him to comply with the demand." Hyung-kook Kim, "U.S. Policy toward North Korea: From Positive Engagement to Constructive Containment," *Journal of East Asian Affairs*, vol. 13 (Spring-Summer 1999), pp. 111–30, especially p. 127. Alexander L. George, *Forceful Persuasion: Coercive Diplomacy as an Alternative to War* (Washington: U.S. Institute of Peace, 1997), especially p. 4. As a label for a particular type of engagement, "proactive engagement" has been used by John Feffer to refer to the form of engagement recommended by the Kim Dae Jung government. See John Feffer, "North Korea and the Politics of Engagement," *Peace Review*, vol. 11 (September 1999), pp. 415–22.

34. Thibaut and Kelley called the two standards the comparison level and the comparison level for alternatives, respectively. See John W. Thibaut and Harold H. Kelley, *The Social Psychology of Groups* (John Wiley and Sons, 1967), chap. 6.

35. Alexis de Tocqueville, *Old Regime and the French Revolution* (1856).

36. Paek Mun-kyu, "Only When a Mosquito Net Is Set Up Securely Can the Infiltration of the Yellow Wind Be Blocked," *Nodong Sinmun*, June 11, 1999, p. 6.

37. Ibid.

38. Memoir of former DPRK air force senior lieutenant, *Wolgan Choson*, August 1999, pp. 62–96.

39. "On Preserving the Juche Character and National Character of the Revolution and Construction: Comrade Kim Jong Il Publishes Work," KCNA headline, June 22, 1997.

40. Secretary Hwang Chang-yop has made this suggestion on several occasions. See, for example, his interview by journalist Hagiwara Ryo in *Bungei Shunju*, February 1999, pp. 324–46. See also pp. 330–33 in Hwang's *Nanun Yoksaui Chillirul Poatta* (I Saw the Truth of History) (Seoul: Hanul, 1999).

41. Lee Young Sun discusses the high costs of unification in "Nam-Puk Kyonghyopui Yuhyonggwa Chonmang" (Models and Prospects of North-South Economic Cooperation), in *Pukhan Kyongjeron* (A Theory of the North Korean Economy), edited by the North Korean Economic Forum (Seoul: Popmunsa, 1996), pp. 385–416. Numerous economic models' calculations of unification costs are presented in Marcus Noland, Sherman Robinson, and Li-Gang Liu, *The Costs and Benefits of Korean Unification*, Working Paper 98-1 (Washington: Institute for International Economics, 1998).

42. Nicholas Eberstadt, "Hastening Korean Reunification," *Foreign Affairs*, vol. 76 (March-April 1997), pp. 77–92. See also Eberstadt's *The End of North Korea* (Washington: American Enterprise Institute Press, 1999).

43. KCNA compilation of DPRK news media commentary on the previous day's statement of the spokesman of the KPA General Staff, December 3, 1998.

Index